Discover
Meditation & Mindfulness

Create a better life through the power of inner reflection

Tara Ward

This edition published in 2017 by Arcturus Publishing Limited
26/27 Bickels Yard, 151–153 Bermondsey Street,
London SE1 3HA

AD000307UK

Printed in the UK

List of Exercises

CONTENTS

INTRODUCTION

Why have you picked up this book? Perhaps you know a little about meditation and like the sound of it. Perhaps you have already practised it on some level. Or you may be aware that you dream a great deal and wonder what those dreams might mean and why you have them so frequently. Perhaps you have heard of spiritual guides before but aren't quite sure who or what they really are. Maybe you just liked the colour of the cover or the cover 'blurb' – or picked it up on an instinct without quite knowing why.

Whatever your reason, whatever you think meditation, spiritual guides and dreamwork mean, the first thing you need to know is the intention behind this book. After all, why should you bother to wade through 384 pages? What will you gain from it?

Quite simply, it is to help you understand yourself and others better. You're going to be encouraged to look at life in a different and more meaningful context, to look beyond the mundane minutiae of the everyday, to delve deeper into why we are all here and what each of us has to learn during our time on Earth. All of this may sound daunting, and you may be wondering how you can possibly do any of it.

None of it is as difficult as it sounds. You start by taking a very personal, inward journey which progresses gradually and gently. You can go at your own pace, looking at different aspects of who you really are as and when you are ready to do so. You will gain an understanding of why you are where you are right now, of why you have certain people around you in your life and of what you can learn from them. A healthy by-product of this greater understanding is that much of the daily routine in your life can become more significant and enjoyable as a result.

After all, how much of your day is taken up with routine tasks that afford you little pleasure? Do you enjoy the process of getting up, getting ready for the day ahead, eating, working, socialising, sleeping? What percentage of your day do you find rewarding and pleasurable? Do you wake up each morning happy to face the day, looking forward to everything ahead of you?

What about all those routine tasks: brushing your teeth, showering or bathing, cooking, cleaning, washing, ironing, emptying the rubbish, shopping, using public transport, ferrying your children from one activity to the next, doing household accounts and paying bills? Do you find enjoyment in any of these activities or do you simply regard them as chores that have to be done, so you get through them as quickly as possible, often feeling tense and irritable in the process? Most people would probably admit to the latter a great deal of the time.

Do you often have moments in your life when you wonder what this thing called 'living' is all about, particularly when you feel so much of your day is taken up with mundane tasks that give you little or no pleasure? Perhaps you often feel that life must be something more than working, eating and sleeping. You may acknowledge that certain boring chores have to be done on a regular basis, but surely there ought to be something in your life that affords you greater reward and a true sense of achievement. You may want to feel good about yourself, other than feeling you are existing on an acceptable level. You may just want life to be more interesting and more important.

The fact is that many people go through life deeply dissatisfied, often without quite realizing why. They may have this vague sense of wanting more, either materially or emotionally, but when they are given more the unhappiness remains. Even a vast amount of material wealth doesn't seem to offer any guarantee of contentment on a deeper level.

Perhaps you are someone who always wanted certain things from your life, say marriage and children and a decent home and car. You may have felt that by achieving a certain status, it would make you feel happier inside. Do you still feel an emptiness without understanding why? Perhaps your goal was having a specific job or living in a particular place. If you've achieved that right now, has it satisfied you? If you haven't, are you sure that you really want what you say you want?

How do you know what you really want? Many of us go through our lives not really knowing. We may settle on a lifestyle because we think it is all we are capable of or because it's undemanding or because we are told this is what we should want or because somehow we fell into it without actually taking responsibility for our destiny. Are any of these good enough reasons for ending up with an unrewarding life?

If you are now beginning to worry about what major changes you might make as a result of reading this book, please rest assured that you are not going to be encouraged to consider adopting an entirely new life through what you learn here. In fact, the reverse is true. You are going to be encouraged to accept and enjoy every single moment of the life you have at present, to acknowledge and appreciate everything that is working well for you and to turn negative, frustrating scenarios into positive, encouraging ones. Can you possibly believe that you might enjoy being stuck in a massive traffic jam? Can you see yourself being happy to clear up after a chaotic party when you have a hangover? What about facing a crowd to whom you have to give a big speech? Enjoying all this and much, much more is available to you.

The techniques we are going to work through will afford you the chance to reconsider what you think are difficult or 'bad' experiences. There is, in fact, no such thing as a 'bad' experience, only how we react to it and what we learn from it. Even then we are not good or bad as a result of that experience. We are simply enlightened or unenlightened by it. You are going to learn how to allow new knowledge to come into your life and help shape your daily existence in a positive way.

If you do end up wanting to make some changes in your life as a result, these shifts will happen gradually, in small, gentle, easy stages and will involve you taking time to appreciate exactly what you have already got. Happiness is not about seeking something outside, it's about being content with yourself inside. Only then can you find out the truth of what is available to you.

Certain techniques can lead you to the truth about who you really are and what you really want in life – the process of stopping, of going 'within' to a quiet place through meditation, of seeking help from our spiritual guides, of paying attention to our dreams and working with them.

The possibilities that open up from understanding yourself and others better are infinite. The repercussions are potentially very powerful. If you can see where you are in life and realize how much more you have to offer of yourself, as well as your greater potential to learn from others and to openly embrace all experiences, then the scope for change and growth is enormous. This means positive change not just for you but also for others.

Perhaps you may feel this isn't something you will be able to do. You may be very immersed in your normal, everyday 'outer' world of work, family and friends and wonder how on earth you can access some other 'inner' world that doesn't seem to reflect any of the things you already know. It may seem too large a step to move forward into a place that is new and strange. You may wonder whether you want to know certain things! After all, ignorance can be a blessing at times, can't it?

However, what you need to know is that, wherever you are right now in your life, the contents of this book and its exercises are relevant to you and can benefit you. The joy of all this work is that you can only progress at your own pace. You will only discover what it is right for you to deal with at this time – nothing more. This is regardless of whatever stage you have reached in your life, irrespective of how satisfied or unsatisfied you may feel with some or all of your existence. One of the facts we will truly be able to embrace during this journey together, is that each and every one of us is unique. Your path in life is yours alone and is completely different from anybody else's.

You are reading this book at this time in your life because it is applicable to what is happening to you right now. Had you read it at an earlier or later stage, you would have responded differently because, whether we are aware of it or not, each day leaves an indelible experience in our memory and shapes how we think, feel and act. Your experiences as you work through the exercises in this book and how you respond to everything are rightfor you at this stage in your life. There is no pressure on you to conform to anything!

Therefore, if you find some of the concepts discussed here exciting and helpful, that is wonderful and it will help you to move forward in your own personal journey of discovery. If you find some of the theories hard to grasp or unbelievable, that simply reflects the stage you are at in your life, and is every bit as valid and positive as the other response! You may reject certain areas because they don't feel right for you or because you are not ready to look at them yet or because they just don't 'ring true'. It may be you decide to work with a few techniques and find that they give you everything you need right now.

There is no rule that says you must accept all of what you read here in order to move forward and discover new concepts. All I ask is that you read with an open mind, ready to stretch your thought processes and that you enjoy the whole journey, irrespective of how you choose to respond!

So what are some of the concepts we'll be looking at during this journey? Let's take a look at some of them now so you can see where they might lead and what you might need to consider.

First, ask yourself what spiritual or religious beliefs you hold as far as any form of greater or higher consciousness is concerned. This is a fundamental issue because during meditation, working with spiritual guides and dreamwork you will need to form some sort of association with awareness of a power/source/entity/energy/deity greater than you. This does not have to take any religious form although it may do. Remember, this journey of discovery is individual and personal. Whether you follow an orthodox religion or whether you have your own private spiritual beliefs, this journey will work for all.

It is possible to experience the power of this work even if you hold no strong views about any form of higher consciousness, although it may not be quite as easy to free your thought processes and to open your mind to other concepts. In other words, you may have to work harder than others, if you hold the viewpoint that life is purely earthly and not connected to any form of higher awareness or universal laws. There is also another possibility here.

One of the many joys of meditation, in particular, is that insights and revelations often come to you when you are least expecting them. If your thoughts of higher consciousness and spiritual laws are either unformed or cynical, it is quite likely that repeated meditations will offer a breakthrough. This is not to imply that you might end up a fervent religious believer or a deep spiritual enthusiast, but it is likely that you will find yourself thinking about life in a different way, trying to work below the surface of everything to understand your existence on a deeper level.

For those of you who may feel very sceptical about the presence of an all-knowing source of higher consciousness, it is suggested that you can use nature and an appreciation of it to enhance your relationship with all of life. Many people who claim to have no spiritual or religious beliefs nevertheless have a great love of nature and find solace in it, combined with a sense of wonderment about its beauty and perfection.

Spend some time improving your relationship with, and awareness of, all that nature offers. Next time you take a walk through a beautiful wood or a stroll along a deserted beach, stop to really see what is around you. Until you stop, you can't fully appreciate it all. Look at the amazing symmetry of a spider's web; how is such a perfect pattern created? Notice the beautiful formation of a group of birds as they fly – how do they manage that uniformity? See the fantastic shape of an old tree. Notice the wonderful colours in a sea-shell. Watch the tiny insects around you; follow a beetle or ant in its daily tasks and notice its instinctive behaviour. Where has their innate ability to do this come from? Think about a wild animal with its young. No one has taught it how to behave as a parent – how does it know what to do?

There are many wonderful facts about nature. Here is just one – and it is true! Have you heard of blister beetles? It has been discovered that they have a unique and ingenious way of feeding on honey. A group of blister beetles gets together and forms the shape of a female bee. This attracts a male bee which swoops down to mate. He quickly realizes the beetles are not the 'real thing' and flies off, but not before the blister beetles have attached themselves to his body. Once the bee has flown back to the hive, the beetles detach themselves from him and gorge on the plentiful supply of honey. Now, how have the blister beetles developed the ability to form themselves into the shape of a female bee? How do they even know its true shape and exact size, let alone how to work together to create this shape? Nature is full of such extraordinary examples of awareness that seem to supersede logical ability. It is all around us if only we stop to look and to learn about it. Start becoming more aware.

Lose yourself in a wonderful cloud formation as it swirls and floats above you. Focus on the rhythmic pounding of waves upon the shore and consider how the tide is a constant and never-ending cycle. Stare up at the moon one evening. How much do you really know about it and what it does? Think about everything else out there in the universe. Think of all the stars and planets, of other galaxies. What else is out there, undiscovered? How did it all come into existence?

When you spend even a small amount of time regularly acknowledging the beauty and perfection of nature, it is impossible not to become increasingly appreciative of what is around us. Our sense of wonderment about it all also increases. How can a butterfly have such extraordinary colours and markings? The same is true of so many creatures: a pheasant, a peacock, a leopard, a zebra. Diving into the sea and witnessing the wonders of sea life is truly inspirational. The beauty of any living thing takes your breath away, if you stop and consider it long enough.

Developing this sense of wonderment and appreciation will help you in your journey towards understanding more about life as a whole. We get so caught up in our own narrow lives that we forget to see the world around us. This is what we want to start doing now. Nature is an excellent starting point from which to expand our thoughts.

In fact, let's now stop and do an exercise to help us relax and to allow our thoughts to spiral outwards a little. Read through the exercise first and then close your eyes and let yourself drift off as described. Or, if you have a friend who is also sharing the contents of this book, you could always take turns and read the exercise out loud to each other.

The camera

Sit in a comfortable seat, close your eyes and relax. Take a few comfortable breaths and wriggle your body about to settle yourself.

Now you are going to take a journey to help free your imagination. You start this journey by holding a feather-light but very powerful camera in your hands. Your eye is trained through the lens of this camera at all times. Your finger is on a button that adjusts the focus of the lens. You are in control at all times. The camera is now in your hands. Your eye is trained through the lens. Your finger is poised on the focus button. Your journey is about to start.

Look through the lens. It is trained upon a tiny ant in the grass. Follow the ant on its journey as it scurries from one blade of grass to the next. Now pull back your lens a little. See a larger beetle in the grass near the ant. Notice how much bigger it is. Pull back further. Now you see a bird next to the beetle. It seems enormous in comparison. Keep slowly pulling back the lens and gaining more perspective as you do so. Keep noticing different creatures to compare the size of each one. See a rabbit, a cat, a small dog and then a large dog, then a horse. Finally focus on the head of a tall giraffe and see everything moving below you. Realize you can't even see the ant in the grass below.

Now pull the lens back even further. Through the lens you see that you are above the giraffe's head. The giraffe is in a large field. Pull back further. The field is surrounded by houses. Pull back further and the vista widens. You can see other fields and other houses, but they are becoming smaller and smaller as you pull back. You see minuscule movements below and think they might be ants. Then you realize they are all people, scurrying about their daily business. They seem so small and insignificant in the distance. You can see mountain ranges below you and large bodies of water. You keep your finger on the focus button and keep gently, constantly widening your frame and increasing the distance between you and the Earth.

You pull back through billowing clouds and keep going. You notice that the Earth is now becoming a round ball in front of you. You can just make out water and mountains but these blur as the globe fast becomes an indistinct sphere. You see the moon. It looks much clearer and larger now. You keep pulling back. Stars pass in front of your lens in a blur, then planets and other galaxies. Keep going. Wait until the focus button stops and you can go no further.

When the focus button stops, have a good look through your lens. What is the image you see? This is personal to you. This is your vision. What do you feel as you look at this scenario? What sensation accompanies this experience? Let yourself enjoy the experience, then let the image drift away and slowly recede into the distance.

Now you want to remember where you are. You are sitting in your chair. Remember what room you are in. Say the day of the week to yourself, then the month, the year. Open your eyes slowly and look at the time. Take a few minutes to re-orientate yourself before you get up or you may feel light-headed.

Did you see an image that you didn't expect? Were you surprised by how easy it was to pull back the lens and see everything in a constantly widening perspective? What sensations accompanied these actions? Was there a point at which you felt you wanted to stop? In other words, were you resistant to certain leaps of focus? What was the point where you finally couldn't pull back any further? Do you think that you might be able to pull back further on another occasion?

The Camera exercise is one you can return to whenever you feel the urge to experiment with it. The only rules are that you have to remain in control at all times, your eyes must remain trained through the lens and your finger has to stay on the focus button. When you try this again, you will find that your last image will probably have changed to something else. It will manifest itself as whatever is relevant to you at that particular moment.

Congratulations; you have just experienced a form of meditation! That wasn't too daunting, was it? You may be aware that you felt more relaxed when you finished. Perhaps your body felt more comfortable in the chair. Maybe your mind felt calmer, less agitated. Sometimes, when you open your eyes after a meditation, everything seems brighter and sharper, more in focus. You generally feel more alive, happier. Whatever you felt was right for you. If you felt little different, remember that is fine, too.

So you have just been through a small meditation. If you haven't done that before, was it what you expected? Often people get stuck in the concept of meditation meaning someone sitting cross-legged for hours, surrounded by strange music and scents, looking as though they must be desperately uncomfortable and deeply unhappy! That is not the sort of meditation we are going to be working with here. Ours is going to be gentle, comfortable, relaxing and nurturing. It's going to be a natural state which you will not want to leave because it will feel so good and so right.

Meditation is fundamentally about deep reflection. It's about going into peace and quiet, clearing your mind of troublesome thoughts and allowing yourself to drift into a wonderful state of relaxation, through which you can gain clear insights into what you really want and who you really are.

As we'll see when we discuss meditation in greater detail in Part One, meditation is an ancient art that has been practised in Eastern civilizations since man first came into being. We're just beginning to catch up in the West and to realize how beneficial it can be. It's not difficult and unnatural. It's a gentle, nurturing process which refreshes and releases.

The quiet inner world that we enter during meditation acts as a reflection of our noisier, outer world. In other words, meditation is about helping us to handle our outer world which, quite frankly, can often be extremely demanding and stressful. So, whatever is happening for you in the outside 'real' world, it will be shown as some sort of reflection to you during your meditation. Does that make some sense of the final image you had during the Camera exercise? How did it reflect some part of your everyday life? If the answer isn't immediately apparent to you, that is fine. Sometimes, the purpose of our meditations and their messages only become clear to us later. The benefits of meditation continue long after the actual process itself ceases. Sometimes, the real benefits only start after the meditation has finished.

Spiritual Guides

So, now that you have gained some insights into how meditation can benefit you and what you have to look forward to in this new process, what else is involved? Where, for example, do spiritual guides fit into this new world and what are they?

We'll answer that question in greater detail in Part Two, but a quick explanation would be to describe spiritual guides as forms of energy who can be called into our consciousness when required, to help guide, comfort and nurture us on our journey in life. Trying to describe in detail what a spiritual guide is takes some time and it would probably be more helpful for you to work your way through Part One first, before delving into the significance of spiritual guides. This is because it is through meditation that we first start to become aware of the helpful energies we can call upon. It is hard to describe or to believe in such a phenomenon without first being able to experience it for yourself. It's a bit like trying to find the words to describe an overwhelmingly emotional experience, such as the birth of a baby. It is hard to find adequate words; you need to witness it for yourself and feel the whole process as a live example. Working with spiritual guides comes into this realm.

Dreamwork

Lastly, what about dreamwork? Where does it fit into helping you to understand yourself and others better?

How often do you dream? Many people only remember vague, indistinct dreams, and then infrequently, while others constantly have vivid experiences and often wake up in the morning feeling as though they have done a full day's work! Perhaps your experiences fall somewhere between these two extremes.

There has been so much conjecture about why we dream and what dreams mean. There are many different schools of thought as far as interpretation of dreams is concerned: you may have heard of the psychologists Jung and Freud and their theories. During our work we aren't going to focus on other people's interpretations, although we will touch upon what they have said. You are going to be encouraged to find out for yourself what your dreams mean to you and what you can learn from them.

Our dreams are as unique as we are. Two people can have a similar dream but the message or what they can take from it may be completely different. The only true interpreter of your dreams is you, because no one else is living your life and can get inside you. You will learn to trust your own intuition and to work with it to appreciate much more about yourself on every level.

You may be worrying that you can never remember your dreams and therefore won't be able to do the exercises in Part Three. This isn't a problem. Many people have to be encouraged to remember their dreams and there are tricks that allow you to open the door into this new world.

Unfortunately, dreamwork has a reputation for looking at the negative and considering dreams as portentous warnings of upcoming events or fears in your life. What we are going to do is to see dreams as a vital and nourishing part of our lives. Accurate interpretation of your dreams can be the gateway to understanding all aspects of yourself on a new level. There is no such thing as a 'bad' dream when you realize what the dream actually means to you. You will also be learning how to shape your own dreams and learning to take control. This will mirror your taking control in aspects of your 'outer' world.

Just as meditation is an inner reflection of your outer world, so dreams can offer reflections, too. They work on a different energetic level of the subconscious; that is to say dreams can offer a deeper level of interpretation as to what may be happening in a given area of your life. This does not mean that dreaming is more valuable than meditation. It is simply another tool of understanding for you to use. Both techniques are only useful if you can learn to interpret them for yourself. This is fundamentally what you are going to learn to do during the course of this book.

So how can these three different techniques be pulled together to create a powerful learning course for your own personal progress, to say nothing of also helping others?

These three forms of self-awareness are inter-connected, as you will see when we work through Part Four. By pulling the different techniques together, it is possible to create a powerhouse of understanding and knowledge. However, as was mentioned earlier, you do not have to end up embracing all the concepts you work with. Not every exercise in this book will prove to be a powerful experience for you. Some you may find difficult; some may leave you cold. You may find meditation easy and deeply insightful; another person will struggle with this and yet will find interpreting their many dreams a wonderfully helpful tool. Some of you will discover literally dozens of spiritual guides flocking into your energy fields to help and nurture you; some of you may struggle to connect with even one!

It is fine for you to like some of what you discover and want to dismiss other sections. However, there are a couple of requests before you continue. One is that you read through the book in order. It has been carefully structured so that each chapter follows through with more detail and explanation of what you are dealing with in these forms of self-analysis. If you decide to skip forward to Part Three and think you will work only with dreams, you will probably find yourself floundering and not understanding many of the references. There are certain steps you need to follow before any of these techniques will work. They are explained in Part One and then worked through to a deeper level during Parts Two and Three. Part Four then takes you into an even deeper realm of work. So please do read through in order.

You will soon discover that virtually every chapter has at least one exercise, often more. It is suggested that you read through each chapter once, then go back in order to work through the individual exercises contained in each. Often you need an overview of the whole chapter and what you are setting out to do before you start working slowly through the exercise.

Don't worry if you feel you want to skip certain exercises and then return to them later. There are only a few that you need to do initially, mostly related to the breathing techniques. Feel free to leave until another time anything that seems too daunting or too emotional.

At all times, as you continue absorbing new concepts, remember to keep expanding your thought processes. If something seems difficult to grasp, ask yourself what element of that concept you find hard to understand or accept. Keep questioning your own set of limiting beliefs. After all, meditation is all about releasing tensions and restrictions, not just physically but also mentally, emotionally and spiritually. Refuse to limit yourself. Set no boundaries as to what you are willing to consider possible. Enjoy this new freedom!

PART ONE:

MEDITATION

WHAT IS MEDITATION?

The first thought people usually have about meditation is the traditional image of a figure, such as a Buddha, sitting cross-legged in the lotus position, eyes closed, hands turned upwards on the knees, often with thumb and first finger touching.

How do you feel when you look at this image? Do you find it inspirational? Does it make you want to learn how to meditate? It's probably fair to say that far from finding this image appealing, many people find it off-putting. If meditation is about relaxing and unwinding, this image personifies the exact opposite, at any rate to most Westerners. After all, the pose looks deeply uncomfortable. The legs appear to be contorted into a deeply painful twist that looks unnatural and positively unhealthy. Why should one have one's hands pointing upwards and what do two fingers touching mean? (There is a very good reason for this and it relates to working with our chakras and energy meridians which run through our body. These energies are discussed in more detail later.)

Relax. You do not have to try to adopt this position for our meditation. You do not even have to sit cross-legged, let alone try to contort yourself into a lotus position. You don't have to place your hands palm upwards, if you don't feel like it. Even closing your eyes is not necessary in the early stages of our meditation. Does that make you feel less daunted?

However, let us clarify something. There are good reasons why the position shown is adopted for certain forms of meditation and it can indeed be a wonderfully powerful and beautiful experience. However, it takes years of practice and gentle manipulation. Generally it comes easier to people in certain Eastern societies, where the constant warm climate helps to naturally loosen and relax the muscles and meditation is part of their culture and something for which they are prepared from an early age.

For now, you just need to remember that you are not going to be asked to do anything difficult or uncomfortable during your meditation sessions. So where has this technique called meditation come from?

Meditation has been practised in different forms for thousands of years. We know that many early civilizations lived their life by appreciation and awareness of various gods and deities. We know the ancient Egyptians used to offer gifts to their gods; the same is true of the ancient Romans and Greeks. An awareness of higher forces was central to their way of life. Nature was linked into this belief, of course. People would pray for rain or sun or whatever was needed to allow their crops to prosper. They would pray for a healthy child or for enough food to eat or for immunity from disease or pestilence. They would build temples and palaces to honour and acknowledge the power and beauty of their gods.

They would meditate and obtain messages and guidance from spiritual energies. Many ancient sages and soothsayers were known to have abilities to communicate with deities through meditation and prayer. They were revered within their society and their advice was constantly sought. Meditation was accepted as a normal and essential part of everyday life, even if not every layman meditated himself.

The more we learn about early peoples, the more we realize that their entire lives were, in essence, a meditation. They lived in appreciation of what they had and, of course, in some instances, in fear of what might come. That fear sometimes led them to behave in a way that we find abhorrent. Most people nowadays would find appalling the idea of sacrificing children or animals to appease the gods and to give them good fortune. As always, anything taken to extremes can seem unbalanced and dangerous. However, the basis of meditation is in an appreciation and awareness of nature and of forces outside human control, and it is these aspects we shall be working with in this book.

It's true to say that various remote tribes in far-flung corners of the world still live their lives through what we could call meditative practices. The fact that we rarely hear about them or gain access to them in any way is perhaps a reflection of our ignorance not theirs.

Modern man's quest to understand the increasingly large array of diseases affecting people in Western society has prompted him to question why it is that various tribes in remote areas of the world enjoy good health and lack of illness. Such tribes are to be found in the Australian outback, northern Mexico, Botswana, Venezuela and Tasmania, and elsewhere. They all live simple lives, eating basic food, in harmony with their surroundings and the forces of nature around them. Whether you want to put a spiritual or religious slant to this is irrelevant. They live in appreciation and awareness of what is immediately around them, unfettered by our obsession with material possessions, wealth and an insatiable urge for always wanting more of everything.

Why do you think so much of modern society, particularly in the West, has fallen into this trap of selfishness and greed and moved so far from any spiritual appreciation and awareness? We have certainly made extraordinary advances in many areas in the last few hundred years; we are justifiably proud of all our technological advancements and the easier life which they afford us. Most people would say it is a joy to have electricity, sewerage, heating, telephones, cars, planes, computers and all the other wonderful inventions we tend to take for granted.

Perhaps a clue to understanding why we have become so 'unspiritual' lies in the phrase 'we tend to take for granted'. How much do you appreciate what you have in life? It takes only a few minutes of watching a news programme about terrible drought, floods, famine and/or wars in another part of the world to make most of us stop for a moment and realize how fortunate we are in comparison. Yet how long does that appreciation last – a few seconds, a minute or two? – before we return to everyday life and forget? Probably you don't give another thought about how blessed you are, until you have another reminder thrown at you.

Most people spend time thinking about what they haven't got and what they think they deserve or need to have. They spend their lives trying to attain these things: more money, better job, larger home and car, etc. In other words, the majority of their time is spent trying to achieve more and never being contented with what they have right now. Is that true of you?

Perhaps, added to that, you have a sense of loss about things in your past. Perhaps you can also say 'if only' or 'I wish' relating to past events which you cannot now change. Do you regret some of the past and wish you could change it? Is this true for you often or just occasionally?

Now consider that there is another way to live. You don't regret the past but see it as a springboard into what is happening now and will happen in the future. You choose constantly to appreciate everything around you, to love what is there, good and bad, and to accept there are reasons why you are where you are right now. You choose to seek out these reasons and to understand what they mean for you. This does not mean that you adopt an attitude of not caring and believing you should never have anything other than what you have. It means that you work towards your future, with complete and utter awareness and appreciation of what you have now.

In other words, you live for the present moment, whilst acknowledging a future ahead of you. This is in direct contrast to living for what you hope for in the future whilst hating the present. Can you see the difference? There is a lovely anonymous saying which sums this up:

The past is history
The future is a mystery
But right now is a gift
Which is why it's called the present.

Meditation is about returning constantly to a state of appreciation and awareness of everyone and everything. It seems very possible that it is our quest for material knowledge that has led us to forget our spiritual roots and why we are here on Earth.

Marvellous though modern technology is (and I for one wouldn't want to be without it), it has complicated our lives enormously. How much simpler it was when small groups of people lived in harmony in rural locations, working the land, and reaping its offerings. Of course, it was also hard work without hot water, central heating, convenience food and modern medication.

Yet nowadays, much as we enjoy our modern privileges, we do live in a constant swirl of activity, a lot of it highly pressured. We rush from checking our answerphones, to answering our mobiles, to logging on for email, to picking up faxes, to communicating and travelling at speed, dashing on and off planes, trains, buses, cars and bicycles, constantly struggling to keep up.

Surely, technological advancement was intended to simplify and improve our lives? Yet the truth is that it has complicated them in almost every way. No wonder meditation has been left behind. We have no time to appreciate what we have now because we are either trying to keep up with it all or too busy trying to create new technology which will end up pressurizing us even more!

Of course, this is painting the average Westerner's lot as being very difficult indeed and we all know there are many people who balance the excessive demands of modern life with a degree of relaxation and appreciation. It's also true to say that most of those people will have discovered a revitalizing, self-awareness tool such as meditation to enable this to happen in their lives.

So, the early stages of meditation involve appreciation and awareness of what is around us. That seems fairly straightforward and you will shortly learn simple techniques to enable you to do this. In fact, let's take a short break now and do a simple exercise to set you on your way.

Read through the exercise below and then pick up your chosen item of food and work your way through the awareness.

Food appreciation

Choose a simple food that you are happy to eat. It can be something as little as a single grape, a mint sweet or a sugar cube, it doesn't matter. Hold it in your hand and look at it.

Where has it come from? Is there a label that tells you? Is it from your country or elsewhere? What do you know about the area of its origin? What about the people there?

> Do you know anything about the manufacture of this item? Whatever the item, it or its ingredients had to originally grow somewhere. Even if it's a sweet, it contains ingredients that come from the earth, such as sugar from canes. Think about all the components that went into this item in your hand. Nature must have played a part somewhere, if it was grown. Rain and sun were important at one stage.
>
> What about the people who either picked this item or put it together or worked the machines that manufactured it? Who packaged this item and where did it go? Who put it on some form of transport? Who then carried it into the shop where you purchased it? How did you pay for it? How did you get it to where you are now?
>
> Consider the item in your hand. It actually has had quite a journey to make it to you. It was nurtured by natural forces at some stage, perhaps processed in some way, and has passed through many hands before ending up in yours. Now, say a silent 'thank you' to everyone who participated in this journey from raw state to finished product. Acknowledge that everything around you has gone through a similar journey. How does that make you think and feel?
>
> Now eat the item, slowly, with awareness and appreciation. Notice how you feel while eating it. Is it different from how you would have felt if you had simply popped it into your mouth without stopping to think about it? Make sure you take your time and eat it slowly.

Was that somewhat of a shock to you – to really stop and think about what was involved in that simple item in your hands? If it was a natural item, did you feel more drawn to eat it? If it was a processed item, did you feel less inclined to want to consume it? Can you see how complicated other items might be, if you were to consider them? Appreciation of everything is a far more powerful and all-encompassing act than you might first suppose. This exercise is an example of meditation as an everyday, vibrant part of living.

Meditation is also more than this. It's about going quietly within to work out more about yourself and others on a deeper level. This then opens up a wealth of benefits.

It means we can learn to accept ourselves exactly as we are. It means we can understand why we are where we are in life and what we might do to shift areas of our life that appear 'stuck'. Again, the simple exercises coming up will show you the way forward with this.

Meditation also means you can learn to accept others as they are. This is hard for most of us. We haven't naturally been taught to do this. For instance, if someone does something unpleasant to you, is it a natural reaction to want to understand why and to forgive that person? A part of you might feel you should respond that way, but your natural reflex action is more likely to be one of anger, injustice or hurt. You might want to retaliate and inflict some of that pain on them. This isn't because you are a 'bad' person; it's simply because you are reacting in a way that has been conditioned into you.

Meditation is about letting go of some of that conditioning and seeing everything in wider perspective. Letting go of long-established thought patterns can take time. You don't have to expand your thinking overnight. This can be a gradual, gentle process that carries you along in its wake, rather than a difficult lesson you try to force yourself to learn immediately.

Meditation was described earlier as 'deep reflection'. By becoming calm and silent and slowly withdrawing our senses from the world, we can reflect on anything and everything in a much more profound way. The deeper the reflection, the more we are likely to learn from it. The secret lies in how well we can learn to withdraw.

For example, think of trying to concentrate on some task, such as reading a good book. How difficult is it to concentrate if we are interrupted in various ways? Imagine the following scenario. You are sitting reading a book and you are really enjoying it. Then the phone rings and you have to stop to speak. You return to your book afterwards and continue reading. Then the doorbell goes and you answer it. Again, you return to your book. A little while later, someone bursts into the room, demanding your attention. You persuade them to leave and start reading again. Someone next door puts on loud music and distracts you. You try to focus again on your book. In the kitchen, someone starts to cook a mouth-watering meal. You find your attention diverted again. You realize you are hungry. Then you notice your mouth feels dry and you realize you are also thirsty. How much of your book have you actually absorbed and digested?

Without some discipline and focus, you run the risk of your meditations also being interrupted and disjointed. If they are, you won't be able to derive much benefit from them. The sad truth is that distractions are everywhere in life and it takes little effort to find them. Sometimes it feels almost impossible to get rid of them.

Meditation is a wonderful opportunity to work on your ability to focus and concentrate. It is possible to shut out distractions and irritations through learning to meditate. By putting on the answerphone, by locking the door into your room, by requesting not to be disturbed, by wearing ear plugs if need be, you could have chosen to concentrate more on your book. How much more would you have relaxed and been able to enjoy the book if you hadn't been interrupted?

The ability for you to sink into deeper states of relaxation and shut out your senses to what is around you is a large factor in determining your success in meditation. We'll be looking at ways of helping you to do this in the next two chapters.

Are you someone who finds silence unnerving? We have become so used to constant noise that shutting it out or eliminating it altogether can be unsettling. Do you always have the radio or some music on, either at home, at work or when you travel? Do you like having the television on, whether you are watching it or not? Are you used to the sounds of people talking constantly, of traffic outside your windows, or of a neighbour's dog barking frequently? Perhaps your washing machine is always going, or the computer is always turned on and buzzing quietly, or your refrigerator makes a constant humming sound. Maybe you are on a flight path of planes or near a railway track. Perhaps your neighbours are DIY enthusiasts and regularly disturb your peace, or someone nearby owns a motorcycle and is often revving it. Start to notice what sounds are around you constantly.

How often do you enjoy the natural sounds of nature around you? Are you aware of bird song? Can you hear the wind rustling in the trees? Are you near a body of water: can you hear waves lapping on a shore or the whooshing of a fast-flowing stream or brook? Are there any natural sounds that you can enjoy on a regular basis, either near your home or work place? If not, think about taking a trip to a park or the seaside and enjoying the peace that it affords.

Try switching off the radio, television or stereo system. Let yourself experience the silence. How does it make you feel? What else are you aware of when you shut off ancillary sounds? Does it make you think about certain things? Sometimes we actually want distracting sounds around us because we don't want to be quiet. We are afraid to sit still because we fear that we might end up thinking about lots of issues that we've been trying to push into the background.

In other words, we often use sounds as a means of covering up how we are really feeling. If you know that you do this, don't worry. Meditation will gently and gradually reveal to you that you needn't be afraid of any of those emotions and worries. It can teach you to let go and release the anxieties blocking your way forward. If you are someone who relishes silence and loves the feeling of peace that it affords you, then you are well on your way to enjoying meditation!

So what else does meditation entail? Let's have a recap. You've been shown that meditation is an ancient form of awareness that has existed since early man. You realize it is about appreciation and awareness of everyday life. Your experiment with a small item of food has already started you on that journey of discovery. You've also heard that meditation is the withdrawing of your senses and a 'going within' process that allows you to understand yourself and others better.

We can take it even further than that. We can say that meditation, when used at a profoundly deep level, is about the revelation of what 'life' really means. That is a serious statement and not to be taken lightly. This isn't to imply that everyone who reads this book will discover 'the meaning of life', but it is quite possible through regular meditation for you to receive extraordinary insights that will help your understanding of life as a whole.

This journey is personal to each individual: there is no single 'right' end result, because there isn't one definitive answer. Just as different religions have different belief systems, so every spiritual believer may come to their own private conclusions as to the purpose of life. No one person is right or wrong, because each individual's personal perception is valid and true for them. A major mistake would be to expect someone else to embrace your belief system.

One of the many joys of meditation is that it is utterly personal to you and no one else can totally share your experience. If you feel that you don't quite understand why you are alive, what your mission on Earth is, or whether there is indeed any purpose to your life or anyone else's, meditation is the means through which you may receive some answers. What is doubly wonderful about meditation is that it is absolutely free and can be practised entirely in your own time!

Let's start this process by looking at the first and most important factor in learning to meditate: breathing.

LEARNING TO BREATHE

You might find this title odd. Surely you already know how to breathe! It's something you've been doing quite successfully on your own since you were born, usually unconsciously. You know you can survive for a number of days without food and water, but breathing is the one undisputed constant you can't do without right up until the moment you die.

Yet how much do you know about your own breathing? You might acknowledge that it varies; sometimes it is shallow, such as when you're sleeping, and sometimes it is laboured and quite deep, such as when you exert yourself through some form of physical exercise. You might remember times when your breath seemed to catch in your throat, perhaps when you were scared, watching a horror film or when you were about to do something unnerving, such as give a talk to your class at school. If you've ever had an asthmatic attack or suffered from some type of breathing problem, then you know how frightening it can be when you have trouble breathing. If you have ever choked on something, you will also know what it feels like not to be able to catch your breath.

However, the majority of the time, we simply breathe in and out unconsciously and constantly, without ever stopping to think about it. Do you know what is physically happening to your body every time you breathe in and out? Have you any idea of the beauty and complexity of your breathing system?

Before we look at breathing in detail, you may want to know what it has to do with meditation. It is through awareness of our breathing that we access every meditative state. That seems a sweeping statement, doesn't it? It sounds too simple. How can something we do all the time possibly be the means through which we meditate? Since you breathe normally every day and up until now you probably haven't entered any meditative state every day, how can breathing accomplish this state of awareness?

The answer lies in the word 'awareness'. Of course, every human breathes every minute of every day, on average about 15 times per minute. However, how often are you aware of your breathing? How often do you notice each breath coming in and going out? The answer is probably almost never! So meditating is about awareness of the breath. Just as we discussed in the previous chapter about meditating being awareness and appreciation of everything, so awareness of your own breathing is the key to learning how to meditate.

The second part of this equation is *how* you breathe. Since most of us never pay any attention to how we breathe, most of us also don't breathe deeply and fully. Meditation is about learning how to breathe deeply into the lungs, enjoying every single in and out movement, rejoicing in the power and beauty of our own breathing system. This close observation of our own breath allows us to slip effortlessly into a deeper state of relaxation and thereby enjoy a true meditative state. The process really is as basic as that. However, learning how to truly observe your breath and to focus solely on that is not quite as easy as it first sounds.

The notion of our breathing being the means through which we access greater awareness is not remotely new. There are many ancient sayings confirming the belief that breathing is the key to all knowledge. In all ancient belief systems you will find references to breathing as being our true vital life force.

You have already been asked to consider a lot of abstract concepts relating to the spiritual and the meaning of life, so you can now take a welcome break and look at something purely physical and factual!

The Mechanics of Breathing

Let's start by finding out what happens to our physical body when we breathe. Have a look at the diagram of our breathing system opposite as you read this.

We take in air through either our mouth or nose. It is best to breathe through the nose. The reason is that the inside of our nose contains a wealth of thin but coarse hairs that act as a filter system, helping to stop unwanted substances penetrating our body's defences. The nose is also a good heater – it helps to warm the air as it travels down through our throat and into our lungs.

Have you noticed on a very cold wintry day how air breathed in through your mouth actually hurts as it goes down into your chest area? The reason is the air hasn't been warmed by your nose. The mouth isn't as efficient a heater, nor can it filter out unwanted particles. For the majority of exercises in this book, you will want to breathe through your nose, unless a cold or sinus problem makes this a physical impossibility.

So the air comes in, preferably through the nasal passages, and works its way down the throat through a tube (known as the trachea) and then finds its way into the lungs via two bronchii or tubes.

The lung area is a powerhouse of activity. The bronchii split off into a complex labyrinth of passages and tubes, called bronchioles. Each bronchiole ends in a tiny little sac that looks somewhat like a bunch of miniature grapes. These sacs are called alveoli and they are there to inflate and deflate with each breath we take in and then let out. That sounds fairly simple, doesn't it?

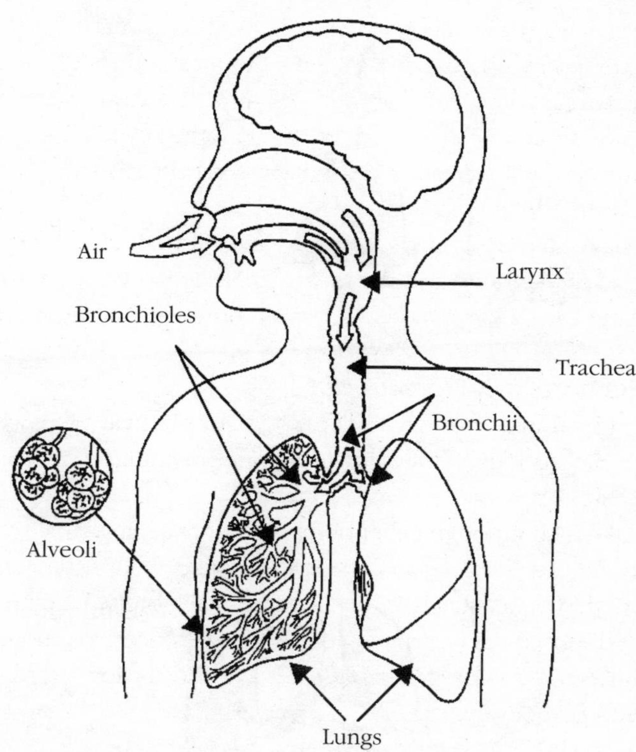

However, once you realize that each lung contains approximately *half a billion* sacs, you appreciate how incredibly complex is the work that takes place in our lungs. It's hard to make our concept of size shrink down to that minuscule a model, isn't it? The fact is that although we have millions of these sacs to inflate and deflate, the majority of us never learn to breathe deeply and fully enough to fill them. Over two-thirds of our alveoli or sacs are never used properly and, as a consequence, over time they lose their elasticity. In other words, most humans only use a third of their full breathing capacity. The other two-thirds is left unused and unwanted and eventually shrivels from lack of use.

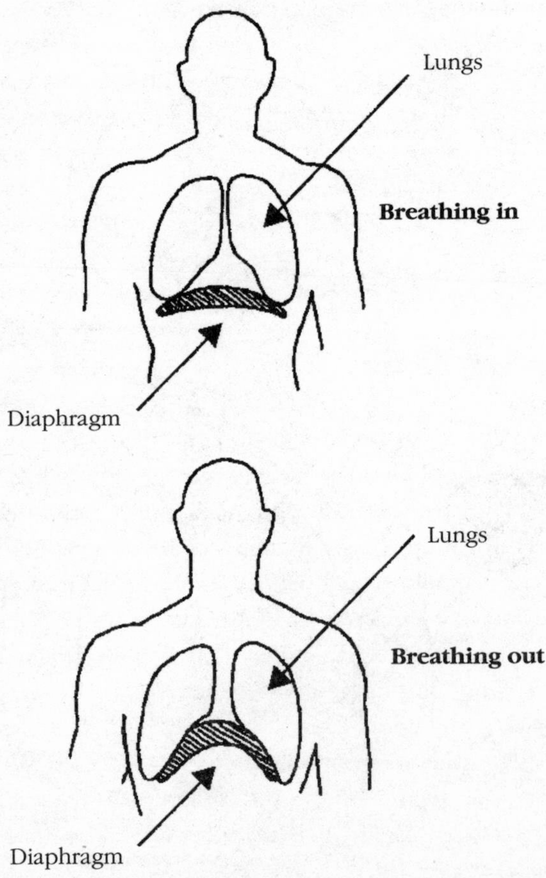

Do you notice that you are unconsciously breathing more deeply as you're reading this? Our brain starts to respond as we absorb the facts and we want to make an effort to rectify the situation.

The reason we don't tend to breathe properly is the result of an under-used muscle called the diaphragm. If you look at the image opposite, you'll see what this muscle does. It lies just at the bottom of the ribcage and just below the lungs and resembles the shape of a piece of pitta bread or an oblong pancake.

Every time we breathe in, the diaphragm flattens out, to allow the lungs to fill up with air. When we breathe out again, the diaphragm assumes the shape of an inverted 'U', helping to squeeze the last of the air out of our lungs. This process is then repeated every time we breathe in and out.

Most of us don't use the diaphragm properly. We tend to go around doing what is called shallow breathing. This means we fill the top part of our lungs with air, but not the bottom two thirds and thus, as the diaphragm is resting on the bottom of the lungs, it is never used fully. Certain professions are exceptions to this. Opera singers and athletes are people who have to learn to breathe deeply. Musicians who play wind instruments also come into this category, as do stage actors. Anyone can learn how to breathe deeply; it simply takes a little practice.

How Do You Breathe?

How do you know if you are breathing deeply or not? Below is a simple exercise to check what is happening with you.

Stand in front of a mirror that shows you the top half of your body, down to your waist. Take a deep breath in and notice if your shoulders lift as you do so. Can you see them rising? If you can, then you are doing what is called shallow breathing. You are filling the top half of your lungs but not the remainder. Don't worry if this is the case for you. Remember, most people do not use their full lung capacity.

Now is the opportunity for you to learn how to breathe deeply and to persuade your under-used diaphragm muscle to work properly. Look closely at the images of the fingers over the chest (see overleaf). Notice that one picture shows the fingertips just touching, the other shows the fingertips an inch or so apart. Now read through the following exercise:

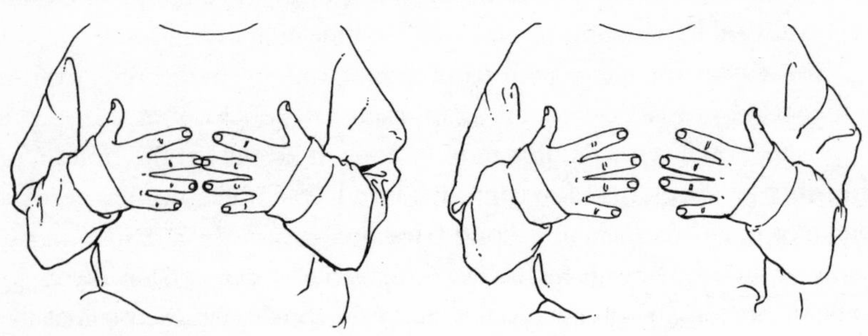

Testing your diaphragm

Stand in front of your mirror. Place your hands over the lower part of your ribcage so that your middle fingers are just touching. Now take a good, deep breath in. Let your ribcage slowly and comfortably expand.

Have your fingertips moved apart just a little? If they have, you are learning to breathe deeply. If they haven't, breathe out and then take a breath in again, but this time watch your shoulders and upper chest. Are they rising again? If so, remember that you are breathing only into the top of your lungs and not further down.

Focus on your lower ribcage again. Don't force your breath but simply imagine all the air coming in and going down into the lower part of your lungs. Let your ribcage expand outward. Are your fingertips moving just a little bit apart now?

Practise for a few minutes, but if you feel dizzy, stop. If you aren't used to breathing deeply, you may feel a little light-headed for a minute. Also, the process of trying too hard can be a strain! Return to this exercise from time to time to see how your diaphragm muscle is progressing.

Don't feel concerned if your fingertips are staying resolutely close together. Remember that all of your life has probably been spent breathing in this shallow fashion. It takes some time for your diaphragm muscle to wake up and realize it has some work to do. After all, you wouldn't suddenly expect yourself to be able to lift heavy weights without training, would you? Likewise you need to give your diaphragm muscle some time and gentle exercise to strengthen it.

Strengthening the Diaphragm

Sometimes just focusing on your fingertips can seem a discouraging business, as no matter how hard you focus the ribcage doesn't seem to want to expand any distance. There are various techniques you can use to help deepen your breathing. Several exercises are detailed below and you might want to practise these on a regular basis for a number of weeks. But remember, if you start to feel dizzy, stop. Resume your normal breathing and don't return to the exercise for at least fifteen minutes.

These exercises basically use a thought process to allow you to breathe fully without any effort. Our mind or imagination can accomplish extraordinary tasks that often defy logical thought. You probably notice this when day dreaming. Some people can simply close their eyes and effortlessly transport themselves somewhere else, even smelling the scents and being aware of a different atmosphere. Even people who tend to apply logical reasoning to most aspects of their lives and are generally sceptical about spiritual matters, would acknowledge that losing one's self in a day-dream can be wonderfully pleasurable and very relaxing. Try the exercise below.

Stomach breathing

> Sit down in a comfortable upright chair, close your eyes and focus on your breathing. Don't try to do anything with the breath, just observe it coming in and going out. You will notice some breaths are naturally shorter than others, some seem longer. Don't try to force your breathing into any regular pattern. Just enjoy observing it.
>
> Now we're going to play a game. Next time you breathe in, imagine that your lungs are actually down in your stomach. You know that they aren't, that they rest under your ribcage, but, just for fun, let's pretend they are under your navel. Enjoy the sensation of the breath going all the way down into your stomach. Remember not to force it, just let

the warm air float all the way down to your stomach area. Follow the path of the breath back up again, from your stomach, all the way up and out through your nose again. Notice how much warmer the out breath is after the inside of your body has warmed it. Keep repeating this process for a few minutes.

Remember you are not trying to breathe deeply during this, you are simply redirecting your breath to another area of your body. Don't force anything. Let the air come and go naturally and easily but keep focusing on the thought that your lungs are in your stomach.

After a few minutes, take the focus away from your stomach and let your breathing return to its natural, shallow state. Open your eyes and focus on some object in the room. Give yourself a moment before you stand up or you may feel dizzy.

Many people find this exercise quite liberating. It breaks with the conventional way of teaching breathing, and by concentrating on something you know isn't true, it becomes an enjoyable game rather than a difficult task to focus on. Make sure you give yourself a break of at least fifteen minutes before you try the next exercise.

Balloon breathing

Sit in a comfortable upright chair and close your eyes. Start to focus on your breathing but do not direct it in any way. Let your breath come and go naturally without forcing it. Enjoy the freedom of observing your breath without trying to control it.

Now imagine that your lungs have ten little balloons inside them, five in each lung. They are tough balloons with thick skins that won't burst. The next time you breathe in, notice how many of the balloons are being blown up. Are they all inflating? If they are, increase the number of balloons in each lung. Make it ten or twenty, whatever number seems right for you. If only a few of the balloons have been half-inflated, then reduce the number to three in each lung, or whatever feels manageable. You do not want to make this exercise hard work; it should be enjoyable. Make sure the number of balloons is right for you before continuing.

Now you want to help blow up all your balloons. Take a deep comfortable breath in and notice how the balloons fill up, easily and effortlessly. Breathe out and watch them deflate again. Does it feel as though they are all working properly? Keep focusing on the balloons in your lungs and keep expanding your breath, easily and effortlessly, until you feel all the balloons inflating and deflating comfortably with each in and out breath. If it becomes too easy, gradually increase the number of balloons and work with that. You may choose to make all the balloons much smaller in size but then add to the numbers. (Remember you truly have over half a billion minuscule sacs in each lung!) Keep enjoying the process.

Then let the image of the balloons fade. Return to your normal, shallow breathing. After a few minutes, open your eyes and focus on an item in the room. Make sure you have returned fully to normal breathing before you stand up.

This exercise is another useful way of playing with your breathing and not trying to force yourself to breathe more deeply. The moment we focus on something in an intense, uncomfortable way, we create all sorts of blocks to breathing deeply and fully. Games are a good way to exercise the breath! Again, give yourself another gap of fifteen minutes before you try the next exercise.

Ribcage breathing

Sit in a comfortable upright chair and close your eyes. Start off by watching your breath as it goes in and out. Don't force it in any way, just let it come and go naturally. Sometimes it's shallow, sometimes the breath seems longer and deeper. Let it be and simply observe how it feels. Take your time over this.

Now you want to think about your ribcage. Notice on the next breath in, how the ribcage slowly expands outwards. Notice as you breathe out, how the ribcage contracts back into the body again. Keep observing this movement of the ribcage without trying to alter it in any way.

Next, you want to imagine that every time your ribcage expands, it is actually reaching further and further outwards. Keep your eyes closed as you do this. You know your ribcage isn't really extending out into the room, but play with your imagination and feel as though it is. Gradually have it expand, without trying to make it happen. Know your thoughts are simply having fun. There is no effort involved. Even have your ribcage touch the walls of the room you are in! Imagine your ribcage as soft and free flowing. See it billowing out around the room, effortlessly expanding and contracting. Notice how it seems to have a life of its own, easy and unrestricted. Play with this new freedom for a while.

When you are ready, return to your normal breathing, and as you do so let the image of your expanding ribcage fade. If you have really lost yourself in this game and want to come back to reality, simply place your hands either side of your ribcage. Recognize how solid and real your ribcage is now. Open your eyes and gaze at an object in the room. Wait a few minutes before standing up.

These are all fun exercises that you can return to from time to time, even after you have attained the ability to breathe more deeply. Periodically, return to the diaphragm awareness and place your hands over your ribcage. Monitor how deep your breath is gradually becoming. Notice which of the above exercises are more effective for you than others. Keep encouraging that diaphragm muscle to work!

You will be amazed at how much more there is to learn about breathing and your own individual relationship with your breathing system. We will keep returning to the importance of the breath and discovering new methods of working with it. Once you start to discover the joys of breathing deeply, it becomes a pleasure to let yourself slip into that relaxed state, and it becomes something you can do easily and effortlessly.

Awareness of Breathing

However, it's important to realize that, no matter how proficient someone might be at deep breathing, no one spends their entire life breathing deeply. We use the deepening and expanding of our breath to achieve greater awareness but we use this only at specific times, such as during meditation. Trying to breathe deeply on a constant basis would only leave you feeling very light-headed and disjointed.

What can be a useful adjunct to everyday living, and an invaluable way of releasing tension, is using deep breathing when you feel pressured or under stress. Just as prolonged deep breathing is a means through which we access higher awareness, so stopping occasionally to take a few deep breaths can benefit us enormously and release pent-up emotions or stresses.

What makes you feel stressed? Everyone gives a different answer to this. You might be someone who finds being in the company of other people quite stressful; someone else will find being alone more unsettling. Perhaps you like working to tight deadlines and having lots of projects on the go at once; in others that induces panic and anxiety. Some people find having to give a talk to a group of people very daunting; others will say it's the thought of taking off in a plane or being in close proximity to a spider or snake that makes their heart thump! Factors that induce stress are personal and sometimes hard to explain. The reasons for phobias and panic attacks sometimes defy logical explanation.

Whenever we are confronted by something we don't like or which makes us nervous or upset, the first thing that usually happens is that we stop breathing for a moment. When we breathe again, we may take one deep breath to compensate for the lack of oxygen for a moment, but we then tend immediately to revert back to the shallow breathing.

Whatever your personal nightmare, or whichever circumstances make you feel stressed and anxious, there is one course of action that will always improve the situation – breathing deeply. This applies irrespective of your state, the reason for it or the degree of your emotional or physical response.

This is a useful tip for you to employ at any time during your day when you feel stressed. Before you go into an important meeting, before you greet a difficult relative or colleague, just as you are about to snap at someone or burst into tears, when you feel at the end of your tether and ready to scream – whatever your difficult scenario, simply STOP.

Sit or stand still for a brief moment and let yourself breathe. It takes only a few seconds. Use one of your quick techniques of imagining your lungs in your stomach, or the balloons in your lungs or whatever works for you, and take several deep breaths. It is impossible to feel quite the same way afterwards if you stop and do this. It doesn't mean this is a foolproof quick cure that will always relieve your problem, but it is a first step towards a solution. Sometimes just stopping to breathe is enough to defuse a potentially awkward situation.

The physical action of stopping and standing in silence and stillness for a moment is important. So often, the actions which we later regret are done on the spur of the moment in a flash of anger, hurt, spite or frustration.

When you stop to breathe, it is impossible to do something without thinking. The very act of stopping to breathe properly slows you down and forces you to think clearly for a moment. That moment is a very precious period of time. It forces you to be aware for that moment. Bringing you back into yourself and looking at what is really happening now is a wonderful way to stop yourself from saying and doing something you may regret later.

If you think this all sounds too easy, try it yourself and see what happens to you. Keep a little diary and note what happened when you didn't stop to breathe and what happened on the occasions when you took a moment to stop and focus on your breathing. Do remember you have to stop fully and breathe deeply. It's no good just taking a second and gulping one breath in and out quickly. Stop. Focus. Breathe. Breathe again. Make sure you are physically still while you do this.

An interesting question to ask ourselves is whether we were born this way. From the time we were born did we always shallow breathe and never know the joy of deep breathing? No, that is not the case. We were born with a natural, unconscious ability to breathe deeply when we needed it. Somewhere along the way we lost the technique. One theory is that all the traumatic events we have experienced teach us to stop breathing deeply and fully. We were born knowing how to breathe deeply, but most of us lose our capacity as we get older.

If you want proof of how you were as a child, watch another young child and see what they do. Have you noticed that if a toddler falls over and hurts himself, before he actually starts crying, he will take the most enormous, long, deep breath? The child instinctively knows he is going to need good lung power to express his emotions; he prepares for it without having to think. If you observe newborn babies preparing to wail because they're hungry or need a nappy change, again you will see their tiny lungs taking in a deep gulp of air, ready to express themselves fully. You can see their tiny ribcages expanding, easily and effortlessly.

The Fear Factor

So what is the process that stops us eventually from breathing deeply when we need to? As children we expressed ourselves freely. What happened? What went wrong? It's simple really: We were introduced to the concepts of fear and danger. Once these new emotions were introduced, we started to go into shallow breathing. We forgot how to express ourselves clearly and easily. Our breath forgot how to express itself as well. As we grow up we learn to hold back our emotions and responses. Each time we do that, we move further down the path of forgetting how to breathe deeply.

Think back to when you were a few years old. Can you remember some of the dangers our well-intentioned parents/guardians constantly taught us to be afraid of? There were so many: fire, electricity, deep water, the oven, hot drinks, knives, every household substance imaginable, roads, cars, buses, trains, strangers, bees, dogs, wild animals. If you think of the list of things we were told to be careful of and with, it stretches into hundreds of items. Each time we were warned, our little bodies sensed something difficult or dangerous. Chances are that each time our little hearts stopped beating for a moment and we temporarily forgot how to breathe deeply. We had a lot of learning to do during our early days and no doubt there were times when our breathing systems choked with fear of the unknown.

It didn't stop as we got older, either! As teenagers we were warned about other dangers: wanting to learn to drive, wanting to go out alone, the opposite sex, the dangers of sexual diseases, the necessity of working hard and doing something with your life. Again, the list is extensive.

As adults we faced further challenges: looking for a partner, finding a rewarding job, making more money, considering whether to have children, working out how best to support your family, etc, etc.

If you consider that through all these encounters, we were constantly experiencing fresh moments of anxiety and stress, it is no wonder that somewhere along the road, we lost our ability to breathe deeply.

The positive factor here is that we can go back and remind ourselves how to do it. It's good to know that it isn't something new that we have never done – it is purely an action we are relearning from our childhood. If you doubt that you have ever breathed deeply and effortlessly, do spend some time observing newborn babies and young children. They really are shining examples of free and easy breathing. It's wonderful to watch the ease with which they switch into deep breathing when it's needed.

Now you have had a good introduction to breathing and what it really entails, we're going to start looking at how you can incorporate short meditations into every aspect of your daily life and the benefits this can bring you.

MINI MEDITATIONS FOR EVERY DAY

We are now going to delve into your everyday life and see how daily, short meditations can benefit you in a practical and enriching manner. Mini meditations are quite quick, don't involve a lot of deep concentration and the amazing results they offer can give you just the boost you need to encourage you into the deeper realms of more prolonged meditations.

As always, with all the exercises in this book, taking a moment to breathe freely and deeply is important every single time you prepare for a meditation, whether it is for a very brief, mini meditation or a meditation lasting for an hour or more. Your breathing is always the key to the door of possibility.

So what are mini meditations? A good way to describe them would be as a moment of appreciation and awareness. They can encompass anything, from an item of food (as, for example, the Food Appreciation exercise we did in the first chapter) to an inanimate object, an animal or a person. A mini meditation can relate to an action you are taking, even something as simple as walking down the road. It can be done as you wash the dishes, do some shopping or sit at your desk at work. A mini meditation is a short period of time that you use to reflect upon something. That something does not have to be deeply profound. You can find a purpose, meaning and good use in everything in daily life, if you want to.

Let's start with something many people find a chore: getting up in the morning. Do you find this difficult? Perhaps you are one of those rare people who wake up each morning full of enthusiasm and energy for the day ahead, feeling cheerful and contented as you bounce out of bed. If you are like this, think of an occasion when you haven't felt that way.

If, however, motivating yourself to get up is hard work, take a few minutes after waking to work through the following:

Waking up

Lie still in bed for a moment. Resist the urge to shut off to everything and take a few deep breaths. Tell yourself you will not sleep. Instead of focusing on what you don't like about getting up, what can you find to appreciate about this moment? Here are a few suggestions (not all of them may apply to you but consider those which do):

- You have spent the night in a comfortable bed
- You can get yourself out of bed without help
- You have had a rejuvenating sleep
- You are protected under a roofed property
- You live in a prosperous country, free from war
- You have a job to go to
- You have friends and family who love you
- You have your health
- Something wonderful may happen to you today
- You have water to wash in and food to eat
- You have clothes to put on your body
- You are alive

Choose just one statement relevant to you and let your thoughts focus on it. Remember to keep breathing deeply and easily. What happens when you focus on one of these aspects of your life? Do you find yourself floating back into the negative with 'Ah, yes, but…'? Pull your thoughts back and focus on what you can appreciate now. Whatever statement you have chosen, let it expand. What does this really mean to you? What is good about your life right now?

When you are ready, give silent thanks for what you have got and then get out of bed, resolving to allow yourself brief moments of awareness when you will appreciate what is in your life right now.

Did you find that quite difficult? Unfortunately, most of us are programmed to remember and focus on the parts of our life that don't work. We find it unnatural and quite a struggle to refocus our thoughts on what we actually like and can appreciate. Our tendency is to ignore what is helpful and positive in our lives. Although it takes some practice, it gradually becomes easier to acknowledge those areas that do work and feel right.

Good Health

Think of when you have been ill, say with a bad dose of the flu. Can you remember how dreadful you felt and the incredible relief when you started to feel better and memory of the illness faded? That time when you realized you were feeling better was quite wonderful, wasn't it? Can you remember the enormous relief and sense of appreciation you felt when you knew you were improving? Try to recall that sensation of overwhelming gratitude and pleasure. For that moment, could you not tangibly experience how all of you felt alive, grateful and content?

However, once you recovered, did you have any lingering sense of appreciation for your good health? Did you go around daily feeling good about the fact that you were healthy and full of energy? Perhaps you did for a day, maybe half a day. Then your life no doubt returned to its usual routine and you forgot to appreciate your current state of health. That is, until you fell ill again and the cycle started to repeat itself!

What might our lives be like if we spent all of our time living in a state of appreciation for what we had, constantly remembering all the positive qualities around and in us? What if every day we focused on what was good and took the time to appreciate everyone and everything around us? For example, how do you think you would feel if you spent the majority of your time acknowledging your good health and were aware of the pleasure and peace stemming from it?

Your first response might be 'But that is unrealistic. No one can be content all of the time.' It's true that human beings are a complex mass of emotions and we need contrasts in our lives to be able to compare and thereby appreciate our circumstances.

Being ill is not a joyous experience and no one would consciously choose that state. How can one possibly embrace something like that? However, feeling ill is a stage that is usually followed by the process of feeling good again. If, when we are unwell, we acknowledge our state as being merely transient and there to teach us something positive about health, then we won't view illness with the same dread and impatience. By taking the time, when you're unwell, to quietly close your eyes, breathe, and ponder on your current illness, you will probably find insights and awareness coming to you. You may be able to see why you have fallen ill and what you have to learn from it. You will then move on to enjoy the grateful process of feeling healthy again, which enables you to truly appreciate the whole cycle.

Re-programming Negative Thought Processes

Of course, it isn't always that easy. We are much more conditioned to focus on what we don't like, rather than what we do. We get impatient and angry and frustrated. It takes some effort to re-programme our thought processes.

Let's delve further into why we should bother to do this. What real benefit is there in appreciating what we have around us on a daily basis and becoming more aware of what is there for us? You need to know, if you're proposing to invest some time in these mini meditations, what all this will give you. The answer is that it can transform an unfulfilling, confused and unsatisfying life into one that is rich with joy, understanding, purpose and love. That's fairly comprehensive, isn't it? So what will it take to kick start this process?

It takes just one step initially. Simply take the time to stop, breathe and reflect. This means really stop, really breathe deeply and really reflect, not do it half-heartedly and hurriedly. Do it fully, completely. By re-programming your negative thoughts, you start to open yourself to the possibility of what is out there for you. All the knowledge and awareness you will ever need is out there waiting for you to tap into it. All that prevents anyone from learning about themselves and life is their inability to slow down, stop, breathe, and see it. Truly, the information is out there already; we simply aren't accessing it most of the time. Meditation is the process through which we can obtain this knowledge.

The first stage of meditation is to put yourself into a receptive frame of mind, so that insights and awareness can come into your conscious thought and you can appreciate them. Unless you open yourself to the possibility of everything, you won't be able to meditate. That is why these mini meditations are your first step into awareness.

It can start with something as simple as a smile! How can this be true? Think of it this way. How often do you smile each day? How often do you offer a smile to others on a regular basis? With modern pressures and stresses, we are more likely to frown or complain or vent anger than we are to smile. Yet did you know that smiling relaxes about a hundred muscles in your face? Many of us hold so much tension there throughout each day – a smile will release that tension. Also, there is now proof that breaking into a smile actually sets off certain chemical reactions in our body that tells our brain we are happy. In other words, the simple process of smiling can make us feel better.

You also know that if you offer a genuine smile to someone, it is hard for the other person not to respond with a smile in exchange. How does the world and your perception of reality around you change when you smile? Practise the next experiment.

Comparing emotions

Think of a difficult or stressful situation. Let yourself feel the emotion for a moment. Notice you will not want to smile! Give yourself a moment or two to worry and feel gloomy about what is happening. Look around the room you are in and notice things. Are they depressing, negative things you pick up on? Really allow yourself to feel the stress. Notice how it affects your body, your breathing, your mental and emotional state. Now choose to let it go. Let the worrying issue recede. Feel it fade into the distance. Take a moment to accomplish this. Notice if you find it hard to let go.

Now, think of something that makes you happy, something that makes you feel really good. Smile. Let it become a big, generous smile. How does it make you feel? Notice the changes you feel inside: physically, emotionally and mentally. Allow yourself to feel happy and appreciative of what you have. Look around you, wherever you are right now. How does everything seem? Can you suddenly see something nice that you hadn't appreciated before? Let yourself rest in that state for a moment. Keep smiling. You may have the feeling of well-being increase and swell inside and around you. Enjoy the moment. When you're ready, stop smiling, but retain that feeling of comfort and happiness you discovered inside.

Which feelings would you prefer to carry around each day? That simple exercise proves the point. What we choose to feel creates our reality and we then live by that emotion. If we choose to see so many moments of the day as difficult, depressing or as a chore, to be got through so we can enjoy something else coming up later, then we are not aware of our present moment and enjoying it to the full.

Remembering to smile often is really a mini meditation in itself. Remember how we said that babies naturally knew how to breathe deeply when required? Babies also know how to smile with ease. The slightest thing can set them giggling, full of joy. By remembering to smile more often, we are simply relearning what we did naturally as a child: enjoying every moment to the full. Some adults have retained their natural ability to smile constantly. They are usually the people we like to be around. Now you can learn how to retrain your own thoughts so that you naturally want to smile frequently. What does it take to make you smile? Try the exercise below.

Smiling

Close your eyes and focus on your breathing. Let yourself sink into a comfortably relaxed state. Take your time.

Now start to think about what makes you smile. Focus on the image of yourself smiling. Consider what you thought about in the earlier exercise when you compared emotions. What made you smile then? Now think about all the occasions in your life when you couldn't help beaming.

It may be when you accomplished something as a child and were praised. What about the first time you rode a two-wheel bike unaided, the first time you tied your own shoelaces, when you started to read? What moments can you remember from your childhood when you did something wonderful and felt terrific? Feel yourself smile as you remember.

Think about your transition from childhood into adulthood, usually a difficult time for most people. What were the good points? Can you remember learning to drive? What about graduating from school or university? What about receiving your first pay packet from a part-time job? Enjoy smiling as you remember.

What makes you feel good now as an adult? How did you feel when you got your first full-time job? Think about falling in love for the first time. Think of a hobby you love. Think about being with your partner. Perhaps you have happy memories of your wedding day or the birth of your child. Really make yourself think about all the aspects of your life which make you happy.

Widen your thoughts now. What else do you love? Do you enjoy walking in a park or by the sea? What effect does observing wildlife have on you? What about seeing a rainbow? How about watching a dog playing in a field? What areas in the world do you find inspirational? Where do you love being and what makes you feel wonderful? Does soaking in a hot bath make you feel good? Do you enjoy massage? What about sexual pleasures? Think of your family and friends who mean a great deal to you. Who is your favourite person to be with and how do they make you feel? Let your mind spiral onto every happy moment you can think of. Enjoy every moment.

Now, when you feel you have remembered every possible moment that makes you smile, think about what you could have around you as a physical reminder, to help you remember some of these wonderful moments. Are there any photos you have which capture that happiness? What about any objects that mean something to you? Have you collected a beautiful pebble or leaf from a memorable walk? Perhaps an article of clothing reminds you of something happy. Scents are also very evocative. Is there a perfume that makes you smile? Perhaps a certain bath oil or soap brings back good memories. A certain colour may be important to you. What do you have in that shade around you? You could buy a cushion cover or a piece of blotting paper for your desk in that colour, or even a pen or notebook.

Do you have a favourite saying that you find inspirational? Write it out and keep it near you. Let your thoughts widen to encompass anything that serves as a happy reminder. Resolve to put these special objects in a place where you will see them often, to remind you to smile. A good place is by your bed when you wake up in the morning, by the bathroom mirror, or kitchen sink, or on your desk or the top of the television. Put a happy photo or inspirational saying in your wallet, bag or briefcase. Put things where you can always see them.

When you are ready, refocus your thoughts on where you are right now. Remember which room you are in, what time of the day it is, what you have to get up and do next. Open your eyes and focus on an object. Give yourself a good few moments to remember your present reality – but remember to keep that feeling of a smile in you as you get up and continue your day!

Remember to follow through with whatever you thought about during this exercise. Go and pull out that old photo album, find that comfortable sweater you have pushed to the back of your wardrobe and place it somewhere more prominent, or even wear it sometimes! You can even walk around your home or work-space and look at what there makes you smile. Are there lots of areas you think you could improve, without having to spend a fortune? Notice what makes you feel good and positive, and start to make those small changes.

Being in the Now

So smiling is a great start but we want to add more to this realm of mini meditations. We want to look at what is around us on a daily basis and how we can become aware of everything in a new and more nurturing way. We want to learn to experience each moment for what it is and not think of it in context of what it might have been or what it could be in the future. Most of us have trouble with this concept of enjoying each moment as it exists. We tend to live more with our thoughts in the future, or sometimes in the past, if we feel either state is preferable to the present. We want to learn how to live 'in the now' and enjoy it.

Let's look into that phrase a little more to understand it better. Being 'in the now' relates back to that earlier discussion we had about concentrating on what is happening now and not worrying about either the past or the future. We referred to this in the context of how 'unspiritual' much of Western society has become through focusing purely on technological rather than personal progress.

A lot of people don't really understand the concept of enjoying every moment as it comes along, because they are naturally so geared up to believing life is about planning for the future and thinking ahead. Perhaps it is to do with affording another child or a bigger house or planning for retirement. Everything becomes about the future.

Yet the future doesn't exist. It hasn't happened yet. You have no guarantees about what will happen to you. You also can't change anything in your past. The only thing that is absolutely definite and real is this actual moment. Of course each moment is changing. What you were reading a few seconds ago happened in a moment that has now gone forever. The only moment that is real is this moment and then that changes immediately into the past. If we don't fully live each moment as it comes, how can we possibly be ready for the future?

What positive changes might we be able to make if we clearly see everything around us now and take full advantage of it to shape our future? Surely it is only if we understand why we are where we are at this present moment that we are then able to understand what we might accomplish in the future and the path we could take to get there?

So, if we can obtain greater awareness and understand better how to find our intended path in life through being 'in the now', how can we achieve that state? We can do it by constantly undertaking mini meditations that remind us who and what we are and how valuable everything we do is, no matter how slight or trivial it may seem.

Let's continue looking at the routine daily tasks that most of us carry out and see how we can give them more meaning and purpose.

We've already looked at how getting up first thing in the morning can be transformed into a pleasant action. What other things do you do that you would classify as a chore, without any joy attached to them? Most people would agree that house-cleaning, clothes-washing and shopping are boring. So how can we transform them?

We'll take one mundane task – shopping – which you can then adapt to suit other actions in your daily life.

Shopping

Start your awareness about shopping by carefully considering what you put on your shopping list. Do you really need all the items you are writing down? What are you purchasing through habit, or through conforming to what modern society tells you that you ought to have? How much do you buy through greed rather than need? How much of the food listed is actually healthy and will fill you with energy and nurture your body? What might you add that will enhance your life rather than complicate it or reduce its quality in some way? Give yourself time to make these assessments. Notice how much your shopping list has changed by the time you finish it.

Now consider where you want to shop. What businesses would you like to support? Whose ethics do you value? You want to walk into that store with a smile on your face, happy to give custom to the people involved. If you don't know what is right for you, then start to experiment. Go into different places and notice how they operate. Find out their policies and think about what really matters to you.

Do you want to avoid genetically modified food? Do you prefer organic produce? Do you care that the food you eat is ethically produced without 'slave' labour or unfair regulations? Do you even know where most of the food you eat comes from? Which countries would you like to support by buying their produce? What ingredients are harmful in the detergents we use today? How do some of these chemicals affect the environment? What can you do about this? What can you buy to reduce these polluting effects?

These are all very searching questions, and you may feel daunted by some of them. How can you find the answers to all these questions? The answer lies very much in being 'in the now'. There is a lot of information available on most of the issues I've mentioned, if you simply go through your day, mindfully noticing what is there for you. Many stores now proudly state they do not use genetically modified ingredients or that their own brand of tuna fish is caught without the needless killing of dolphins. There is so much people and institutions are trying to tell us, but often we walk around as though blinkered, not noticing anything other than our own immediate selfish needs. Now is the opportunity for you to start changing.

You may also be thinking that you simply do not have time for all this extra 'work'! Remember it doesn't have to happen all at once. Make small changes. Decide on just one action to begin with, such as not buying detergents containing harmful chemicals that pollute our fragile environment. Increase your awareness as and when it feels right for you.

Notice, when you do your shopping, how differently you feel. Realize that you can acknowledge and bless the people involved in the chain of actions that brings you the products you buy, starting with those who oversaw the creation of the raw ingredient right the way through to the person who sold you the final product.

Also be aware of the affluence of the country you live in, compared with so many countries in the developing world. As you walk around the different shops and acknowledge the wealth of produce available to you, remember others who have so little or virtually nothing.Take the time to send them a prayer of love and support. Allow their suffering to enable you to appreciate what you have. If this process also makes you want to support charities who help those less fortunate countries, that is another positive step you can take if and when the time feels right for you. Awareness of others is the starting point of compassion. Without initial awareness, we will not act.

Turn the simple act of shopping into a completely aware 'meditation' of seeing what is happening here and now and using it to reassess how you want to live your life. And remember to smile!

Although the above exercise is called Shopping, it really can be adapted to suit any action you undertake. It is purely how you approach the task ahead of you that determines what you will get out of it. Every single thing becomes meaningful, important and valuable when you stop to think about it. Can you see how washing clothes might become a meditative act? How about meditating as you clean the house or plough through a routine job at work?

As you walk down the street, can you see the opportunity for appreciating everything around you? This applies even if you live in a deprived area. There is always something to appreciate, even if it is the cracks in a pavement through which a beautiful wildflower is poking its head. A paint-peeling tower block can still be beautiful when you stop to remember that many people don't even have a roof over their heads, let alone a watertight building in which they can live. There is nothing in life that can not be transformed into a positive action or emotion, if your attitude is that you are seeking true awareness of a situation.

As an ultimate test, how about being aware of emptying your own rubbish? This is a task few people would say they enjoy. It is smelly and disagreeable and we do it as quickly as possible, often holding our nose in disgust and tensing our muscles as we do so. Is it even remotely possible to enjoy this job? It seems a tall order. So try the exercise below next time you empty the rubbish.

Rubbish awareness

For one week, before you throw anything into your bin, think about what you are planning to put into it. How much of what you throw away could be recycled? Do you know what is available in your area to be put to good use? Most of us know about the obvious – glass, paper, cardboard and tin – but there are others. Many charities appreciate old clothes, shoes and blankets; even aluminium foil may be useful.

Have you ever thought about starting a compost heap with your vegetable and fruit parings? They do not have to take the space, time and money many people claim they do. You can end up with wonderful compost that enriches your soil and helps everything to grow. If you don't have a garden, how about offering the parings to a neighbour? Would they appreciate them? Make sure you are helpful if they appreciate your offer. Check what they want and don't want.

Do you need to use all the plastic products you have at present? Can you refill certain bottles or cut down on items that aren't strictly necessary? How much of your waste is from processed products and foods that aren't providing you with the nutrients you need? Can you find the time to eat more fresh vegetables and fruit, and not rely so much on processed products? How will this reduce the amount of rubbish you produce?

With every item you prepare to throw away, be aware of any use it might be put to. Can an empty margarine carton become a container for something? Is that houseplant really dead or could you take a cutting and have it regrow into a strong, new plant?

When you have assessed that everything in your bin really needs to be there, notice how much smaller the amount has become as a result of your awareness. As you put the rubbish outside for collection, think about the people who dispose of it. Acknowledge that they are providing you with a useful service and silently thank them for their work. Realize also that you are offering them employment by having even a small amount of rubbish. Think about the fact that a great deal of pure rubbish can be recycled to provide compost for future growth.

Notice how the awareness of what is rubbish and what isn't makes you rethink your lifestyle, how you eat and how you live. Apart from helping you to re-assess your own needs, it is enabling you to shift your perception of the whole planet.

You may find this exercise demanding at first. It sounds like a lot of extra work, doesn't it? Recycling different things, taking various items to different areas, asking people if things are of any use. It is only more work initially; once you establish a routine, it becomes as easy and normal as any daily task.

The distinct advantage you now have is that you are acting with awareness and a clear conscience. If you know that you are creating the minimum of waste, you know that you are doing your bit to help the planet and reduce our increasing pollution problem. One of the benefits of acting with awareness is that it affords you a greater sense of inner peace through acting responsibly and carefully.

Why do you think our planet is becoming so polluted and we are doing such irreparable damage to so much of it? Greatly increased population is one of the major factors, but there is one other important consideration. Ignorance.

Many people truly don't realize what damage they do every time they take certain action. They don't stop to think that detergents, sprays, disposable nappies, and careless rubbish create enormous pollution and threaten our long-term survival on Earth. Why do they not stop to think? Because they have never been taught to stop, breathe deeply and consider what they are doing. They are too busy trying to cope with their own demanding and stressful lives. It doesn't occur to most people that they perpetuate their own stress and anxiety by not stopping to breathe and think. It is a vicious cycle that we in the West are only gradually coming to acknowledge and to do something about. You are now starting on your own path of awareness through reading this book.

If you feel your own life is too hectic at the moment to allow you to make all of the changes that have been suggested in this chapter, don't castigate yourself. Choose just one simple act which you know you can fit into your schedule and know that you are doing something to improve matters. You can always do more as and when you find the time. In the meantime, continue practising awareness of everything around you on a daily basis. The more you become aware of, the more you realize what there is to be aware about!

One of the realities you will face, even after you have repeated the exercises in this chapter a number of times and started to develop your own personal state of awareness and appreciation, is that being aware isn't necessarily enough to make shifts in the bigger areas of your life. No matter how much you may be able to appreciate the positive aspects of life around you, still there will be areas where you feel stuck. Appreciating and being aware of what you already have, doesn't necessarily help you with other problems.

Mini meditations are just the start of understanding meditation and what it can do. Now we are ready to look at deeper and more prolonged forms of meditating. Before we start to practise, there are a few things we need to do to prepare ourselves for the next stage of our journey.

GETTING READY FOR DEEPER MEDITATION

You will already have realized that the mini meditations you have been practising don't require any preparation, apart from taking the time to focus on your breathing and to deepen it.

As we think about working at a deeper level with meditations, we have a few other factors to consider. Please do read through this chapter carefully and make sure you adhere to all the guidelines. They are there to nurture and protect you. If you don't bother with them, you will find yourself unprepared for the process of deeper meditations and the experience may not be so pleasant.

So what are we going to be doing next and why do we have to prepare ourselves for it in a certain way? You may remember that meditation was described earlier as being about the discovery of an inner peace and stillness. With mini meditations, this sense is not as pronounced. You were working much more on an external level of appreciation and awareness. To go within and to discover a profound stillness and peace requires another level of concentration and prolonged focus. You need to ease yourself into this new experience by giving consideration to a number of external aids that will help you.

Take a look at the list on the following page. This is going to be your check list for all future meditations. It's important that you follow each of the actions, especially in the early stages of learning to meditate. We're going to work through each point and look at why it is necessary. Awareness of what each action entails will allow you to accept each condition and to enjoy working with it, rather than fighting against it.

MEDITATION CHECK LIST

- A QUIET, UNDISTURBED LOCATION (LOCK DOOR, IF NECESSARY)

- WEAR LOOSE, COMFORTABLE CLOTHING

- BE ALCOHOL AND DRUG FREE

- A COMFORTABLE POSITION IN WHICH YOU CAN SIT/LIE COMPLETELY STILL

- CLEANSE BEFORE YOU START MEDITATING

- REMEMBER TO BREATHE!

- PLACE A GLASS OF MINERAL WATER WITHIN EASY REACH

A QUIET UNDISTURBED LOCATION

This is essential. To access the wonderful world of inner awareness requires a degree of concentration. You can't concentrate if you are constantly being interrupted. We discussed this when we talked about trying to read a good book while perpetually being interrupted. You simply can't focus when external forces are conspiring to distract you. You must have a quiet space where no one can disturb you. If you can't trust someone not to come in, such as an animal or young child, then make sure you can lock the door. Put on the answerphone, switch off your mobile phone, make sure everything is geared towards your not being interrupted. Make sure other people in the building know that you do not want to be disturbed.

Initially, until people get used to what you are doing, it might be a good idea to put a sign on the door: 'Meditating – Please Do Not Interrupt'. For people who haven't experienced meditation, it can sometimes be difficult for them to understand why you can't just stop for a minute to answer their question or to help them with something. They aren't trying to be awkward, they simply don't know what it entails as they have never tried it.

The other reason why you want to be alone is because meditating can sometimes produce surprising results. You can feel as though you have entered another universe and it may take you a few minutes afterwards to adjust to the real world. If you are interrupted while you are in an altered state of awareness, this can jar quite badly and leave you feeling unbalanced. Meditation is about being gentle with yourself: going into the meditation, during it and as you withdraw from it. Any interruption during these vital stages will detrimentally affect your sense of well being.

You might also find certain meditations leave you feeling emotional afterwards; this might take the form of a 'high' or euphoria, or you might find yourself feeling quiet and subdued, needing to mull over the insights you received during meditation. Whatever your state, you may feel vulnerable for a while and want to be alone to rebalance yourself before facing the external world again. These sensations are normal and common.

Creating a Space for Meditation

So what makes a good meditation 'room'? Not everyone has the luxury of being able to create their own private space. If you only have the option of a bedroom or study, you will already have certain decor that you will probably not want to change. It doesn't matter in the sense that you can meditate anywhere, as long as it is private and you will be undisturbed.

If you do have a choice and there is a room you can have to yourself, then the key to a meditation room can be summed up in one word: simplicity. You want to create a space that is conducive to you slipping quietly into inner peace and awareness. What symbolizes peace to you? Most people would say white or pale pastel colours. The plainer the room the less likely you are to be distracted by the things in it.

Perhaps you might want to add something that is spiritual for you. This might be a representative of nature such as a vase of fresh flowers, a beautiful stone or piece of driftwood. Perhaps you prefer a painting or poster of a rainbow, body of water or a forest. If you are fortunate enough to have your own space to decorate (and it need only be very small, just big enough for you to sit in comfortably) then give serious consideration to the few items you put in there. Sit in awareness in your room for a while and let your own wisdom come to you and show you what is right for this space. The simpler the better.

WEAR LOOSE, COMFORTABLE CLOTHING

This may seem quite unimportant but the fact is that you want to help yourself in every way possible to sit quietly and relax into your meditation. There are always things to distract you as you start to focus on your breathing and uncomfortable clothing is an easy diversion. Anything that cuts into the neck or waist stops you from focusing on your breath. Avoid a fabric that is scratchy or makes you feel claustrophobic, but also make sure you are warm enough. As no one else will see you when you meditate, this is your time to relax and to be exactly as you want to be.

Wear those really baggy trousers that are loose around the waist, put on that stained jumper which is so soft and warm, choose the old socks with holes because they are comforting. You are not going to enter a fashion show, you are just going to be yourself in a totally relaxed state, so you might as well make the most of it.

It's best not to wear anything on your feet whilst meditating. You want to be as unrestricted as possible. The feet are also useful as a means of grounding yourself when you bring yourself back to reality afterwards, and it's easier to feel grounded without footwear. We'll discuss how this works later.

If colours are important in your life, think about those too. Do you find certain colours more soothing than others? If you find bright red stimulating and exciting, it might not be a good choice for clothing as you meditate.

If you find you are drawn to particular clothing when you practise meditation, then feel free to keep certain items purely for that purpose. No one else needs to see you in them and you can be comfortable and cosy in your own space. It will help you to relax even more.

BE ALCOHOL AND DRUG FREE

This is a must. Alcohol and drugs do not mix with meditation. Even one glass of wine or a strong headache tablet can set your mind working in a way that is not remotely compatible with altered states of awareness. Never, ever drink or take drugs and then try to meditate.

Why is this so important? One of the experiences you may have during meditation is a sense of being protected, nurtured and guided by other energies around you. This is not to say you will have a sensation of a ghost suddenly being in the room with you. We are talking about something much more subtle, gentle and intangible. Often it simply manifests itself as a faint but lovely feeling of warmth and comfort that slowly comes over you and permeates your body. It is a great joy when this happens and once you've experienced it, you can't wait for the next time.

If you mix alcohol and/or drugs with meditation, you run the very real risk of attracting energies that are not so nurturing. Alcohol and drugs distort the mind, but don't enhance it, and that very distortion can leave you vulnerable to disparate energies which, while harmless, may have a deeply unsettling effect upon you.

Unwittingly, you could end up communicating with what we might term lost souls or unformed, incomplete and confused energies, and these may unbalance your own energy systems. Sometimes they can be hard to get rid of, too. If you are under the influence of drink or drugs, it may be virtually impossible to shake off their presence until you are sober again. To save yourself this unwelcome experience, please ensure you are alcohol and drug free. Don't worry if you aren't quite sure what is meant by 'lost souls' and their effects; all this will make much more sense when we work at deeper levels with our spiritual guides during Part Two.

It is also easier not to meditate with a full stomach. It isn't a strict rule that you can't meditate after a large meal, it's simply that your stomach will be extremely busy digesting all the food. This can take your focus away from your meditating because chances are you will find yourself constantly being diverted in thought towards your rather heavy and bloated stomach. A light meal is better. Preferably, though, wait several hours after eating before you meditate.

FIND A COMFORTABLE POSITION IN WHICH TO SIT/LIE COMPLETELY STILL

During mini meditations, being still physically wasn't something you had to focus upon. Now, as you enter deeper meditative states, you want to try to maintain a motionless, comfortable position. This may not always be possible, but it is your aim.

Whether you choose to lie or sit is a personal decision. The main problem with lying down is that it is so tempting to go to sleep, particularly if you are tired when you start meditating. The only way to know if this is going to happen to you is to try it one day and see if you succumb.

Sleep is a wonderfully regenerative act but it has nothing to do with meditating. The only way to derive benefits from meditating is to remain fully alert and awake throughout. Sleeping through any meditation renders the meditation itself useless. You may enjoy the sleep, but it's simply not the same thing!

If you want to experiment with lying down for meditation, then try

adopting the position shown above. It is suggested that you lie flat on your back, with your legs stretched out and a distance apart. Your arms should rest straight out on the floor and a foot or so away from your body with the palms facing upwards. Your head should be in a straight line to the rest of your body and you should be looking up at the ceiling. This position puts least strain on your body, whilst allowing it to be in alignment.

If you think you run the risk of falling asleep, then opt for the sitting position – see the illustration on page 66 for the suggested position.

This sitting position is advised because, again, the body is in natural alignment. You can see there is no undue stress placed on any part of the body and by sitting upright, not hunched over, you are giving your lungs the opportunity to do their work freely and effectively. Notice how the hands rest comfortably in the lap (preferably palm upwards). The head rests easily on the neck and the shoulders are down and resting comfortably. It's best if you can keep a right angle between your upper and lower legs and for your upper legs to be parallel to the floor. Look at the diagram to see how this works. Again, this is to place as little strain on your body as possible. If you need to sit on a thicker cushion, or even put something like a telephone directory under your feet to make this work, then it's a good idea to do so.

If for whatever reason neither of these positions is comfortable for you, don't worry. Meditate in whatever way is possible for you. It is the fact that

you have a clear intention of learning how to meditate that is of paramount importance. Although certain positions are naturally more conducive for meditative states, you can meditate in any position so long as you are able to relax and focus on your breathing without feeling restricted in any way.

Remember, your intention is to be completely still during meditation. You want all the help available to allow this to happen. Any part of your body that starts to ache will detract from your focus during the meditation.

Spend some time practising lying in the position shown. Is it comfortable for you? Is your back relaxed and stretched out fully along the floor? Are your neck and head relaxed and feeling comfortably heavy and loose? Try placing a thin, soft pillow under your head and see how that feels, but do make sure it is not bulky. Do you feel the definite urge to drift off to sleep?

Now try sitting in an upright chair and adopting the position shown in the illustrations opposite. Does it feel comfortable? Notice if your shoulders or neck are tense; give them a gentle shake and try to relax them. Make sure your hands rest loosely in your lap and that you are not clasping them together. Ensure the seat of the chair is not too hard and uncomfortable. Place a soft cushion underneath you if necessary.

Experiment with the different positions. Tell yourself you will lie still for five minutes and set an alarm to go off. See what feels right for you. During that time do nothing but focus on your breathing and observe the breath going in and out. During the exercises coming up later, you can decide which is the right position for you. You may find that some exercises seem to lend themselves to sitting, others to lying. It is a very personal choice.

CLEANSE AND EMPTY YOURSELF BEFORE YOU START MEDITATING

This doesn't refer to cleansing in the physical sense, although it's a good idea to make sure your bladder is empty before you start meditating, otherwise that can become another distraction.

This cleansing refers to letting go of the everyday worries and stresses that may be a part of you when you prepare to meditate. If you want to attain stillness and go into a state of inner peace and awareness, you will find it hard to do this if you are constantly thinking about everyday problems. You have to learn how to let them go for the period of time that you are meditating. It may seem like a difficult task, but once you practise the art of releasing tension, it becomes a discipline that you adopt easily. Some people find it quite easy to shut off from anxieties; often these are the people who can leave their work behind at the end of each day and enjoy a good evening socializing with family and friends. Other people are natural worriers and everything seems to crowd in on them all the time.

Whatever category you fall into, it is now time to learn two cleansing techniques that will serve you well before, during and after meditating. In fact, this cleansing can be a useful adjunct to everyday living and you can enjoy its benefits on endless occasions when you need to let go of something that is unwanted and unhelpful.

The cleansing sanctuary

Close your eyes. Focus on your breathing for a moment but don't force it in any way. Wait until you feel your breathing slow down and deepen before you continue.

Now you are going to discover your own personal technique for cleansing away anything unwanted that is around or inside of you.

You are going to create a cleansing sanctuary that is your own personal space. It belongs solely to you and it will be to your own personal design. This is the opportunity for your fertile mind to create something wonderful. You may know it doesn't exist in the real world, but here in the wonderful realm of your imagination anything is possible and you are going to enjoy the creation process.

What do you find most cleansing and comforting? It may be warm water from a bath or shower or fast-flowing, cool water from a stream or river. It could be hot sunlight or perhaps soft, gentle rain. Maybe you just want to imagine pure, brilliant white light streaming down from above as a spiritual or religious cleansing. This is your chance to create what is most powerful for you. Give yourself some time to think about what is most appealing. Choose a scenario that you find both comforting and nurturing.

When you have created an image you like, strengthen your relationship with it by making it as vivid as possible. So if you like the thought of a shower or bath, see it clearly in your mind's eye. Where is it? What size? What colour? Put big, fluffy towels and wonderful smelling soap into this space. Make it as real for you as possible. Take your time during this process. Enjoy it. If you have opted for rich sunlight or gentle rain, where are you when this cleansing takes place? What are your surroundings? Make them as clear as possible. Feel as though you can smell, touch and hear your cleansing space, as well as see it. If you like the thought of pure white light from above, where is its source? How does that make you feel? Where do you choose to be when this cleansing takes place? Create it. You may find that immersing yourself in a fast-flowing brook is all you need to make yourself feel cleansed and rejuvenated, free from worries. Then see the river clearly and where it is located. What is the bank like and the surrounding area? What are the colours and smells? Don't rush this process of creation. Savour it.

When you feel your cleansing sanctuary is vivid and really powerful as an image for you, then slowly place yourself into it. Stand under that shower, sit in the sunlight, walk in the rain or experience the pure white light. How does it make you feel? You should feel all your worries, fears and problems ebbing away, being washed away or dispersed in whatever fashion you have chosen. This should be a real sensation for you and it should be deeply comforting. If you can't receive any tangible sensation of cleansing from it, then your cleansing sanctuary is not yet working for you. It should always give a feeling of peace and safety. You should feel calm, renewed and refreshed after time in your cleansing space. Work with this image all the time to make it even richer in imagery, even more powerful in its cleansing ability. You will use it often, so ensure it feels as wonderful as possible.

This cleansing sanctuary is your retreat from unwanted energies. You can use it at any time before, during and after meditations. It can be used on a daily basis when you want to quickly wash away something unpleasant.

It is always there for you. Look after it well and keep it clean and pure. Never let anyone else into your cleansing sanctuary. It is solely for you. Enjoy it.

Did you find this exercise easy or difficult? It is one of the most important you will ever do, so make sure you don't rush it. Give yourself time to repeat the cleansing process on a number of different occasions. Work with different images – see what works best for you. You will know when you have found the right one. You will immediately feel safe and comforted as you visualize yourself in your cleansing sanctuary. You will find it easy to create; the moment you think about cleansing yourself, the image will be there for you, strong and clear. Every time you step into it, you will be filled with the same, reassuring sense of peace. Don't worry if it takes you some time to reach this stage. Enjoy the creation process.

The second cleansing technique works more specifically on outside influences. You may find sometimes that your cleansing sanctuary doesn't rid you of what you don't want. You may know that you have issues or influences that may be outside of you and feel separate from you, that you want to be rid of before you can enjoy meditating. How do you work with those outside forces and get them to disappear? Below is a technique that may help you.

Cleansing outside forces

Close your eyes and focus on your breathing. Take some time to relax and unwind. Retreat into your cleansing sanctuary for a few minutes and enjoy its benefits. Make sure you are relaxed and settled before you continue.

Now acknowledge the outside influence or emotion that is affecting you. You may know logically that it is a part of you, but it just doesn't feel as though it is, and when you move into your cleansing sanctuary, it isn't there with you to be cleansed away. Really think about this energy and focus upon it.

Now you want to try to give it a physical presence. What does it look like? Giving it a physical shape makes it a more tangible, recognizable force for you to deal with. How would you describe it? Is it a black thick mass or a discordant pulsing light? Does it feel very close to you or far away? Is it dense or does it move and change shape? Is it a hot or cold sensation? Does it have a colour? What about size – is it small and intense or large and heavy? Give it a recognizable physical status. Does it now feel more real to you?

What is the most effective way to get rid of this unwanted shape? Think carefully and really focus on this issue. What would it take to make it disappear?

Let your mind start to create possibilities. You know it didn't vanish in your cleansing sanctuary but can you create some other space that would work in this instance? Is there some other shower or bath that would get rid of it? Put the sunlight, rain or pure white light into another setting and see whether that works for you. Maybe you want to create another kind of fast-flowing brook that swirls it all away. You could also visualize a roaring fire that burns the unwanted image into ashes. Create a helium-filled balloon and put the physical shape into that; see it float up into the sky above and disappear. Or picture a bird picking up the mass in a bundle and see it soar up into nothingness. You might like the image of a rocket into which you pack the unwanted matter and you then watch it being blasted up into the cosmos. You might want to create something completely different that is personal to you.

The only condition is that you must find it a powerful yet comforting, helpful image. Avoid violent images such as guns or knives; the technique needs to calm and soothe you, not agitate you in any way.

Remember to make the setting as powerful as possible. If you have opted for a bird, make sure it is as real for you as if it were sitting in front of you now. Give it size, shape, colour, even a personality. If you use a roaring fire, where is the fire? What size? What surrounds it – open air or is it in a particular room? What colour is the helium balloon? What size is it?

Really take your time in visualizing this new cleansing technique. It is a vital area to which you will want to return on many occasions. Make sure you get to know it well and that you enjoy using it. Ensure there are no negative images here, only positive, nurturing energies.

When you are ready, you want to place the physical shape you have created into this new space. Really watch it disappearing and enjoy the process. Watch it wash away through the plug hole/see it burn to nothing/have it evaporate into the sunlight/concentrate on the bird, rocket or balloon as it takes off into thin air and eventual nothingness.

Give yourself a moment to appreciate this disappearance. Really acknowledge that it has gone. Feel cleansed and released by the action you have taken. Enjoy resting in a new sense of peace and contentment, feeling freer and lighter. You might want to go back into your own cleansing sanctuary now for a moment of quiet.

Ensure you give yourself time before you either continue with your chosen meditation or return to reality. Don't rush either process.

Did you find it easier to create this second cleansing technique because part of it seemed less connected to you? Sometimes it feels easier to rid ourselves of something outside our own body. Did you find it hard to give a physical shape to the problem? With practice, this becomes a natural action, and one that can be quite enjoyable. Making something real physically helps you to make the issue real and solid for you. Often by seeing it clearly, we can then deal with it better. If you have never thought about releasing unwanted energies and influences before, it can be quite a liberating experience but it also strange because you are unused to it. You may want to change your cleansing technique a few times before you find one that really works for you. You only know what is powerful by creating it in your mind's eye and then observing your response to it.

You may also discover that certain emotions and feelings need different techniques. You might find, for example, that anything relating to one area of your life, such as your work environment, might always require the arrival of your bird to get rid of it. You may notice that fears about family always need to be dealt with by throwing them into the flowing river. This is such a personal area that you never have to discuss it with anyone and it can change and adapt as you learn more about what works for you.

As we go further into different forms of meditation, you will appreciate even more why these two cleansing techniques are invaluable. Keep looking at your cleansing techniques and constantly refining them. The more vivid they are for you, the more beneficial you will find them.

Of course these are also techniques you can use on a daily basis, whatever your situation. If you are squashed into a crowded train or bus, take a quick dip into your own private sanctuary. If someone has bombarded you with unreasonable behaviour and it's left you feeling stressed, take a moment to wash away their influence on you. Perhaps you are nervous of a person or situation you are about to face – stop for a moment, breathe and cleanse away the emotion, using your newly learned techniques.

In fact, it is a good idea for you to practise cleansing anywhere and everywhere, as often as you like. This can be a quick process. You don't have to close your eyes and lose yourself in another world. You can do it with your eyes open, once your cleansing spaces are really powerful images for you. Is something that doesn't feel good happening? Practise letting it go. Are you spending needless time fretting over some situation? Wash it away. Do you feel angry with someone? Give that anger a tangible shape and then release it.

Of course, this isn't to say that you will find it possible to rid yourself of every single thing you don't like or want, but by experimenting with it you will learn which issues in your life you have the immediate power to release. Some may appear to go and then return later. Sometimes, by giving a shape to something, you understand it fully for the first time and you can then truly release it. As we work with different meditations, you will also learn other techniques for looking at difficult issues in your life.

REMEMBER TO BREATHE!

Perhaps this seems the most trite of all the check list items. Yet it is the most important because you will accomplish very little if you don't focus on your breath. It is there as a constant reminder for you because even though you may intend to remember the significance of your breathing at all times, there will still be plenty of occasions when you will forget about it completely.

How often did you remember to breathe during the two exercises above? If you remembered even three or four times, you did well. Most people start off focusing on their breathing and then completely forget about it. You need to return to the power of your breathing throughout the meditation process. Without an awareness of it you will not be able to move onto a higher level of meditating or get to grips with a particular issue you may have been avoiding or misunderstanding. For many reasons, breathing is always and forever your golden key to meditation.

Within this awareness of breathing, is also your reminder to let your physical body relax as much as possible during meditation. We carry in our bodies an enormous amount of physical tension. Remember how we discussed earlier about a simple smile being able to relax around a hundred muscles in the face? Well, our body is composed of approximately 656 muscles. How many of those do you tense during each day and how many do you forget to relax properly when you don't need them and they're not in use? When we walk we use about two hundred different muscles. Do you remember to release them when you sit or lie down?

Here is a basic exercise to bring about awareness of your muscles and then teach you how to relax them.

Relaxing the muscles

Sit or lie down and close your eyes. Breathe deeply and let yourself relax. You are going to build a system of awareness around your body, rotating your consciousness, allowing yourself to feel the tension in each part and then learning how to release it.

Start with your right foot. Focus on nothing but this foot. Crunch up your toes and feel the tension seeping through the foot and up your leg. Now take a deep breath in and as you breathe out, relax all the muscles. Enjoy the wonderful sensation of the tension leaving this part of you. Breathe in and out again if you can still feel the tension in the right foot.

Repeat this process, working slowly through the body as follows: right lower leg, right upper leg, right hip, right side, right shoulder, right upper arm, right lower arm, right hand. Now work through the left side with all those parts of the body: left foot, left lower leg,left upper leg, left hip, left side, left shoulder, left upper arm, left lower arm, left hand. Remember to focus only on one part of your body at a time. Now move to the buttocks, lower back, middle back, upper back, neck, back of the head, top of the head, the face, upper chest, chest, stomach. Then tense the whole body and relax it. Do this several times.

Now, mentally go through your whole body and ask yourself where tension remains. You can do this quite swiftly if you are really focusing. Is your jaw still tight? Release it. Are your shoulders still aching? Release the muscles. Always release on the out breath. Really feel it happen as you exhale.

When you have thoroughly gone through your whole body, lie there quietly for a few minutes, appreciating your newly relaxed, physical body. Notice how much more ready you feel to enter a meditative state. Give yourself a moment to return to reality before you get up and continue your daily life.

This is such a useful exercise to do even if you aren't planning to meditate. It's a wonderful way to unwind after a hard day. If you do it every time before you meditate, it will improve both the depth and focus of your meditation.

HAVE A GLASS OF MINERAL WATER WITHIN EASY REACH

It is common to find yourself becoming quite dry and thirsty during meditation, particularly as you gradually slip into longer and longer periods of time when you remain still and silent and sink deeper into altered states of consciousness.

As you come out of the meditation and open your eyes, it is a good idea to drink some water, to help rebalance. It is also a good opportunity for you to sit quietly and reflect upon what you have learned from the meditation. Often insights come slowly after you have finished; you need some time just to be quiet and digest what you have gleaned. If you rush to get up and continue with your day, you run the risk of feeling disjointed and out of sorts. Learn to be gentle with yourself when you finish. Sit for a few minutes silently appreciating what you have learned from your meditation. Use this time constructively and slowly sip a glass of mineral water.

Sometimes you may find it hard to return to earth after a meditation. You might feel as though your head is still up in the clouds somewhere and although it's a lovely feeling, you need to get rid of it before you continue with your day. This process of returning to earth is also called grounding yourself. Below is a useful exercise for you do after you finish meditating.

Grounding yourself

Close your eyes and focus on your feet. (If you choose to meditate lying down, bend your legs so that the soles of your feet are resting flat on the floor. If you are sitting, make sure your legs are not crossed and that your feet are resting flat on the floor.) As you concentrate, realize how heavy your feet feel. They seem to be like lead, solid and secure on the floor. It would be hard for you to lift them.

Now imagine that the soles of your feet have long roots growing out of them and that these roots are anchored deep into the earth below you. Feel the long roots coming out of your feet and going deep into the ground.

As you focus on your feet, you will slowly feel yourself sinking back into your whole body again. You will become aware that all of you feels comfortably heavy and relaxed. Notice which parts of you are touching the floor, chair or bed and realize how solid they feel.

Focus on your breathing again as you open your eyes. Become aware of how differently you feel now you are grounded. Wait a moment before you get up.

This grounding exercise is useful on many occasions, not just when you finish meditating. Any unpleasant or uncomfortable experience can make us feel as though we are slightly out of our bodies and not quite 'here'. If we feel extremely nervous or scared, we can withdraw physically. Shock can also do that to us.

You know that focusing on your breathing can always help to ground you again, but focusing on your feet is also another effective way of returning to planet earth after your levels of consciousness have been resting elsewhere. Just ensure that you keep breathing deeply as you do the grounding exercise.

You have looked at what you need to know before you enter the next phase of meditating. Remember to keep looking back over the check list and make sure you are following all the suggestions. Give yourself time to adjust to the concept of cleansing, and experiment with the different ideas suggested. Don't be afraid to branch out and find something different which works well for you.

Now you are ready to start looking at meditations in a different light. This is going to entail a little more discipline and focus from you, so take your time as you work your way through the next chapter. If you feel you want to spend more time on your mini meditations before you proceed, that is fine.

When you are ready, continue with the next chapter.

GOING INTO THE STILLNESS

This is where you start a new stage of development. You have practised your mini meditations and learned to cleanse yourself and let go of outside influences. Now you are ready to experience meditation at a deeper level.

During this chapter, you are going to find the part of you that contains the stillness we were discussing earlier. This stillness is a wonderfully quiet, peaceful place within that you will go to each and every time you meditate. Everyone has this place, even though you might now be wondering if maybe you don't! Everyone's place is individual to them, too. Your path of discovery will be different from anyone else's and your place of stillness will be personal to you. So, your next task is finding that place. We are going to use a number of exercises to allow you to get there.

To begin the process, we are going to use a new technique to focus on your breath and to show you how to deepen it even more. Your breathing is your first step to allowing you access to this haven of stillness and peace. You may feel that by practising the techniques you have truly learned how to breathe fully. Perhaps your fingers are now moving apart when they're placed on your ribcage and your shoulders are no longer lifting. If so, that is wonderful! Even if this is the case, do experience the exercise below and use it as a new means of focusing on the breath.

In and out

Close your eyes and focus on your breathing. Initially, you just want to observe the breath, nothing more. Settle yourself and give yourself time to focus. If you want to go into your cleansing sanctuary and get rid of anything unwanted, if you want to use your own personal technique to stop other thoughts and emotions from distracting you, that is fine.

Now, as you focus on your breathing you are going to use two simple words to increase your focus. Every time you breathe in, say silently to yourself 'in'. Every time you breathe out, say silently to yourself 'out'. Keep doing this. Say 'in'. Say 'out'. Every time another thought comes into your head, other than these two simple words, acknowledge it but then immediately dismiss it. Let it drift away into nothingness. Nothing exists beyond the words 'in' and 'out'. Keep concentrating for several minutes.

As you do so, notice how your breathing is changing, imperceptibly at first perhaps, then more obviously. It is deepening and slowing down. Notice how much slower and how much more of a gap there is between your saying 'in' and 'out'. Take your time as you do this. Keep letting other thoughts drift away. Don't hold on to anything except 'in' and 'out'.

When you are ready, slowly open your eyes and take some time to focus on an object and reorientate yourself. Sip your water and sit quietly for a few minutes.

Were you surprised by how many thoughts kept coming into your mind, other than 'in' and 'out'? Did you find it somewhat frustrating? We don't realize how easily and frequently our thoughts hop about from one area to another, until we actually stop and acknowledge it, until we rest in a state of awareness about what is really happening to our minds. For most of us, our normal state is to be thinking about a number of different issues all at once, whilst physically engaged in doing something else that is often not even related to what we are thinking about. How easy it is for us to become distracted; the slightest thing can deflect us. Stilling the mind is not as easy as it first might have seemed. Below is another exercise to help your concentration.

Playing with numbers

Close your eyes and focus on your breathing. Acknowledge each breath coming in and going out. Give yourself a few minutes to settle comfortably.

Now when you next breathe in, say 'one'. As you breathe out, say 'one'. Breathe in again and say 'two'. Breathe out and say 'two'.

Continue this process. Notice how easy or difficult it is for you to remain focused on the numbers and to count correctly. If you get confused and aren't sure which number you are on, return to 'one' and start again. When you successfully get to 'twenty', stop counting.

Now you are going to start again, but this time you want only to think of the number you are currently using. Can you focus solely on the number you are saying, without having your thoughts travel on to the next number or the number you have just said? Can you regard each number as a number and not give it any other significance? This isn't as easy as it sounds! Try it for yourself.

The only rule is that you must focus just on the number itself as you breathe in and out; nothing else is allowed to come into your mind. Every time another thought or number comes into your mind, start again at 'one'. How many attempts does it take to get to 'twenty'? Can you not get to twenty at all? Don't get irritated if this is the case. Everyone finds it hard to concentrate in the beginning.

You can vary the way you play with numbers. You can start with any number you like and count downwards. Pick a random number such as '87' and count backwards from it. See how far you can get. Return to the same number and start again when you have to. You can start at another random number and work your way upwards. Choose a high number, such as '999'. Keep focusing on different numbers that will test your ability to concentrate.

Always remember to give yourself some time to readjust when you finish. Sit for a few minutes before you get up and continue your day.

Playing with the numbers is a fun and effective way of improving your concentration. It doesn't matter if you constantly have to keep returning to your original number. The more you practise, the easier you will find it to focus on the numbers. There is a great sense of achievement when you realize that you have succeeded in going through twenty or so numbers without a break in concentration.

Next, we're going to look at how something as simple as a candle flame can not only increase your concentration but help you work towards discovering the centre of stillness inside you. For this, you will need a lit candle anchored securely in a holder. To help you focus, it's best if the candle is plain, preferably white.

Do ensure it is firmly held in a container and not going to fall over and cause damage. You will be closing your eyes at times during this meditation, so it's extremely important that it's safe and you can relax without any worries. You will need to sit upright for this exercise.

The candle flame

Place the lit candle comfortably in your line of sight, directly in front of you. It's helpful if you dim other lights, or pull the curtains or blinds so that the candle flame is a clear focus for you and stands out against its surroundings. Try to ensure the candle is not in a draught either. If the flame is flickering wildly it will make your work harder. Place the candle where the flame just waves gently.

Now close your eyes and spend a moment or two focusing on your breathing. To do this, use any of the techniques you have learnt so far and which you find helpful. Don't rush the process. When you feel relaxed and ready, open your eyes and let your focus rest on the candle flame.

Just gaze gently at the flame; don't strain your eyes or stare intently at it. Become fully aware of the flame. Acknowledge its beauty. Notice its different colours and how it flickers gently. Realize how unique a candle flame is and that you have never really appreciated it before. Lose yourself in the flame. Let your gaze soften and blur slightly. Feel your awareness melt into the flickering flame itself.

Focus on nothing but the flame and feel as though you are part of it and it is part of you. You might want to let your eyes close as you do this; you will still see the flickering flame in your mind's eye. If you feel the flame is starting to fade, open your eyes again and focus on it for a while. Nothing else exists but the warm, flickering flame.

Now allow your awareness of the beauty and warmth of the flame to come into your own body. Imagine this soft, comforting flame coming slowly into the area of your heart. Feel it warm and enrich you, making you feel safe and comfortable. Now let it travel around the inside of your body and enjoy its nurturing presence. Notice where it seems to want to rest.

When you are ready, let yourself feel its glow expanding and filling you. See or sense its wonderful golden hue spreading slowly through every part of you, making you feel warm, relaxed, safe and contented. Enjoy the sensation of peace that comes with it. Everything is all right in your world. Enjoy that knowledge.

After a few minutes, see the flame withdraw from your body, leaving you with the comforting sensation of a wonderful, warm glow inside. Realize the flickering flame is in front of you on top of the candle. Slowly open your eyes and focus on the flame. Give silent thanks for its unique beauty, which you have only fully appreciated for the first time today.

Now concentrate on what today means: what day of the week it is, what time it is, what else you are going to do today. Gradually reorientate yourself and come back to earth.

Did the flame provide you with a feeling of well-being? If you found it a powerful image, return to it on a regular basis and enjoy its beauty and comfort. Most people find a candle flame an inspirational energy that immediately makes them relax. If, for whatever reason, you find the flame unsettling, then try working with the image of a real flower that you find beautiful. Perhaps that may make you feel wonderful. Try the next exercise.

The flower

Place a beautiful single flower, in water, in front of you. Now close your eyes and relax yourself, using the technique you find most helpful. Work with your breathing and feel it deepen and slow down. When you're ready, open your eyes and focus on the flower head.

Really look at it, without straining, and enjoy its wonderful beauty. Realize how special each flower is and what a work of nature flowers are. Enjoy its texture, its colour. It may even have a scent you can appreciate. Let yourself be filled with wonder and appreciation for this wonderful offering from nature.

Let your consciousness melt into the flower itself. Feel what it is like to be a part of nature. Enjoy this comforting sensation. Be aware of what it really means – to be part of the constant ebb and flow of life in all its cycles and seasons.

When you are ready, close your eyes and bring the consciousness of this magnificent flower into your own body. Feel it melt into your physical being and travel into the heart of you. Enjoy its pulsing softness and beauty. Acknowledge how wonderful it makes you feel and the sense of peace which it gives. Wallow in the feeling.

Wait until you feel ready and then let the image of the flower return to the flower in front of you. Withdraw it from your physical body and open your eyes, to see it there in front of you. Give silent thanks for its beauty and to nature, its creator.

Reorientate yourself slowly.

You can, of course, put anything symbolic into this exercise. The simpler the image the more powerful it usually is. Do you have a beautiful seashell that you love? Try meditating on that. A stone, crystal or piece of wood can also be effective.

You may feel from the exercises you have done so far that you have touched something new and deep within you, a place you haven't quite found before which feels quiet, peaceful and comforting. You might feel the opposite – as though you can't really warm to anything you have tried to do so far and that nothing is really touching you or making you feel differently. Remember, whatever is happening for you is just fine. There are so many different exercises to explore in this book and you will discover what works for you when the time is right. Keep working gently through them and enjoy the experience of what they do for you, no matter how little your response may seem.

Now you have experienced the different techniques above, try the exercise below. This is a step into the stillness we have been talking about which heralds deeper meditation. Ensure you go through the Check List (see page 60) and then settle into your comfortable position. Read through the exercise first, and then when you are ready, begin.

Going into stillness

Close your eyes. Wriggle your body gently into a comfortable position. Start observing your breath. Don't alter it in any way. Notice if you are feeling relaxed or tense. Let yourself go into your cleansing sanctuary for a while. Cleanse and renew your energies. Feel yourself literally melt into a comfortable state of relaxation.

Now return to your breathing. Feel each breath coming in and going out. Use whatever technique you wish to lengthen and deepen the breath, such as the stomach, ribcage or balloon breathing exercises. Try the numbers or use the 'in' and 'out' technique. Give yourself time to adjust and let the deeper breathing feel natural and unforced.

Now you are going to shift your focus from each in and out breath to another area. You are going to feel your focus going to a point deep within your body – the part of you that is peaceful, still and quiet. You are going to find this area for yourself. It is hidden deep in the middle of your body, below your ribcage and around your navel area. This is the very centre, the very core of you. It is a wonderfully calm, soothing place. You can take your time to find it.

Start by taking your focus from your breathing to the area just below your ribcage. Then let your focus slowly shift from the ribcage to a little further down, towards your belly button. Keep exploring. Take some time to find this area. You may think you have found something and then it starts to move around a little within you. Sometimes it may slide up towards your heart, then it may seem to fall further down into your lower stomach area. Give yourself time to find the stillness. There is no rush. (Some people start to worry at this stage and feel they haven't got this vital point of contact. They worry that everyone else has but they are different. Relax. Everyone has this centre of stillness. In some it is buried more deeply than others, but it is always there. Take time to explore this new part of you. You will find it for yourself.)

Wait until you can feel the contact. It will probably manifest itself as a slight sensation of something different happening to you. It may be a pleasurable tingle or gentle tickle inside. Perhaps it will feel like a warm glow or a welcome sensation of a cool breeze flowing through you. Everyone feels it differently. Some people even have a scent in their nostrils or a beautiful sound such as tinkling bells in the distance. Give yourself time to find out what your natural reaction is to this new world. Don't rush.

Now let yourself sink into this place. It is so inviting it is easy to do this. Drop slowly into the wonderfully warm, soft enveloping sense of peace. Let yourself really relax into it. Realize how comforted, safe and contented you feel here. Remember to keep your breathing deep and regular. Just let yourself wallow in the pleasure of this new place. Rest here for quite a while. Make a mental note of where this place is within your body and know you will come here again.

Then, when you are ready, withdraw your concentration from this area. Let yourself come back to your breathing and focus on each in and out breath. Focus on your real life again. Where are you sitting? In what room? What time of day is it? Slowly, bring yourself back to awareness of the present. Notice how heavy your body feels. Slowly open your eyes and focus on an object. Sip your water and wait a while before you get up.

How did your physical body feel after that experience? You may have felt wonderfully relaxed and supple, or you may have noticed your body felt tight and slightly achy afterwards. You may have felt strange when you first opened your eyes. Perhaps your surroundings felt extra bright, or everything seemed more colourful. Perhaps you just felt a bit 'unreal' afterwards. You may have felt you didn't really find this stillness or sense of peace. You may just have felt relaxed, or maybe you know you didn't find what you were supposed to. Whatever your experience, that is fine.

Going into this state of stillness is a very personal journey and you can't rush it. You might be the person who finds this place with ease, as if going into a wonderfully familiar place which you hadn't quite appreciated before. You might have already experienced this deep sense of peace and contentment before, but not realized that it actually resides inside you and that you can go into it whenever you choose. You may have a glorious sensation of 'coming home' and feeling settled and comfortable.

Maybe you feel more uncertain about what is happening to you. You may feel a slight sensation of something different and wonder what it means, or realize something else is there but somehow you can't quite access it. You may feel frustrated, sensing that it keeps eluding you, and yet knowing it is within your reach, if only you can just find it. You may have had a brief flash of this state of stillness and then not been able to stay there. Whatever you feel, you are doing well. Please stop to acknowledge what you have accomplished. You are learning so many new techniques and whatever you have picked up so far and made work for you is an achievement. You are doing well. But there are still plenty more exercises for you to try!

Let us look at another meditation that may help you find this state of stillness you are seeking. When you were doing the Going into Stillness exercise, you were learning how to work inward into silence. Now we are going to look at how we can start with an awareness of outer influences and slowly retreat into the silence. Some people find this a more helpful means of attaining a state of stillness.

The retreat

Start off by settling yourself comfortably in your meditating position. Close your eyes, and relax into your deeper breathing.

Now you want to take your awareness to outside sounds. Really listen to see what you can hear outside your immediate space, outside the building or space you are presently occupying. What are those distant sounds? Try to identify them. Can you hear a plane flying? Perhaps there are sounds of traffic. Is there a dog barking down the street?

Perhaps birds are twittering in the trees. Can you hear the hum of machinery, or the sounds of wind or rain? Maybe some construction work is taking place nearby. Perhaps someone is playing music or a television is turned up to full volume. Perhaps you can hear people walking down the street, chatting. Whatever you hear, try to identify it and then let it fade from your consciousness. Make sure you have fully identified all the distant sounds you can hear.

Now move a little closer in to your own surroundings. What can you hear just outside the room you are in? Is there the hum of electrical appliances? Are floorboards creaking or is there a whirr of heating or air conditioning? Maybe you can hear a pet moving around the house or even snoring. Really listen to the sounds outside your room. As soon as you recognize them, let them float away.

Now bring your focus to the room you are presently in. What sounds can you hear in the room itself? Is there the ticking of a clock? Perhaps a breeze is blowing through the window. Does the electricity in the room make a faint humming noise? Again, listen intently to anything you can identify within the room itself but try not to hold on to the awareness of the sound. Let it fade away.

Now start to bring your awareness closer in to you, just around your body itself. Become aware of the space your physical body occupies and tune in to that. What can you hear? Concentrate solely on your body. What is that new sound you now hear? Focus. If you listen closely enough you will hear it. It is a gentle, repetitious thudding sound, faint but persistent. Can you hear it? The more you focus, the more you will become aware of it and the louder it seems to become. Thud. Thud. Thud. Do you recognize the source?

It is your heartbeat. Listen to it. Enjoy it. This is your very life source, work your body does day in, day out, to keep you alive and healthy. Appreciate the sound. Really become aware of it. Move your awareness within your own body to access its centre. Take a journey into your heart area and appreciate the strength and beauty residing there.

> As you move inside, be aware of other sounds within your body. Can you hear your stomach gurgling as its digests? Can you feel your veins pulsing gently in other parts of your body? Realize what a powerhouse of activity takes place constantly in your own body. Give silent thanks for its divine existence.
>
> Now move deeper into the very core of your body. Can you find an area that is deep, dark, silent and still? Gently explore with your conscious thought. As you do so, let the other sounds in your body fade into the distance. Become aware gradually that there are no more sounds. No sounds remain. Only silence. There is only wonderful silence – pure, clear silence that is infinitely comforting and peaceful. Nothing exists here but stillness and a wonderful sense of nothingness. Rest in this absolute silence and stillness for as long as you like. If any thoughts come into your head, let them fade away. Enjoy the sensation of nothingness. Savour it.
>
> Then, very slowly, bring your awareness back to the everyday sounds around you. Realize that the clock is ticking. You can hear the wind in the trees or the rain on the window. Really focus on everyday sounds again. Gently, open your eyes and focus on the room you are in. Sip your water. Take your time to return to present day.

Was that an easier route for you to take? By accentuating what is outside, you can sometimes find it easier to retreat to your inner world. If that was also difficult for you as an exercise, don't worry. Time will help you to work with your new awareness.

If you are really struggling still, you might want to stop and consider if you are breathing deeply and spending enough time focusing on this aspect of meditation. It can be tempting to rush the breathing and relaxation, because you want to get onto the section where something actually happens and you experience something new and exciting. However, you won't give yourself the opportunity to move into this new realm unless you have prepared yourself with the deep breathing first. You might want to return to some of the different breathing techniques mentioned earlier before continuing.

Are you also remembering to physically relax your body as shown in the Relaxing the Muscles exercise on page 74? It's easy to forget this in our rush to move forwards. We are also good at fooling ourselves into believing that we really are relaxed and that it's unnecessary to go through all the parts of our body.

There simply is no substitute for awareness of our breathing and learning to physically relax, as well as mentally and emotionally releasing our worries. These steps are necessary before you can progress.

So, you want to be able to move comfortably into this newly discovered stillness before you continue reading. You want to know that within a few minutes of focusing on your breathing, you can have your physical body relax, your mind empty itself of thoughts or problems, and you can slip effortlessly into your new world of inner peace and stillness.

It doesn't matter at this stage if you can't sustain this state for long; you will only be able to learn that through continually practising different meditations. Right now, all you want to do is to acknowledge a deeply appealing state of stillness and to know you have been there, no matter how briefly. If you can practise enough so that it becomes quicker to get there and easier to remain there, that is wonderful and will improve the quality of your meditations enormously.

The next area we are going to look at is how sound can enhance the way we meditate. Whether you are still finding it difficult to access this inner stillness or whether you can sink into this state comfortably, we're going to discover how powerful and helpful different sounds can be.

SOUND AND SCENT IN MEDITATION

You have been learning about how we need to withdraw into silence in order to meditate deeply, so it may seem confusing now to talk about using sound as a means of doing this. However, anything used as a focus can help you to meditate. We are going to explore ways of concentrating upon sound and then losing ourselves in it.

The sounds we can make ourselves have long been used in meditating. Making a sound and repeating it constantly is known as a 'mantra'. Most ancient forms of meditation use mantras, as indeed do many of the more modern, Western forms of meditation, which regard them as the main method through which inner calm can be discovered. Whether or not this is true for you can only be determined by trying out some sounds for yourself.

Your Sound

Because making a strange noise and continuously repeating it might feel odd to you, it is doubly important for this type of meditation that you are in a quiet, and will not be undisturbed. You might also want to ensure that no one else is within earshot.

First, choose a sound and then, breathing deeply and comfortably, utter that sound out loud, slowly and sonorously. The sound will last as long as your breath. Stop only to refill your lungs and then continue. Does this feel rather strange to you? Perhaps you are wondering how this can possibly be a powerful experience.

Now try something else. Take a comfortable, deep breath and then hum a low note quietly to yourself. Pitch the note near the bottom of yourregister so that it resonates inside you. How does that feel in your body? Can you feel a sort of tingle or vibration deep inside? Take another deep breath and quietly hum a high note near the top of your register. How different is that as a sensation within your body? Did you notice different parts of your body react to each note? Did you find the high note or the low note more comfortable?

For meditative purposes, it is accepted that a lower note is more in harmony with your body and that it is easier to relax with a lower note than a high, piercing one. So, apart from choosing your lower register, what else do you need to create an effective mantra?

First, it's better not to use a real word. Although some words, such as 'peace' or 'calm', might sound very comforting, the problem is that you may be tempted to think about their meaning and what the words mean to you. The purpose and power of a mantra lies in your ability to lose yourself in its rich, sonorous sound and the way it vibrates around and through your body. If you are thinking consciously or unconsciously about the word, it stops the mantra from doing its job.

Secondly, a mantra should be no more than one or two syllables. It is the simplicity of the sound that will help you to focus. You want something you can repeat continuously without effort and conscious thought.

Thirdly, certain consonants are more helpful than others for meditating. Let's do another experiment to help prove this. Quietly utter the 's' sound to yourself. Now say the 'n' sound softly to yourself. Which feels richer and vibrates more? Try saying the 't' sound. Now say the 'w' sound. You'll probably agree that the 'n' and 'w' sounds vibrate through you. The 't' and 's' sounds seem sharper, higher and less resonant.

So, you want to find a word that has no recognizable meaning, that has only one or two syllables and that consists of consonants which resonate in a rich, comforting way in and around your body. Creating a mantra is a very personal matter, so it is good if you can discover your own word for yourself.

However, you may want to choose one of the following or use one of them as a guideline. You may want to put two of the syllables together.

SUGGESTED MANTRAS

MAH - NUM
VO - HUM
RAHM
LAH - NEE
SOHM
WONE
VEE - NONG
PRAH

DA - YAM
RAH - MAH
SHAH - LOON

There are many others you can create. Choose another sound altogether if it feels right for you. The only way to know which sound works for you is to try them all or create your own while in a relaxed state. When you are ready, work through the following exercise.

The mantra

Choose the word you will concentrate on and then close your eyes. Use your cleansing and breathing techniques and allow yourself to sink into a comfortably relaxed state. If you can find your inner core of stillness, let yourself fall peacefully into this.

Now see your word in your mind's eye. How does it look to you? How does the word make you feel? Take a deep breath and speak it slowly and sonorously to yourself. It can be spoken quite softly if you like. Let the word continue until you have finished the breath. If there are two syllables, try to balance them out equally in your breath although you may find this difficult at first. Just keep making the sound until your breath runs out. Then take a comfortable deep breath in and repeat the process. Do this at least three times with the word. Notice what feelings and sensations come to you at this time. Where do you feel the vibrations in your body?

Remember, if you experience anything unpleasant, wash it away from you. If at any time you feel over-powered or too emotional, simply stop and cleanse. You can continue on another occasion if you wish. If you are enjoying the process, then continue.

Really feel the word vibrate through and around you. Lose yourself in the word, completely. Feel it spread outwards from you in a wonderful glow of energy. Let yourself merge with the sound and then become nothing but the sound itself. You will find that you are unaware when you are breathing in because the sound seems continuous as its vibrations spread ever wider and intensify. Stay in this state for some time.

When you are ready, slowly prepare to withdraw from your word. To do this, start chanting the word more slowly and more quietly. Gradually, make it softer and softer. Let it gently fade into nothingness. If this has been powerful for you, then you may find it is quite difficult to let the vibrations of the sound disappear. Give yourself some time for this to happen. Cleanse it away if you need to. Don't rush the process.

Let yourself sit in the stillness for a while. Enjoy the silence. Now you might want to discover if there is a mantra out there for you which is personal and right for you. Focus on this possibility. Ask for help. Say you would like to be given your own private mantra that will work powerfully for you. See if anything comes to you. Sit quietly and wait with your eyes closed. Keep concentrating on the possibility of there being a word that is meant just for you and that will be revealed in your state of higher awareness. If nothing happens, it doesn't matter.

However, you may find this mantra coming to you. It may come like a whisper on the wind and you may actually hear it. You may see it in front of you, in your mind's eye. You may find yourself saying it without even realizing it. If you do receive anything, give yourself the chance to work with it. See how it feels for you. Go through the process of seeing it, speaking it, immersing yourself in it and truly becoming one with the mantra. Notice if there is a tangible difference with this new word. Enjoy it. When you are ready, cleanse it away thoroughly. Take your time.

When you open your eyes, you may find that the room suddenly feels very bright and clear. It may seem as though it is pulsating with light. You may notice you are tingling with a vibrant energy you haven't felt before. Ensure you give yourself plenty of time to readjust again. Sip your water very slowly. Sit quietly for five minutes before you get up.

It is unusual for this exercise not to have a powerful effect. It is impossible to ignore the effects of sound. Whether you personally enjoy mantras and choose to use them regularly is another matter.

Some people simply find them too powerful, too invasive, particularly in the early stages of meditation. They can seem to consume your body and make you feel uncomfortable, especially if your own energy is very sensitive and vulnerable. You may find a lot of emotions creeping up on you that you weren't expecting. If you aren't comfortable with mantras, that is fine. You do not have to use them in order to meditate. You can use other relaxation tools.

If you found them comforting and powerful, then do use them as a regular means of meditating. You can chant throughout the whole meditation and see how that works for you. You may find wonderful insights and images coming to you through the waves of sound. Try out different mantras to see what the effects are on you. Each word has its own energy and meaning that will become personal to you. Some people use a particular mantra to look at a specific area of life. See if a certain mantra makes you want to meditate on one particular aspect of your life. You might want to start a Mantra Diary to keep track of your experiences.

You might find that you want to use a mantra to help you to sink into your relaxed state and you may then choose to slowly let the mantra fade as you withdraw your senses and prepare to enjoy meditation. It doesn't matter how you work with the mantras as long as you feel comfortable and secure with them.

Using Outside Sounds

There are also other sounds you might choose to have around you while you meditate. It does not have to be you making the sound; it can be an external force. In fact, you might be the sort of person who finds this more relaxing. You might prefer to focus on your breathing and let other sounds wash over you without your having actually to make them.

So, if you choose an outside sound, what might you enjoy and find soothing? This is, of course, very personal and you will have to experiment and see what works best for you. Some people are naturally much more in tune with what they like to have around them sound-wise because they are always aware of what is there. Other people have a natural ability to shut off from sound and to retreat when it suits them. For instance, some people find the continuous, recorded music that plays in hotel foyers and shops irritating and distracting, while others are completely oblivious to it. Perhaps you don't mind the dog barking next door or the hum of a computer or fridge. You may, though, find these sounds deeply aggravating.

Now is your chance to learn about what sounds you find therapeutic. Let's start with certain sounds of nature. Do you like the sound of the wind rustling the leaves of trees? Perhaps waves pounding on a seashore or the rush of a powerful waterfall make you feel good. Bird song can be wonderfully uplifting and relaxing. Other sounds of creatures are also gradually being accepted as helpful to meditate upon, such as the calls of whales or dolphins.

There are plenty of man-made sounds as well. What about drums beating or rattles shaking? These are used in many Indian and Shamanic practices. The ringing of bells is used by Buddhists to bring about awareness. You might prefer the sound of flutes or harps. Some of the synthesized 'new age' music can be beautifully dream-like in quality.

There is no one clear solution here for you. You need to try different sounds for yourself. So much is available for you to experiment with; new age music has become widely accepted and appreciated in our western society. Do make sure you listen to this music before you buy it, whenever possible. It can be expensive and until you hear it for yourself, you've no sure way of knowing what effect it will have on you. You might think you will like dolphin noises because you love dolphins, but until you hear a recording of their sounds for yourself, you can't know if they will be helpful for you. They might end up making you feel uncomfortable. It's better not to make assumptions but to actually allow the sounds themselves to vibrate around you and through you. Then you will know what is right for you.

During your meditations try experimenting with different types of sounds and see what works. You can do very simple tests. Open the window and let noise from outside come in and see how you react; depending upon your environment, this could be quite interesting! Buy a small wind chime and place it in a breeze by a window. See what that feels like to you. You can even get a glass jar, fill it with dried beans and shake it. What does that sound feel like to you? If you like it, why don't you record it onto your phone or your computer and play it back.

You may be surprised that certain noises really are helpful and comforting. Let yourself enjoy the learning process of sound and its effects and take your time. There is always some new sound for you to experiment with. The sound of a brush going through long hair can be beautiful or the purr of a contented cat. Try to become more aware of what effect the world of sound has on you. If you are regularly practising your mini meditations and being 'in the moment' more and more, you will find this easier to do.

Scents

Now let us look at the power of scents during meditation. Appreciation of scents and their power has existed since early man. You may have heard of aromatherapy: the art of using essential oils to nurture and balance our energy system, primarily through scent. As aromatherapy has only been rediscovered quite recently in Western society, you may not realize that it is actually an ancient form of healing.

An interesting discovery in 1975 confirms this. At this time a skeleton dating to nearly sixty thousand years ago was unearthed in Iraq and beside it were found concentrated deposits of pollen from plants; these same plants are still grown and used for medicinal purposes by Iraqi farmers.

This appreciation of scents and their beneficial properties can be found throughout man's history. A number of Central and North American excavations, dating back to 3000BC, have revealed a variety of seeds from medicinal herbs. A Chinese emperor, Kiwang-Ti, wrote a medical textbook in 2000BC acknowledging the healing properties of various scented herbs. It is well documented that the ancient Egyptians were deeply committed to using different oils and that they believed these were actually gifts from the gods. A scent such as myrrh, for example, was burnt as incense because they believed it pleased the gods. It was the Greeks who then invented distillation, the process by which essential oils are extracted from a plant and true aromatherapy as we know it today began.

The Romans appreciated the hedonistic pleasures deriving from scents, as did the Arabs. In his 'Book of Perfumes and Distillations', written in 850AD, Yakub al-Kindi of Baghdad details how to distil musks and balsams. In medieval Europe at the time of the Great Plague, pine, cypress and cedar were burnt as incense in sickrooms and hospitals. The white settlers who colonized North America discovered that the Native Americans used many scented natural substances whose properties helped in the treatment of various ailments.

In the last one hundred years or so, appreciation of the power of scent has enjoyed a resurgence of interest, particularly in the West. Much of this is due to research by French chemist René-Maurice Gattefosse, medical doctor Dr Jean Valk and biochemist Marguerite Maury who, between them, looked more closely at the scientific and medical benefits of applying aromatherapy to different conditions. Their work has done much to validate the physical power of scent and to give it the scientific seal of approval.

As you will appreciate from this very potted history, scents have played a major role in our awareness of well-being. It's important that you believe in the therapeutic qualities of scents and how you might work with them. Simply buying a synthetic perfume and spraying that about your meditation room will have little effect; in fact, it could be detrimental, as many people are allergic to synthetic scents, which often contain a number of man-made chemicals.

So what scents are going to be helpful for you? Now is the time for you to start experimenting. Certain flowers have very powerful odours; which ones do you like? Make a habit of sniffing the flowers you come across. (This is another wonderful way of living your life in daily awareness. When you stop and smell a flower, it's impossible not to be filled with appreciation for its beauty.)

If the area in which you live is very barren flower-wise, then notice what trees you have around you and, when they come into flower, stop and smell their flowers. You can also go into florist shops or stop and study the flowers sold on stalls. Certain flowers, such as freesias and lilies, have very strong aromas which can literally fill a small room with a glorious scent. Do you like the sweet perfume of lilies? Perhaps you prefer the delicate scent of roses.

When you next take a walk in a park or forest, stop and smell the plants. Certain house plants – scented geraniums, for example – can make wonderful additions to your meditation room. Simply brush your hand delicately across a geranium and the scent will linger on your skin. Give yourself time to experience this new appreciation of the world of scent.

When you have exhausted all the flowers and plants around you, turn your attention to different kinds of incense. Fortunately, many shops nowadays sell individual incense sticks, giving you the opportunity to try a variety of scents without incurring great cost. Buy just one or two and burn them in your room as you meditate. Notice what happens and which scents you react favourably to and which make you feel uncomfortable. You might find it useful to keep a Scent Diary, to monitor your reaction to these new odours.

If you find that you are responding positively to different scents, you might consider investing a little more and to work with more advanced concoctions. A good health or new age shop will be able to provide you with incense sticks that have been specially prepared with natural odours known to enhance meditation. Of course, this is still a personal experience. If you are very sensitive to scent, you might try one of these and find it a cloying, unpleasant odour and prefer to return to something else.

Essential oils are also a wonderful way to enhance your appreciation of smell. The drawback here is that pure oils can be expensive; there is little value in buying the cheaper synthetic alternatives, as they provide few benefits as far as relaxing for meditation is concerned. If you want to try essential oils, make sure you buy quality oils which only contain the pure essence of a product; if the label says 'perfume' you will know it is synthetic.

Again, essential oils can be strong and you will need only a few drops put onto a cotton wool ball to scent a small area. There are also certain oils you would want to avoid in special circumstances, such as pregnancy. If in doubt, always consult with the shop before purchasing. Never put pure essential oils directly onto your skin; they are too powerful and can cause skin irritation. Before massage, any essential oil is heavily diluted into a carrier oil, such as grapeseed or almond oil.

Essential oils are used neat only when burnt in an incense burner or diluted in bath water. If you want to invest in an incense burner, this is an excellent method through which you can scent a room. Again, make a note of how you react to different oils and really observe how your meditations differ when you try different oils. Do some make you want to meditate on different areas of your life? Is there a specific feeling that always comes over you when you use a particular oil?

Of course, you can use your incense burner for many purposes other than meditation! It can be used for cleansing, to rid a room of unwanted smells. You might want to have it burning away while you take a bath, to relax you. Perhaps you want a romantic evening with your partner; you can choose a scent for its aphrodisiac qualities to enjoy together. You may need lifting out of a feeling of depression, and want to burn a suitable oil in your work space.

Your relationship with different scents is personal and it is good for you to develop your own individual preferences. That is why a Scent Diary can help you gauge how you are responding and make you aware of what works for you and what doesn't.

However, there are certain flowers and essential oils that are said to have specific purposes and produce particular effects. This does not mean that you will necessarily respond in the way suggested to all of them, but it might be useful for you to try some of the scents listed below and note your reactions to them.

FLOWERS/PLANTS

Apple blossom: divination; health and romance
Carnation: self love; physical passion
Garlic: protection; health
Scented geranium: affirming appreciation of life
Goldenrod: protection
Honeysuckle: youth
Hyacinth: gentleness; femininity
Jasmine: self-esteem; psychic development; dreamwork
Lavender: inner guidance; spiritual contact
Lilac: travel; past lives
Lily: spiritual love; purity
Rose: awareness of the heart and love; beauty

All the flowers listed have quite strong scents which should make it easier for you to have a clear response. They are also only available during certain months, so your exploration of flower scents can take you through an entire year. Don't worry if your reaction is not the same as what is listed. These are general observations of effects and it is a very healthy sign if your reaction is entirely different; you are truly experiencing scent for yourself, rather than being conditioned by a set of beliefs.

If you are looking at the more complex world of essential oils, then below is a suggestion of just a few of the less expensive oils which you might find beneficial in the ways listed.

ESSENTIAL OILS

Cedarwood: enhances connection to spirit
Chamomile: for inner peace
Clary sage: balances mind and emotions
Eucalyptus: clears negativity
Lemon: increases energy and encourages clarity
Marjoram: calms agitated mind
Neroli: opens heart and enhances creativity
Rosemary: helps increase spiritual awareness
Rosewood: enhances meditation
Vetiver: aids stillness (known as the 'oil of tranquillity')

There are several hundred essential oils on the market today, so you will realize that what is above is a very small selection indeed. You may be fortunate enough to find a shop that has samples of these oils which you can sniff. If you go to an aromatherapist for a treatment, ask if you can smell some of their different oils and see how you respond. You won't necessarily want to buy the oils until you are reasonably certain they will benefit you.

Again, the oils don't have to be used purely for meditation. You might want to put a few drops of an appropriate oil into your bath water. For instance, if you are tired in the morning, try adding some rosemary to pep you up. If you return home deeply stressed after a difficult day, use some marjoram. If you really enjoy the power of essential oils, there are many good books available on the subject which go into each oil in considerable detail and will give you a good reference guide for the future.

As you continue with your meditations, also continue developing your relationship with sounds and smells, as this will increase your ability to sink into your newly discovered world of stillness and peace. Really work at finding your perfect combinations.

Keep trying out different mantras. Then keep looking at good combinations for you. Perhaps it is bird song in the background with vetiver essence around you. Maybe you prefer harp music and the smell of lilies in your nostrils. Dolphin sounds with chamomile essence may be right for you.

Perhaps you need to tailor the sound and scent according to what state you are in when you start meditating and you will need to work out what is right according to your immediate needs. Use mantras for a while and then stop and notice how differently you feel. Do the same with different exterior sounds and all the different scents. Keep being aware on a daily basis of what is really happening to you and allow yourself to use sound and smells as a helpful balancing tool. Continue using these new tools of awareness as complements to all the new techniques you are about to explore.

Next we are going to look at some of the other tools available to us, not only to help us retreat into our inner world but also to help us discover what is available to us once we are there. We're going to start off with the simple but very powerful use of words.

THE POWER OF A WORD

So what will this new world of meditation offer? It is one thing to experience this pleasurable sense of calm and peace and to enjoy it. But what more is there to gain from it? What good will it do, apart from leaving you feeling pleasantly relaxed?

Some people might say that simply to find this stillness is enough and that is all meditation requires. You find your peaceful core and you go into it each time you meditate and simply see what happens. That is indeed one way of meditating and simply to do nothing but rest in your inner stillness can be very refreshing and energizing. You can receive insights and advice simply through doing nothing but being there.

You might choose to do this for the next little while and enjoy yourself enormously in the process. That is fine. There is no need for you to rush through what is a pleasurable stage of exploration, working with the new tools you have been learning about, relishing this state of inner peace which you have only recently realized was there.

When you are happy to move on, you are ready to explore this chapter, which is about how we can work at a deeper level of awareness once we are in our meditative state and how focusing on a simple word can help our thoughts spiral onto new levels. You will already have seen how a word in the form of a mantra might help you. Now we are going to look at known words and see how awareness of something we recognize can take on a greater level of significance when we are meditating.

The 'A' Word

To start with, we are going to compare the difference between our level of awareness when we are not meditating and our awareness when we are. This is to enable you to realize that this inner stillness does indeed possess a great strength and offers more than your everyday state of awareness. In other words, we really want to prove that by taking the time and trouble to access this inner world, you will truly reap some definite benefits that would not otherwise be available for you.

Try the following two awareness exercises. For them you will need two blank sheets of paper and a pen.

Awareness exercise 1

Without stopping to breathe deeply or to think too much about it, ask yourself what the word 'awareness' means to you. Jot down your answers on one of the pieces of paper. It doesn't matter how silly or inconsequential your thoughts seem, just write them down. Put down everything you can think of, whether it seems particularly relevant or not. When you have finished, take a moment to cleanse everything away. Use the techniques you have recently learnt to do this.

Make sure you have cleansed thoroughly before you continue into the next exercise. Try to do this as soon as possible after finishing exercise 1.

Awareness exercise 2

Now, take the time to close your eyes, relax your body and breathe deeply. Get ready to enter your world of stillness. If you want to use a mantra, external sounds and scents to aid this process, that is fine. Let yourself sink into that sensation of peace and comfort. Wait until you are settled there before you continue.

Now say the word 'awareness' silently to yourself. What do you feel? What sensation comes with the word? What images? Let yourself play with the word, have it dance in front of you. Enjoy the information you are receiving. Rest in this comfortable state for as long as you like. When you feel you have learnt what you can from the word, slowly withdraw from it. Cleanse yourself and slowly return to reality. Write down what you have learnt as soon as possible before it slips from your consciousness.

Now compare the two exercises. How much did you write while you were in the first state? Was what you wrote enlightening and helpful? Did the information come to you quickly and easily? Now look at what you found out about the word 'awareness' while you were in your meditative state. What insights came to you then? Did you feel as though you were finding out this information for yourself or did it feel that you were being given it from another source? How much more did you discover from the second exercise? Compare the quantity of what you wrote in each exercise.

You will have found out that however much you gleaned from just thinking about this word, by meditating upon it the word was revealed to you in a new light. In other words, you were in an altered state of 'awareness' when you received these insights.

Apart from wanting to write down more after you meditated, you will also find that the content of what you discovered through meditation shows that your awareness progressed to another level. You may be amazed that you could possibly know so much about a simple word, and be touched by the profundity of what you have learned. This experiment should prove to you that what you are doing in meditation is indeed powerful and beneficial.

Working with Different Words

Now we're going to expand what you were doing above and see how working with different words really can open up a whole new world of awareness. Do you often feel that you don't understand the true significance of words, that they elude you in a maddeningly abstract way? This can be true of even relatively simple words you think you ought to know, such as 'peace' or 'stillness'. We are going to continue using words as a wonderful means of showing you what else you can learn about yourself and others. Spend a little time meditating on some of the words listed below and see what each one tells you about aspects of life.

WORDS FOR MEDITATION

Peace
Stillness
Cosmos
Truth
Honesty
Happiness
Money
Power
Conscience

Life
Universe
Purpose
Destiny
Meditation
Infinity
Fate
Time
Duality
Knowledge
Love

No doubt you can think of words of your own and add them to the list. Do make sure that when you meditate, you take yourself fully into that state of stillness before you continue. You might like to write your chosen word in large letters on a piece of paper and prop it up in front of you. Whenever you feel lost or stuck, you can then open your eyes and look at the word for fresh inspiration.

The next exercise shows how you can meditate powerfully upon one single word:

The word

Close your eyes and settle yourself comfortably. Relax, breathe deeply and let yourself enter your inner stillness. Rest there for a moment and then, when you are ready, open your eyes and look at your chosen word.

What is the first thought that comes into your head? Ask yourself why this is your response. See if a personal experience has triggered this reaction. Then let the feeling drift away. Say the word out loud or say it silently to yourself. What else does it mean to you? Do certain images or sensations come with it? Let yourself flow with those reactions, but try not to become deeply involved with any of them. If you have feelings you don't want, remember to keep washing them away as you have been taught. Let as many thoughts as you wish come and go.

If you are struggling to get anything with this word, you may be trying too hard. Let yourself play with the word instead. Have it dance it front of you. Close your eyes and imagine the letters stretching outwards and then inwards again. Have it become bold print or capitals or a beautifully flowing scroll. Bounce the word up and down like a ball. Sniff it. Eat it! You are free to respond however you wish. No one will know.

Ask the word if it would like to talk to you. Have the word or a letter in the word assume the shape of a person and see what the person says to you. Enjoy the sensation. Remember to keep observing your response to this word without becoming deeply engrossed in it. Does a certain colour or shape seem to fit this word? What other image might be appropriate? See what scenario comes to you as you focus on the word.

Now make the word become more personal to you. Where does this word manifest itself in your life? Are you comfortable with this? Where is it lacking? Where might you like it to be? What would you have to do to make this happen? How realistic a possibility does this seem to you right now? You may find yourself becoming emotional if some of the issues this brings up are very sensitive to you. Remember to go into your cleansing sanctuary if you want to. Remember how to cleanse away anything you don't want.

When you are ready, withdraw from the word. If it has really come alive for you during the meditation, you may find it difficult to let the word go. Use one of your cleansing techniques to get rid of it. Burn it, wash it away, have it float upwards in a balloon – whatever is powerful for you. Cleanse yourself again before you open your eyes.

Did you find yourself wondering how on earth you knew so much? Did you have a sensation that perhaps you were getting some information from outside sources and that you were a pupil being taught? Perhaps you had the feeling that you knew this all along but you had to pull it deep out of your unconscious mind before you could access it properly. Maybe you feel you didn't get what you wanted from the word. That is fine. You can return on any occasion and 'play' with the word again.

You might find it helpful to keep a Word Diary of what you discover during these meditations. Some of what we meditate upon can be lost to our conscious memory shortly after we finish meditating. Of course, the knowledge is still inside of us but we often choose to secrete it away and not call upon it regularly. This is also dependent upon how much we fill our minds with normal everyday problems and stresses. If we decide to give other matters priority, our minds will gradually push what we learn in meditations back into our subconscious and we may not use what we have learnt as effectively as we could.

Are you still doing your mini meditations? How often do you stop to be aware of what is there for you during your daily routine? When did you last eat mindfully and slowly? Did you pause to appreciate your life before you got up this morning?

Remember, all this work at a deeper level also wants to be balanced with your normal, everyday life. Meditating works on so many different levels and although as we travel more and more into our deeper world of inner awareness, it is exciting and powerful, we need to remember to balance it with our daily life.

Are there areas of your daily life that you would like to understand better? You can use meditation to help your understanding of them. You may remember our discussion earlier about the beauty and significance of simple, everyday tasks and how even washing or cleaning can become meaningful if you do it with total awareness. Perhaps you are still struggling with this and can't find any pleasure in your daily routine. Why not use the act of meditating to improve your understanding?

Everyday Meditation

The technique of using a single word to let your mind spiral onto other levels can also work in improving your toleration of mundane jobs. Are you struggling with the daily washing or a work task or the routine of collecting the children from school each day? Whatever you want to give extra meaning to, simply meditate on the action.

At this stage, it is probably easier if you use one word or two to identify the action, such as 'collecting children' or 'washing'. If you try to complicate it with long sentences you are going to be throwing a lot of emotions into the meditation and any insights you receive may be confused and jumbled as a result. To create powerful and helpful meditations, you need to make the concept you are meditating on as simple as possible.

If you are meditating on a personal subject, and are struggling with it, for whatever reason, remember that you will have to keep putting aside your own negative feelings during the meditation. If it is an emotional issue for you, then it is natural that your own emotions will be uppermost as you start. This is where the cleansing techniques become so valuable.

You will soon discover that it is your own preconceived thoughts about how everything ought to be which get in the way of you moving past the ordinary and progressing into the layers of deep subconscious thought, which is where our true wisdom and knowledge lies. Meditation teaches us just how human we are, and how our individual traits can sometimes stop us from achieving greater awareness.

The paradox is that we have to embrace our human behaviour before we can move past it to the higher levels. That is why you are constantly being reminded about awareness of everyday matters and how to bring this into your meditations. By truly embracing our very human responses to everything, we can learn how to let go of them during meditation and understand life on a much deeper level.

Do spend time assessing your everyday life through meditation. See what insights come to you through meditating on very simple words such as those below: There are probably quite a few of your own words that you want to add to this list, so feel free to do so!

DAILY WORDS

Washing
Cleaning
Ironing
Cooking
Career
Marriage
Partner
Child
Parent

Sibling
Mortgage
Rent
Home
Garden

Let yourself enjoy the experience of meditating with each word and notice what insights come to you. Do you find you are developing the ability to view areas of your life in a different way? Of course, some areas you will always find more challenging and frustrating than others. When these crop up, don't worry. If nothing really helpful or insightful happens in an area which you desperately want to understand more, let the emotions wash away and know that shortly you are going to learn some more techniques to help you deal with the heavier issues.

If you acknowledge that you can get so much from a single word, what else is there waiting for you to discover it? For instance, what about the possibility of a visual image helping to bring about a state of altered awareness? Let's move forward to look at this new area.

VISUAL IMAGES IN MEDITATION

During this section, we're going to be looking at different visual images and assessing what impact they have on you. We are talking about physical images now, not the sort you create in your imagination, although, as you will discover, one can directly affect the other.

Just as you have been discovering what you truly feel about different sounds and smells, now is the opportunity for you to find out what visual images you find helpful and enlightening. We've dealt with this already in talking about colour and what you would like to have around you in your meditation room. You have also been encouraged to create certain visual images in your imagination, to help elusive emotions or anxieties become more vivid and real for you.

Choosing an Image

First, you are going to consider what visual images help you to relax into a meditative state. After that, we will look at different, more complex images that may help you once you are in a meditative state.

We will begin by thinking about what images you find relaxing. Just as with mantras, you don't want to find yourself getting too caught up with the meaning of the image. If there are people in your image, chances are you will start thinking about what is happening to those people in the image. The simpler and more appealing the image is, the better. The best way to start this voyage of discovery is to visit art galleries or picture shops and really look. Personal taste in art is just that – personal! It is impossible to define what is a suitable picture for meditation because we all respond differently to the same image. Because of this wide diversity in artistic tastes, there is a wide diversity in art. The joy of this is that you are sure to find something that is right for you.

As well as strolling around art galleries, start looking at art in the homes of your friends and family. Do you immediately like some pieces and dislike others? When you are waiting in the dentist's or doctor's waiting room, study the walls. Do they relax you or make you feel more tense than ever?

Art is everywhere: in restaurants and shopping centres, in newspapers and magazines, even in graffiti on buildings. Go into a card shop and study the pictures on cards, or look at posters in poster shops. Get out your old photo albums and see if there are any pictures without people which you find interesting. Take your time and really think about what you like.

When you feel you are developing an understanding of the art you like, think about images in the context of meditating upon them. It's one thing to see a photograph of a newborn baby held in a man's large hands and think it is wonderfully touching and emotionally uplifting, but will it actually help you to relax into the inner stillness that you regularly seek in meditation? It may be you like an image because it is thought provoking. That doesn't necessarily make it a suitable candidate for relaxing into meditation. Continue enjoying your exploration of art, but become much more aware of what you find truly relaxing.

Relaxation in terms of visual images is heavily linked to colour; most people find pastel shades much more relaxing than sharp, bright colours. Do the images that soothe you most have colours that are muted and harmonious together? The colour green is known to encourage growth, harmony and loving thoughts; blue is found to have a very cooling and calming effect. Isn't it interesting that much of nature consists of differing shades of those two colours: grass, trees, sky, water? Have you noticed that many of the images you find comforting have blue and green in them?

Soft pink is also known to have a calming effect, and is often used in institutions where violent and aggressive behaviour is a problem. It has been discovered that a disturbed person will quickly become less agitated when he or she is put in an empty room painted entirely pink. Soft warm purples are considered beneficial for enhancing spiritual awareness. Are you drawn to any of these colours?

If you have only chosen bright reds and oranges so far, carefully consider whether they will properly soothe you for meditation. This is not to say that you are wrong for choosing them; you might have found the picture of a setting sun painted in rich reds and oranges to be the most inspirational image for you. It is just a suggestion that generally soft muted colours might be the most calming and relaxing.

Perhaps by now you will have chosen an image that you find helpful. Obviously, if you've found it in an art gallery you won't necessarily be able to have that image in its original form. However, you may find a postcard or reproduction of it available at a reasonable price. It can also be a good idea to look around second-hand shops and charity shops where you may find some good bargains. You might find your perfect image in a magazine or in an old photo. Greeting cards have some wonderful images on them nowadays, too. You needn't spend a fortune getting something right for you.

If you have a camera, why not invest in a roll of film and take photographs of objects or scenes that appeal to you? If you can't have a vase of sweet-smelling lilac in your room in winter, you could at least have a wonderful photo of it! Try photographing very simple images such as a lone tree or a single flower. A spider's web glistening after rain or a butterfly on a bush can be beautiful images. Take your time and go exploring for pleasing subjects.

Relaxing images can also be found in the surface of items that you might well have around you already. Have you noticed how beautiful the grain in wood can be? Perhaps you have a wooden table or chair that is unpainted. Take a good look at it and see if the grain of the wood has a wonderful pattern of swirls. A simple wooden bowl can be a wonderful object of focus and relaxation. The same is true of a piece of driftwood, a stone or crystal. Even a small crystal can be so beautiful that you can lose yourself in appreciation of its unique form and colour. A seashell is also an object of enormous intricacy and appeal. Look at a single leaf on a plant. Even the skin on a piece of fruit can be beautiful.

In your daily mindfulness of everything, take time to appreciate what is around you. See where there is a possibility of an image that you can use for meditation.

When you have chosen your image, prop it up in front of you and prepare to practise meditating upon it. If you are still feeling uncertain as to what you want to use, then you could select from one of the following and see how that works for you: a small crystal, a vase of flowers, a picture of the sea, a photo of the moon, a postcard of a tree (or other object of nature).

It doesn't matter if you don't find the image you choose as inspirational or relaxing as you would like it to be. You need to experiment to find out what touches you most deeply.

Visual meditation

Start by relaxing and concentrating on your breathing. You might want to close your eyes while you do this. You don't have to wait until you enter into your inner stillness because you are going to let the visual image do this for you; just ensure you are relaxed and comfortable first.

Now open your eyes and let your gaze rest on the image or object you have chosen. Don't stare at it; let your gaze be soft and slightly hazy. If you find thoughts coming into your head, keep washing them away. You don't need them now. Empty yourself of responses to what is in front of you. Just let it rest there without judgement or meaning. This is all you have to do. Simply enjoy its beauty.

As you keep your eyes focused on the image or object, notice that it seems to be coming nearer. It may feel as though it is becoming part of you or that you are approaching it and merging; it doesn't matter which. Let your consciousness slip slowly into the image. Feel yourself slide down into the swirls of the wood, or the petals of the flower or the intricate design of the shell or beauty of the object in front of you. This may be a gradual process and may take a long time, or you may feel yourself swept away on a wonderful wave of awareness. Whatever happens for you, it is right.

As this happens, you may find your eyes closing. You will find yourself sinking comfortably into your familiar world of peace and quiet, your private inner core. Let yourself slide quickly and easily into this state. You may notice that your image or object has come with you and is still visible in your mind's eye.

Ask silently why it has come with you into your inner world of silence and retreat. See what it is you are meant to learn from its presence. Spend some time together and enjoy its comforting presence. Let any pictures or sensations come and go in waves of awareness. Don't try to hold onto anything. Rest there for as long as it feels right for you.

Then slowly withdraw. Come back to your everyday world gradually, releasing the image or object from your mind's eye as you do so. Use your cleansing methods to get rid of everything you don't want. Wait until you are properly grounded again before you continue.

If you found The Flower exercise in the chapter 'Going into Stillness' helpful, this exercise may have seemed quite easy. If you found it hard, then it may simply be that you chose an inappropriate image for you. Repeat the exercise, several times if need be, trying different images and seeing what effect they have. If you find that your thoughts keep intruding, you probably haven't found the right image.

However, when it is right, you will be able to enjoy that lovely sensation of letting yourself float towards and then into the image itself. It is a freeing experience, and one that is hard to explain. When you do find an image or object that is right for you, think about whether you want to keep it in your meditation room. If it is a picture, you might want to consider having it enlarged, to make it even more powerful. If it is a small crystal, you might want one that is slightly larger.

Images don't just have to be there to help you sink into your inner stillness. You know that a mantra is a sound used to help create focus. There is also a geometric image, called a 'yantra', which is used to create visual focus in meditation.

A yantra is a complex symbol, Indian in origin, which reflects ancient laws of universal awareness and cosmic knowledge. This is not as daunting as it may sound, and you don't need to be an Indian guru to be able to work with yantras. The idea behind them is that they contain hidden meanings of life and the laws of universal activity. However, you don't have to tap into all that meaning to receive something valuable from it. You can simply enjoy the beautifully intricate patterns and let your thought processes come and go as you focus on them, enjoying whatever information you receive as a result.

Balancing the Sides of the Brain

To prepare ourselves for yantras, we are going to start with a more basic geometric pattern that will get our brains working in a slightly different way. We are going to get our brain to work on a double image and encourage

it to flick back and forth from one side to the other. The balancing of the two sides this achieves will enhance our ability to meditate.

Did you know that the two halves of our brain perform very different functions? Some people naturally use one side more than the other; usually the left dominates. Let's take a look at what each half contains and you can decide for yourself which half you think dominates in you.

The left-hand side of the brain is known to control our logical and linear outlook on life. This is the part of us which analyses things and which is responsible for our speech. It is very much about our ability to think clearly and scientifically about everything. People who naturally veer towards scientific and mathematical subjects will use this half of their brain a lot.

The right-hand side of our brain controls our more emotional and esoteric side, the emotional responses or feeling and insights that we can't necessarily explain using plain logic. People who are heavily involved in the arts, such as musicians, actors and artists, are likely to use the right-hand side of their brain more.

It is believed that through using both halves equally we can attain a healthier balance in our lives. This means that whilst we can be very 'earthed', logical and scientific about everything, we can also learn to acknowledge and work with the less tangible and more spiritual things in our lives. Meditation is greatly helped by balancing both halves of our brain.

Now take a look at the two images above. Focus on one image at a time, starting with the image on the left. Cover whichever image you are not looking at, so that you are not distracted. Notice how your interpretation of the image keeps shifting. At times the smallest square in the centre will seem the closest to you and it will look as though you are gazing down onto the top of a square cone. A moment later, your perception shifts and it seems as if the smallest square is far in the distance and you are inside and at the bottom of the cone looking up. Let your perception shift back and forth between one and the other, not trying to control your thoughts in any way. First the left half and then the right half of your brain are being used. When you have finished, close your eyes for a moment and let the image fade away. Wash it away using your cleansing techniques.

Now focus on the image on the right, the one with the circle and square. Again, don't force your thoughts, just let your awareness float back and forth between the circle and the square. At times one will dominate and then the other. It is not possible for both to be equally dominant at once. This shows that your brain is switching from one side to the other, balancing as it does so. Close your eyes when you have finished and wash the image away.

Do you notice a slight throbbing sensation in both halves of your brain? This shouldn't feel like a slight headache; if it does, you have been concentrating too hard and forgetting to breathe! You should just be aware of your brain having been used in a slightly different way from usual. Go back to these images periodically and look at them again, but don't strain your eyes and remember to keep breathing deeply.

These two images are not the yantras used for meditation purposes. They are scientifically designed geometric patterns with equally spaced repetitive elements that overlap at certain angles. Your brain and your eyes try to fill in the intersections, producing a sort of shimmer as they do so.

There is also a useful breathing technique that can help to balance the two halves of our brain. It is quite a simple exercise that feels initially as though it might not be very powerful. The proof comes after you have finished the exercise and realize that you feel quite different. This exercise balances the energies through both halves of our body, too, not just our brain. It sounds more complicated than it is; once you get into a natural rhythm, you will find it quite easy to do.

If you suffer from sinus problems or have a cold or a blocked septum, you will not physically be able to do this exercise. However, the alternative is not to hold your nostrils but simply to imagine that you are breathing through just one nostril and then the other. The thought processes alone can be very powerful, even if the physical body isn't able to follow the action through.

Alternate nostril breathing

Close your eyes. Place your right hand over your face so that your thumb can close off your right nostril and your little finger and the finger next to it can comfortably close the left nostril. Your index and middle fingers can rest lightly against your forehead.

Now you are going to close off your right nostril and breathe in through your left nostril. Close your left nostril and breathe out through your right nostril. Still keeping your left nostril closed, breathe in again through your right nostril. Close off your right nostril. Breathe out through your left nostril. Still keeping your right nostril closed, breathe in again through your left nostril and then repeat the process. After a little while you will find it is easy to get into a comfortable rhythm.

As you follow the pattern, count to two slowly as you breathe in and then again as you breathe out. Gradually increase this to four as you breathe in and four as you breathe out. Once you can breathe in and out comfortably to the slow count of four, you can introduce a pause between each in and out breath. Count to two slowly in these pauses. Here is a summary of the exercise:

Breathe in through left nostril to count of four
Hold for two

Breathe out through right nostril to count of four
Hold for two

Breathe in through right nostril to count of four
Hold for two

Breathe out through left nostril to count of four
Hold for two

Work slowly with the numbers and don't push yourself. You can eventually build up to counts of six and three if you practise enough and are relaxed.

You won't appreciate how well this works until you experience it for yourself. This is a very powerful exercise, based on yogic techniques, which can really help balance your energies before you start any meditation. It can be used very effectively if you are feeling stressed or out of sorts and desperate to relax whilst at the same time feeling you can't! Spending just a few minutes focusing on the alternate nostril breathing really helps to calm, ground and focus your thoughts.

The Yantras

Now we are going to work with yantras. There are hundreds to choose from, but we are going to look at just a few examples. People who are used to meditating may find it easy enough for a yantra to be the means by which they sink into meditation, but it is not usually an effective method for the inexperienced. Prop up the image shown on the next page and begin the exercise.

First yantra

Close your eyes, focus on your breathing and let yourself relax. Wait for a few minutes before you open your eyes. Now look at the image. Let your focus be soft and hazy; don't stare too hard at it. What does it say to you?

Initially, you may find this difficult. It may seem as though it's just a pretty pattern and there is no actual meaning within it. This is a common experience in the beginning with yantras, so don't worry if you feel lost and uninvolved with the image. Try some of the suggestions below.

Which part of the image are you drawn to first? Let your concentration be pulled into that area. As it is, notice what feelings and sensations come over you. If you find your thoughts wandering onto an element of your life, let them do so and then gradually pull your focus back

again to the image. Notice where you are drawn to next. Let your focus be pulled from one area to another. Let yourself feel whatever emotions or sensations come up for you; don't try to pull away from them. Remember to keep breathing.

If you haven't done so already, spend some time focusing on the series of triangles in the middle. Let your focus come and go, as you did with the earlier diagrams to balance the two halves of your brain. Notice the myriad of differently shaped triangles for you to discover. Let a particular pattern become vivid for you and see what information comes to you.

Now concentrate on the outside square and slowly work your attention around it. What does each side feel like to you? Does each section have different emotions? Repeat this process with the two circles and their petal-like displays. Notice if your emotions or sensations change. Do you feel that different parts of your body respond to different areas of the image?

Spend a little time focusing just on the black dot right in the centre of the image. Let yourself be pulled into it and notice how this makes you feel.

When you are ready, look at the image as a whole. Observe all facets of the image and see how they fit together as a jigsaw. Become aware of the beauty of the pattern. If you feel you want to close your eyes and you can still see the image in your mind's eye, then see what information comes to you from that.

Withdraw when you feel you have learned all you can. Take your time to withdraw, release the image from your mind and then cleanse and ground. Wait a few minutes before you get up.

Did you find that a difficult exercise? Many people do initially. Meditation with yantras can be a slow practice but a deeply rewarding one. It can seem as though you are simply looking at a nice shape and you can't see anything in it that is worth investigating further. For others, it can be a truly awe-inspiring experience where the pattern seems to dance and move in front of them and they find themselves effortlessly transported to other realms of awareness.

We're going to look at what some of the symbols in this yantra mean, so you can gain some spiritual awareness of what the image represents.

This yantra is an overall depiction of the totality of our existence, so that we may understand our own unity within the cosmos as a whole. In other words, this yantra shows our journey from being a physical body in the earthly world through to true spiritual enlightenment in the highest realms of consciousness. Let us break down the image in more detail to get a clearer understanding of this concept.

First, we'll take the outer frame. This deals with the physical self. Each section represents our passions, which often prevent us from understanding higher spiritual truths. You will see that sections are numbered from 1 to 8, and that each one represents a quality:

1: worldly desire
2: anger
3: avarice and greed
4: infatuation and fascination
5: obstinacy and false pride
6: jealousy
7: earthly rewards
8: our deficiencies and blameworthiness

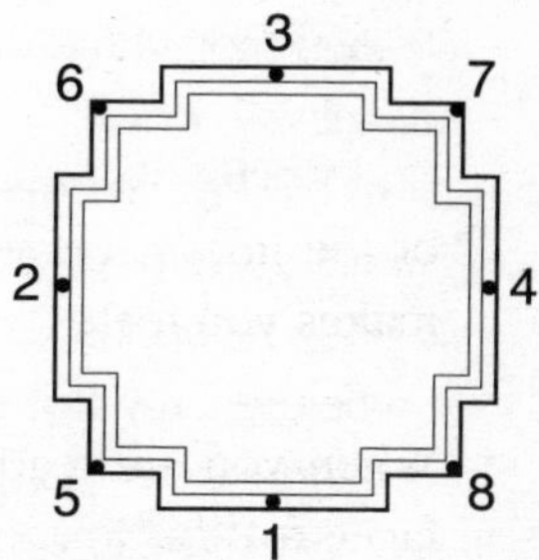

As you can see, taken together these sections identify many human emotions with which most of us can readily identify. Did meditating upon the square make you want to focus on various emotional issues in your life?

Within the square on the yantra, you can see a circle with sixteen petals around it. These relate to the everyday means through which we access our human emotions: the ten sense organs (ears, skin, eyes, tongue, nose,

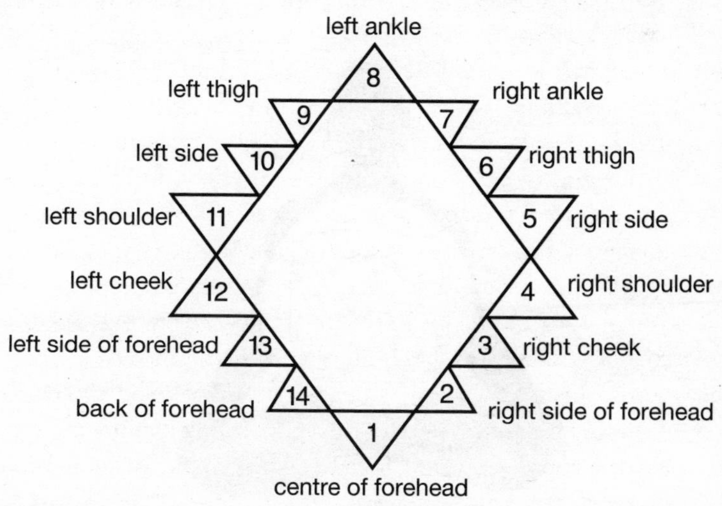

mouth, feet, hands, arms and genitals), the five elements of life (earth, fire, water, air and ether) plus our fluctuating, always trying-to-control-us mind. The circle with eight petals refers to further aspects of our physical self, such as speech, grasping, locomotion, evacuation and enjoyment, and emotions we need to understand, such as rejection, acceptance and indifference.

We then move on through the series of different triangles to appreciate the means by which we can release some of these restricting human emotions binding us to all earthly existence and how we can move forward to spiritual awareness. This is achieved, firstly, through awareness of our subtle body, as opposed to our earthly body, and focusing on points of the body where energy flows; these are similar to the energy meridians used during acupuncture. If you look at the triangular shapes on page 121, you will see how these areas are sectioned within the yantra.

Further triangular configurations refer to spiritual energy and how, through controlled breathing techniques, it can be used by us to create higher awareness. The concepts then become finer and more complex, making it harder for a Western mind to relate to, but basically these symbolize our ability to release opposing physical emotions – such as pleasure/pain, heat/cold – and move beyond them to a higher realm of consciousness. The dark circle in the very centre of the image depicts the true spiritual self, unfettered by earthly, physical existence, living in total harmony with and awareness of all cosmic laws and higher consciousness.

That definitely sounds unearthly, doesn't it? Don't worry, you are not expected to attain these levels of consciousness. Most Westerners don't have the years of understanding and experience to allow them to do this. Nor do you have to try, but it is good to have some idea of where prolonged meditation can lead you. Your intention is purely to use a yantra as a way of finding out more about yourself and the universe in general. If through meditation you can discover more about how your existence fits into the cosmos as a whole, that is a wonderful added bonus but certainly not essential. Once you have a clearer picture of what that First Yantra is saying, try returning to it. Meditate upon it and see what your experience is like now you understand that much more.

When you have done this, you might want to consider the two additional yantras shown on the preceding page and below. No additional explanations have been included for these; they are there for you to draw your own conclusions. There is no absolute truth attaching to the yantras, and what they symbolize is open to personal interpretation. They are there to be used as a personal awareness tool. Meditate on them when you have the time and feel that it is right. You may want to leave the yantras until you have meditated more on a regular basis and ease yourself into their deeper meaning when it feels more natural for you to do so.

We are now going to move forward and look at how we might deal with some deeper personal issues. We are going to do this by learning awareness of the subtler energies around us which we can use in a constructive way to increase the effectiveness of our meditations.

TOOLS FOR DEEPER MEDITATION

You may have become very aware that, although you seem able to look at certain issues in meditation and you can find methods through which you can start to resolve them, the more difficult, long-term issues are not responding as powerfully as you would like. For example, you may feel as though you can go about some of your daily tasks with a lighter heart and a greater appreciation of their value, but has meditation really helped to shift your deep-seated concerns about bigger issues in your life such as relationship or career problems?

The reason you may answer 'no' to this last question is because to work at deeper levels, you need to have better 'digging' tools to access the information you want. To draw a useful analogy, so far you have been working with handmade tools such as pickaxes and hammers to delve into your meditations but more major, long-standing issues require some powerful electrical drills and diggers!

You have already learnt a great deal about your breathing and how it is the fundamental tool through which you can access greater awareness and a deeper state of relaxation. We have discovered that the breath can be deepened in a way we hadn't previously realized. Now is the right time to consider our whole body and how it can work in a more holistic way.

In the last chapter, part of the complex explanation of the meaning of the First Yantra involved how we could use our subtle body as opposed to our physical body and how we used energy meridians in our body to do this. You may have wondered what all that meant, unless you have experienced or studied acupuncture or acupressure or other sciences relating to the subtle body.

The Subtle Body

So let's look at this 'subtle body' in further detail. You know something about your physical body and what it can do, but have you ever thought of yourself as being more than purely physical? In your early stages of meditation, you will no doubt have discovered that this quiet inner core you find inside yourself doesn't actually seem to be a tangible area, but more a feeling or sensation which comes over you. Yet you now don't doubt it is there because you are able to access it on a regular basis. The fact that there is no actual physical area which provides you with this sensation doesn't seem to matter much, does it? The subtle body, as opposed to the physical body, comes into this same realm. We may not actually see it, but it becomes completely real once we experience it.

So what is the 'subtle body'? A helpful way to put it might be to describe ourselves as energy as well as physical matter. Our subtle body is basically our energy system. Think about this in terms of what you sense from other people. Do some people give off comforting energy and others make you immediately feel uncomfortable? When someone is angry, does the space around their body feel very different from when they are calm? When someone is in love, can you sense or almost see a golden glow of pleasure around them? Think about the effect of being around someone who is permanently 'on edge' and distraught. Now think of being in the calming influence of a gentle and wise figure who is always smiling. Would you say that all these attitudes give off very different energies and that you can almost tangibly feel these energies, even though they aren't visible to you in a physical sense?

Have you sometimes entered a space and been struck by how pleasant it feels without any obvious reasons for it? Likewise, you can also go into a room and suddenly feel very uneasy, without any obvious physical indication as to why you feel this way. Just as with people, you are immediately drawn to some rooms and you feel you want to return to them, to enjoy the feeling of that space. So what are you tapping into when you have these responses?

The simple answer is: energy! Everything we say and do gives off a subtle energy. If the emotion is very strong, we can actually pick up on it and want to react to it. If you are now beginning to doubt this, because you believe the physical appearance of a person or room prompts a particular response, then it might help you to know that blind people pick up on this energy without having the ability to see.

You can prove this point for yourself by performing a simple experiment. You will need to find a willing friend to help you explore the energies people give out. However, if they are cynical about meditation or spiritual energy, you might find them a poor subject. Try the exercise below one day when the opportunity arises.

Tuning in to energy

Sit opposite each other, just a few feet apart, and close your eyes. Both of you need to take a moment to focus yourselves and to breathe deeply. Both of you should keep your eyes closed throughout.

Now one of you chooses to be the Giver and the other the Receiver. The Giver concentrates on a particular emotion while the Receiver sits quietly and relaxes. The Giver needs time to let the emotion become real and vivid to them. They might find it helpful to concentrate on a powerful memory to help them. However, the Giver at no time speaks or articulates the emotion, they simply feel it and let it seep out of them in an energetic form towards the Receiver. Ensure you work with strong emotions such as anger, peacefulness, joy, sadness.

When the Receiver is ready, they then tune in to what is coming at them. Remembering to keep their eyes closed, they simply focus on what they feel coming at them in waves from the Giver. They then check with the Giver if their feelings are accurate. Both of you then need to cleanse the emotion away before you continue.

Have another try or swap over so that the Giver becomes the Receiver and vice versa. You may find one person is more sensitive to picking up energy than the other. The only rule is that you must always remember to cleanse afterwards and ensure that the last emotion you choose is a positive one that leaves you both feeling good.

You will probably be amazed to discover how easy it was to sense the other person's emotion. If you struggled, it may be because you weren't taking the exercise seriously and spent more time laughing than focusing! Sensing energy is just like any other technique; it can take some practice before you are proficient at it. However, it is not a difficult skill to pick up. Some people are naturally more sensitive than others, but everyone can learn to increase their awareness.

Now is the time for you to practise this awareness of subtle energies on a regular basis. Find time during the day just to close your eyes and briefly feel what is around you. What can you sense from other people's energies when you stop for a moment, breathe deeply and tune in to what they are feeling? The more you practise, the easier it becomes.

Do some fun experiments, such as closing your eyes briefly when there is a particular atmosphere in a room and experience how it actually feels. The moment before someone enters a room for a surprise party is a good example; you can really enjoy the feelings of suspense, excitement and nervousness all rolled into one. Closing your eyes often intensifies the experience. It also enables you to really 'be in the moment' and to fully savour the energy around you. Do you notice that your skin literally tingles with the energies in the room? Try doing this with very different emotions and start to notice how you personally respond.

Do you find tension quite an exciting energy to tap into? It may be emanating from a contentious scenario such as a row in full flow or a pending argument or nervousness about an upcoming challenge. Some people actually enjoy the energy this creates; others find it very stressful and want to shy away from it. Some people find loud, pulsing music energizing and uplifting; others find it tiring and irritating. You may love quiet, gentle people; others may find them very frustrating. Start to become more and more aware of which energies you find appealing and which you find yourself disliking.

So, how does awareness of this subtle energy system affect our ability to meditate? The subtle body, also called the aura, is like a personal data bank containing all the information about you; it is your constant shadow and it reflects everything you are. By learning how to tap into your own aura, you can learn to understand who you really are. This process isn't always an easy one. Just as we find certain emotions easier to pick up on than others, so our own energy system, or aura, as we'll now call it, has certain elements that are easier for us to tap into than others. Some of them are really hard to fathom out. Why is this so?

The Aura

Our aura is actually a complex series of layers and some of these layers are relatively easy to tap into because their energy is quite dense or heavy.

However, the higher we travel in our subtle body or aura, the lighter and finer the vibrations become and it becomes more difficult for us to tune into. To explain this, think about the energy that anger gives out. That is quite loud and clear as an emotion, isn't it? However, how about awareness or aloneness as an emotion? Either would seem to be a more subtle energy, wouldn't it? How easy would it be for you to sit opposite someone and pick up on the emotion of being alone? You might find it quite difficult. This relates to how difficult it can be to tap into some of our finer energies. However, the finer and lighter our energies are, the more in tune we are with spiritual truths and awareness of who we really are and why we are here. It therefore makes sense that we want to learn how to tap into our own aura and to learn more from it.

Before we continue, it is important that you acknowledge the existence of your own personal area. If you can't believe in it, how can you work with it? The word 'aura' might be a relatively new word to you and you might find the concept of an unseen energy system quite hard to work with. You might acknowledge that people give out and receive energy from others, but who is to say that our own aura contains everything about us? Why is it not just energy that comes and goes? Who says each aura belongs to one person and comes and goes from that person?

The best way to prove this is through seeing an individual's aura for yourself. Not all people see auras, although you can train yourself to do so if this is important to you. Try the experiment below one day when you have some uninterrupted time.

Your aura

Arrange a full-length mirror in front of you and a plain, white light behind you. Make sure the area behind you is as dark and plain as possible. It is hard to see auras against patterned backgrounds.

Now sit or stand quietly in front of the mirror for a few moments. Focus on your breathing and look inwardly for a while, ignoring your own reflection. You might want to close your eyes for this, although if you are standing you might find this makes you feel unbalanced. Calm and still yourself.

> When you are ready, open your eyes and focus on the area just around your head. Let your gaze soften, don't stare too hard. Can you see anything? Remember to keep breathing and don't try too hard. Can you see a vague light? Perhaps it is like a fuzzy white haze or a golden glow. It may encompass the whole head or only seem to be there in sections. It may seem like the light that a candle flame gives off. You may see nothing at all. Concentrate on the area around your head for a while.
>
> Then let your focus be drawn to other areas around your body. Can you see anything near your heart area? (Like the head, this is another part that can give off and receive powerful energy.) Let your focus shift to different areas of your body and notice when you can see anything. Don't worry if you can see very little.
>
> When you have finished, remember to wash away anything you didn't like. Take a moment to ground yourself when you have finished.

Did you see anything? With some practice, most people can at least see a vague sort of glow emanating from their head. Some people see a lot very quickly; others take longer. You can also do this exercise with a willing volunteer. You might find it much easier to see someone else's aura than your own. Always remember to have a white light shining on them and have them sit or stand against a dark, plain background.

Every living form has its own aura, so you can also do this with an animal or a plant. Again, this can become something you enjoy doing in your spare time: exploring the world of auras and what they mean to you and learning how they manifest themselves in your consciousness. Some people see different colours around people; others can distinguish between different layers as they emanate outwards from the body becoming lighter and finer in texture.

You might also find it helpful to feel your own aura. Your aura is around all of you at all times; you can't get away from it or separate it in any way from you, so it is always there to work with or play with. A good way to become aware of your energy is to use your hands. Try the next exercise.

Hand energy

> Take some deep breaths and relax. Take your time. Now hold your hands up in front of you, palms facing each other, but about eighteen inches apart. Have your fingers straight but close together rather than spread open. Now slowly, very, very slowly, move your hands in towards each other. Really take your time over this, do it gradually and with complete awareness.
>
> Before you get very far, you will feel a slight pulling sensation, as if there is something happening between your two hands. You may want to move your hands apart a little. Now move them in again. What can you feel? Slowly, very slowly, move your hands closer and closer together. At some point, you may actually feel as though you can't move them any closer together; it may feel as though a force is keeping them apart. This is your own energy, your own aura.
>
> Play with your aura, feel it bounce back and forth between your hands. Try to pat it into a round ball. Let it stretch outwards until you can't feel it and then move it in again. When you have finished, give your hands a good shake and release any restricted energy.

Could you feel that quite strongly? It's a good way to acknowledge there is some interaction of energy taking place, although you can't actually see it. If you do this exercise again sometime, you may actually be able to see some light playing back and forth between your hands.

It might help you to realize that the existence of these subtle energies and the human aura has been known about and worked with on many levels since time immemorial. Drawings dating to the days of our cavemen ancestors show images depicting light coming from around people's bodies, indicating an understanding of the human aura. There are constant references to the subtle energy systems in ancient Indian, Chinese, Greek and Egyptian cultures. These peoples not only acknowledged its power but constantly looked at how they could work with it in a positive way to increase the health and spiritual awareness of the living. Many of the practices in which this energy is used are now becoming accepted by Western medicine, such as acupuncture, acupressure, reflexology, aromatherapy and many others. The fact we are only gradually relearning about the aura here in the West doesn't make it less important, it simply means we must work harder to relearn what our ancestors already knew.

I remarked earlier that our aura is a kind of data bank of personal information and contains all of us in energy form. So how might this be distributed? Detailed studies of the human aura have been conducted by a number of eminent scientists, physicians and physicists, such as Karl von Reichenbach, Walter J. Kilner and Dr Robert Beck. They were intent upon proving its existence scientifically and also on understanding the information the aura might contain. More recently, highly respected researchers such as Barbara Ann Brennan and Carolyn Myss have explained the human aura in terms Westerners can understand and have allowed us to work more effectively with it as a result.

The human aura is known to contain at least seven separate layers of energy, each one connecting to the other and each one becoming finer and lighter in intensity as it radiates outwards from the body. The aura is a lifetime's study on its own, so what is offered next is a very condensed, simplified version of its relevance to us. However, simply by understanding the human aura at its most basic level, we have the opportunity to understand more about our spiritual selves.

The Layers of the Aura

Below is an outline of each of the seven layers of the aura. The first layer is closest to the physical body and is the part that most people see initially when they start focusing on auras. The others radiate outwards sequentially.

First layer

The physical self; about being earthed and grounded, enjoying all physical activities and pursuits and everything to do with 'earthly' living.

Second layer

The emotional self in relation to one's life; about self-expression and self-love.

Third layer
The mental self; to do with rational thoughts and our ability to rationalize.

Fourth layer
Conditional love; how we feel about others and how we relate to them. Here the energies start to become lighter and finer and harder to see.

Fifth layer
Divine will, the releasing of personal ambitions and emotions; about our ability to see life as part of a larger picture and to understand where we fit in.

Sixth layer
Divine love; unconditional and all-encompassing love, allowing us to understand everything in the larger context of universal laws, rather than through earthly attachments.

Seventh layer
Divine mind; about fusing with all spiritual awareness and becoming one with universal truths and laws. Described as a state of bliss.

This is a fairly comprehensive explanation of what we might find within our own auras, even though some of the higher layers may refer to ideal states we can only imagine rather than actually feel at this stage. It does at least give you an indication of what you can aspire to during meditation.

Each layer of the aura is virtually a blueprint for one aspect of our lives. If we look at what may be malfunctioning within one of those areas, we can, through deep meditation, shift the problem, release it and move forward. So how do you get into these layers of the aura to work with them?

The answer lies in discovering the door into these layers of energy. There are seven doors you can use to enter the aura. These doors are called chakras. You may never have heard of this word, which means 'wheel' in Sanskrit. The existence of these chakras has been known for thousands of years and many techniques have been developed to help nurture this awareness.

The seven chakras are basically the entrance into the human aura. They are located at specific parts of the human body. We mentioned earlier the practice of acupuncture, which is the art of inserting needles into parts of the body to release blocked lines of energy. Our body is a very complex criss-cross of energy lines; it is believed that there are more than seventy two thousand separate lines of energy running through the human body at all angles. Each of the seven chakras is located at a point where twenty-one lines of energy cross the body. (There are also 21 minor chakras represented by the crossing of fourteen lines of energy, but here we shall only be focusing on the seven major chakras.)

It is through our increased awareness of the chakras that we can gain access into our subtle body, our aura, and thereby understand a great deal more about the purpose of our life on every level.

Before you read through the chakras, it is necessary for you to understand that this ancient knowledge and appreciation of the chakras was traditionally passed down from ancient wise men, or gurus, to their disciples. They were considered so sacred that no information was ever written down; only by working with each chakra, it was thought, could you possibly understand its true meaning. No words could do justice to the degree of awareness available through them or the profundity of that experience.

The difficulty in trying to interpret them in a way that makes sense to Western minds is that it tends to trivialize their importance and their impact on spiritual awareness. Many of our words sound quite trite and inadequate because experiencing the chakras is just that: an experience. Some experiences are very hard to put into words. When you have had a wonderful meditation, would you not find it hard to explain? You might try using words like 'peace' or 'stillness' or 'calm' or 'contentment', but they seem rather inadequate for what you are trying to describe.

Similarly, we use words to describe the power of the chakras which are fundamentally inadequate because there are no known words to explain such an experience; it is beyond worldly definition.

If you look at the illustration on the next page, you will see where the seven major chakras are located in the human body. In fact, the entrance to each chakra is just outside the physical body, but for our purposes it is described as part of the physical body in order to make it easier to relate to. You will see the chakras are cone-like in shape and some open back and front through the body, while others have only one opening either upwards or downwards. When we receive subtle energies, such as someone else's emotions, these unseen energies enter our aura through the chakra openings. They swirl in through the open cone and are then distributed through our aura, affecting different parts of us.

You will see that all the chakras are inter-connected and flow into and through each other. The base chakra, for example, isn't just connected to the first layer of the aura and the second chakra to the second, etc. Each chakra has a cone or opening through each layer of the aura, so each chakra is not only connected to all the other chakras, it is also connected to all the layers of the aura.

The chakras make up a very complex system of energy awareness which you can spend a lifetime studying. In fact, the yogis of ancient civilizations would have spent an entire life studying just one of the chakras, content in the knowledge that there would be other lifetimes in which they could continue learning about the other chakras.

It's useful to know that the chakra is often likened to the lotus flower; a multi-petalled profusion which is meant to symbolize the multi-dimensional significance of the chakras. A lotus flower is also used because it is a stunningly beautiful flower which will grow in the muddiest and dirtiest of waters; hence the analogy that from the least likely of physical circumstances true spiritual beauty can triumph and flourish. This analogy also implies that however unclear your own present perception of spiritual awareness, it need not be an obstacle to your ultimate progress because from 'muddy' thoughts, sudden clarity and awareness can blossom. You may find this an inspirational thought.

Below is a run-down of each chakra and its significance. You will notice that each chakra relates to each layer of the aura. The Western interpretation is to attach a colour to each chakra to make it more identifiable, as well as to relate each one to a physical organ in the body. There are many more interpretations which could be added, such as an animal affiliated to each chakra and the number of lotus petals for each, as well as associated actions and elements. They are not all listed here; through meditation you may discover these for yourself.

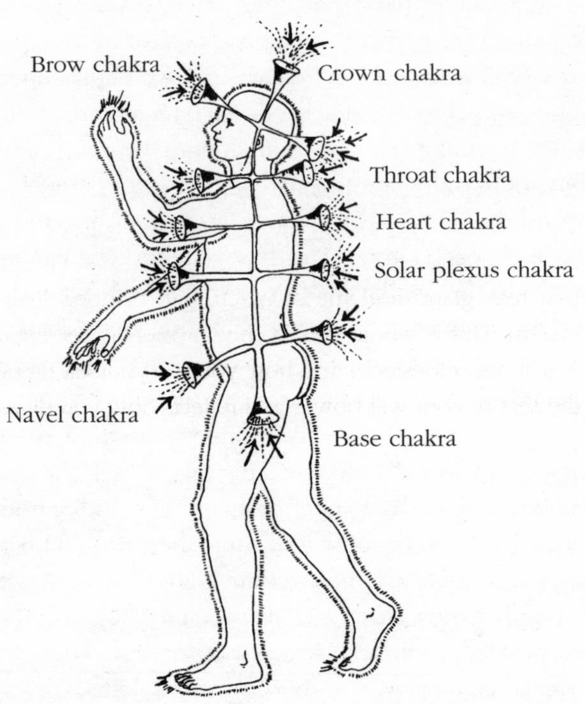

Base chakra

Located at the base of the spine and opens downwards to the ground. Its associated colour is red and physically it is related to the spinal column, the adrenal glands and the kidneys. This chakra is about your physical sense of being and your appreciation of earthly life, such as loving food, sexual relations and all physical activities. It is often called the 'root' of you, because it shows how rooted you are in all earthly matters. It is also about your instinct for survival, your 'flight or fight' metabolism.

Navel chakra

This is found just below the navel and opens front and back through the body. Sometimes it is known as the sacral chakra. It is associated with the colour orange and is connected to the reproductive system and our immune system. This is about our sexuality, but not simply referring to the sexual act itself. It deals with how well you form relationships with others, whether sexual or not. It is about your emotions in relation to this. Given that sexuality is a difficult area for many people, this chakra needs special sensitivity and gentleness.

Solar plexus chakra

This is situated just below the breastbone, slightly to the left. It opens both front and back. The colour given is yellow. It is affiliated to the pancreas gland and the stomach, gall bladder, liver and nervous system. This is where you store your mental perception of yourself; it is about self-esteem and how you see yourself fitting into life. It is the seat of your will-power and reflects how you digest information.

Heart chakra

This is found in the middle of the breastbone and above the chest, and opens both front and back. It is connected to the colour green and associated with the thymus gland, the heart, blood and the circulatory system. This is about love; not just your ability to love yourself and others, but also how you love the universe as a whole. The subtle energies start to change here and become lighter and finer. The heart chakra is often considered the hinge or link between the physical and spiritual worlds: the point at which true spiritual awareness can start to develop.

Throat chakra

This is located at the hollow of the throat and has two openings, front and back. The colour sky blue is connected to this chakra, which relates to the thyroid gland, bronchial tubes and vocal organs, lungs and alimentary canal. This is about how we hear inner truths and learn how to speak them. It reflects what we feel about our professional life, too, and how we can expand our awareness on every level. This is about integrity of speech and living through higher awareness.

Brow chakra

Situated in the middle of the forehead, this opens both front and back. Purple is the related colour and it's connected to the pituitary gland, lower brain, left eye, ears, nose and nervous system. This is often called our 'third eye' and is about our vision to see, not in a literal sense but in a much wider, truly spiritual and universal context. As the energies become yet finer and higher, so these concepts become harder to grasp without literally experiencing them.

Crown chakra

This is found at the very top and centre of the head. It has only one opening, upwards to the sky. It is associated with the colour violet, although it is sometimes also referred to as white, since the crown chakra symbolizes true purity at all levels of consciousness. The body parts it is connected to are the pineal gland, upper brain and right eye. As this is the highest and finest of all the subtle energies, it is the most difficult to explain. It is related to a state of pure bliss, a sense of understanding and awareness that transcends all earthly words. It is supreme connection and merging with the divine. It is a state to which one can aspire, without necessarily understanding all it encompasses.

Have you found all this description quite daunting? Perhaps you have found it exciting and thought-provoking. You have to remember that you are dealing with ancient awareness on a spiritual level which has virtually been forgotten by Western societies. It takes a while for us to grasp these concepts and begin to work with them. Through meditation you have already taken the first steps.

You may not have realized it at the time, but when you were meditating on different areas in your life and different issues that have affected you, you were unconsciously tapping into some of these chakras and working with them. In fact, the base and crown chakra are open at all times; it isn't possible to close them. You receive energy in different forms through both these chakras. All the other chakras close but can be opened when strong emotions are aroused. Let's look at some examples to clarify this for you.

When you work with grounding yourself and feeling the roots coming out of your feet, you are in fact pulling the earth's grounding energy up through your base chakra and letting it fill your subtle body with grounding influences. When you have felt particularly high, as though your head were in the clouds somewhere and you were transported to another, higher realm, then you were experiencing spiritual energy coming down through your crown chakra and filling your aura with the pure white light of love and awareness. When you had a sudden rush of love during a meditation because you were focusing on a concept that filled you with compassion, your heart chakra was being activated. So, as you can see, you have been working with your chakras, it's just that you weren't aware of it before!

What we are now going to do is take some time to learn how to meditate on our chakras and see what an enormous difference this can make to our understanding of life on all its different levels. You might want to take a moment to reread the descriptions of the chakras before you go to the next chapter.

DEEPER MEDITATIONS

At this point, it is important for you to realize that working in a more intense manner may bring up issues which arouse strong feelings you hadn't previously acknowledged. It is therefore particularly important that you acknowledge the power of cleansing and using your sanctuary as and when you need it. You are always in control during meditation and you can decide to get rid of whatever you don't like. It's very important that you acknowledge this is your right and do not hesitate to let go of anything you choose not to have.

The best way to work with your chakras is to open them all up during meditation and then to bring your focus to one particular chakra. It is quite likely you have already been opening some, if not all, of your chakras during meditation anyway, because this will occur naturally when you are in states of higher consciousness.

Here, we are going to look at the additional power that is created by consciously focusing on them. As you start, remember that you have already been working with these chakras unconsciously, so it is not as new a realm as you might fear and you are simply choosing to focus directly on them to enjoy an added strength and awareness in your meditations. It's important that you don't become too obsessed with trying to literally feel each chakra and its power and thereby forget to breathe deeply and relax. Chakra awareness comes gently and gradually when you handle it with sensitivity and love, rather than pushing for an instant response.

So we will start with learning how to consciously open all your chakras and to enjoy the new sensation that comes from this heightened awareness. As with all meditations, make sure you follow the usual guidelines; if necessary, refresh your memory and look back at the check list given on page 60. To help you prepare for meditating upon the chakras, it is strongly recommended that you spend a few minutes doing the Alternate Nostril Breathing you were taught on page 117. It's a particularly effective exercise to help prepare you for these higher realms of awareness.

Opening your chakras

Settle yourself comfortably and close your eyes. Remember to take your time to breathe deeply and relax. Let the cares of the day roll away from you. Wash away what you don't want and don't need. Allow yourself to sink into a wonderfully relaxed state.

When you are ready, you are going to start with the base chakra. This is at the base of your spine. Simply bring your focus to this part of your body. You can either imagine it as part of your body itself, or slightly outside of your physical body; it doesn't matter which. Let your concentration be taken to the area without effort. Remember this chakra only opens downwards to the ground and it is never closed. Tune in to this area. What can you feel? This is personal for everyone. It may be a slight tickle or a feeling of sensitivity. Perhaps you may feel a little heaviness in the area or a pulsing of light or energy. Decide what it feels like for you. Think of the colour red if you like, to help you focus. Now feel how it is moving. Is it like a gentle swirl, a circular movement; or is it pulsing, like a heartbeat? Wait until you have acknowledged this chakra before you move on. Do not stop to delve deeply into it at this stage.

Now go up to the navel chakra, just below your belly button. There are two openings, front and back, so make sure you focus on both areas. Can you feel a little tickle as the chakra starts to open? Perhaps it is open already. Can you speed up its vibrations by encouraging it to move a little faster? Focus on the colour orange. Does this chakra feel very different from the base? Wash away anything you don't want.

Move up to the solar plexus chakra, which is below your breastbone and slightly to the left. Don't struggle to find the right spot, just let your thoughts take you naturally to where it knows it needs to go. Use the focus of the colour yellow to help you. Remember, this chakra opens both front and back. Give yourself time to feel it opening. Every chakra feels different, so don't worry if there is no repeated sensation when you concentrate on each chakra in turn. Just let yourself feel whatever is happening without judging.

Now move up to the heart area. This is where the energies start to change and become finer and brighter. Focus on your heart area and remember this chakra opens front and back. Can you sense more happening in the front area than in the back? Try to balance the flow between the two. Sometimes the heart chakra can seem the easiest chakra to open because we are aware of the beating of the heart which allows us to focus more powerfully. Let the colour green come into your conscious thought and feel it flowing through the heart chakra. This can be a very soothing sensation.

Now move up the hollow of your throat and concentrate on that area. Feel the chakra opening front and back. Notice if the feeling makes you want to swallow or clear your throat; it's fine if it does, either way. Focus on the beautiful blue of a clear sky and let the image come and go through your throat chakra. The energies are finer again here, so don't worry if it seems more difficult to feel anything.

Now continue to your forehead area and concentrate on the spot in the middle. Feel the chakra opening front and back. Don't push for any sensation; just keep focused on this area and notice whatever you feel. Bring the colour purple into this area and see how that affects the chakra opening. The brow chakra is called the 'third eye' by clairvoyants, who focus on it to attain higher energies. This chakra may feel much lighter and less tangible than some of the other chakras. Just enjoy whatever you are feeling without straining for more.

Now move up to the seventh chakra, the crown chakra, which is at the top and middle of your head. This has only one opening, upwards to the sky. It is always open, but you want to feel it open a little more. Focus on it and notice what you feel. Did you know that 90 percent of our body heat escapes through the top of our head? The crown chakra seems to be powerful on physical as well as etheric levels.

After focusing on the crown chakra for a few minutes, let yourself slip into your cleansing sanctuary. Now you are going to cleanse your whole aura, by letting the water or light come down through each chakra, starting with the crown, and very gently and thoroughly washing away anything you don't want. Take this process very slowly, and enjoy it. Carefully go through each chakra in reverse: crown, brow, throat, heart, solar plexus, navel and base. If there seem to be areas that are resistant to the washing process, don't worry. Know you will return to any needy areas in the future and work with them. Feel your cleansing sanctuary working on a spiritual level that leaves you feeling refreshed in a different way. Notice how much lighter and brighter your energy feels as a result.

When you have finished cleansing, sit quietly for a few minutes, noticing how you feel now that you have consciously opened all your chakras. Enjoy the sensation of all your energies feeling more alive and receptive to everything around you, both physically and spiritually.

Now you want to close down. Opening up can be a wonderful sensation but it's essential that you also learn how to close down properly. As you have been reading, you will already have been opening some or all of your chakras unconsciously during meditation and you now need to know how to close them down again, so you are properly protected and grounded before you continue in the everyday world. Go straight on now to close down.

Closing your chakras

Cleanse by using your usual technique. Feel anything you don't want being washed away with your light or water. You want to ensure nothing unpleasant remains in your energy field before you close your chakras.

Now, starting with the base chakra, feel the chakra gently slowing down under your focus. Remember this chakra always stays open to a certain extent, but it will have become much more active during your concentration. Feel it gradually slow down. You will still sense it pulsing or moving slightly but know it is now moving in a gentle, less energetic way.

> Move up to the navel chakra. Concentrate on this area and feel the chakra slowly close, both front and back. It is useful to create your own image for this, to make the action more powerful. Imagine the petals of a flower folding up or a door closing or whatever you find works best for you.
>
> Continue this process up through the solar plexus, heart, throat and brow, remembering to close each chakra both front and back. When you reach the crown, remember that this chakra stays open at all times but you want to slow down its energies. Feel it pulsing at a lower rate or shining less brightly. Use the image that is most helpful to you.
>
> Sometimes after closing your chakras, you can still feel slightly light-headed from your new state of awareness. Remember to use your grounding energy exercise and focus on your feet. Pull up the grounding energy and feel it coming up through your physical body. Notice how heavy your body feels in the chair. Always use this as a grounding tool before you get up again when you are working consciously with your chakras.

Did you find this a powerful exercise? You may feel that you have entered another dimension of awareness now you have discovered conscious recognition of your chakras. If you found it difficult and frustrating because you felt very little, that is also fine. Chakra awareness is a gentle, gradual process and although some people find it easier than others, there is no rule about how everyone should feel about their chakras. It is such a personal discovery and if two people were to try to share their experience of the chakras, it would be like two different worlds of awareness. The wonderful aspect of working with your chakras is that it is utterly personal to you and it can become very powerful as a result. As you continue working with the chakras, you will realize for yourself how true this is.

Through working with your chakras, your own aura grows and expands. This is also why closing down carefully is very important. Since you actually spread out your energies during work with your chakras, you must focus on contracting your energies back again afterwards. Closing your chakras will help this process. You may find as you work more deeply with meditations and chakras that sometimes you end up feeling quite vulnerable. This is because you are working more and more into understanding your own spiritual energies and your true purpose in life. Therefore it's important you create added tools for protection.

We are now going to look at an effective means of making you feel more secure after a sensitive meditation. This is a technique you can use at any time, whether finishing a meditation or stuck in a crowded bus or train or feeling bombarded by someone else's energies. You can use it any time you want some extra protection. If you are with other people, they will not know what you are doing but they may unconsciously sense something is happening and back away slightly to give you more room. The more you use this technique, the more it becomes an extremely powerful means through which you can protect yourself.

Cloak of protection

You are going to create your own invisible cloak of protection that you can call upon at any time to wrap around you.

Sit quietly and close your eyes. Breathe deeply. Let yourself settle and become still. Slip into the state of inner silence that you love and are beginning to know well. Sit quietly for a few minutes.

Now, silently ask that you be given your own personal cloak of protection. Wait for a little while. Don't expect instant results. Gradually, something will be shown to you. You will see it, feel it or sense it. It is your own personal cloak of protection, so it will be something that is right and powerful for you. It may come in the shape of brilliant light that surrounds you and gives you a feeling of safety. You may be given shimmering armour or a fabric that is waterproof and warm. You may think nothing is happening and then, with your eyes still closed, look down at your body and realize that your cloak of protection is already there, waiting for you to acknowledge it.

Whatever you put on, it should immediately make you feel good. You shouldn't feel heavy, restricted or claustrophobic. It may not have any earthly connection so it may be a sensation rather than a physical image for you. All that is required is that it makes you feel safe and insulated from any unwanted outside influences.

This cloak of protection does not shut you off from everyone. You can still give out your energies and receive back what you want to receive. But nothing unwanted can bombard you. Nothing unpleasant can get through.

The cloak of protection is yours forever. Call upon it any time you need it and release it whenever you don't. Practise letting the cloak go. Feel it slip from your consciousness. Has it gone? Call it back again using your thought processes. If this was rather slow in happening, continue practising. Have the cloak come and go at your will. Notice how wonderful it feels every time it is put around you.

When you are ready, remember to come back from your meditation. Thank the realms of higher awareness for offering you this new form of protection, then withdraw slowly. Ground yourself and give yourself some time to refocus your energies. Open your eyes slowly, sip your water and wait before you get up.

You can keep this cloak with you after you finish meditations, particularly if you feel more sensitive than usual. You might simply wake up one morning and feel more vulnerable than normal and decide to wear it for a while. If you find yourself in a situation that makes you feel uncomfortable, use it. This might be when there are energies around you that are uneasy or feel threatening in some way. If you feel claustrophobic because too many people are expecting too much of you, pull your cloak around you for a while. You will discover endless uses for your cloak of protection once you practise wearing it. In fact, you will wonder why you haven't discovered it before!

As we prepare to work with the chakras in a meditative way and see what they have to teach us about ourselves on a more profound level, there are a few important points to raise. Hopefully, you will find this new area wonderfully rewarding and inspirational. It will reveal new aspects of your life that you may never have thought about before. You may discover new depths of relaxation and stillness that have positive repercussions in all areas of your life. You may discover new insights about much more universal concepts that eluded you previously. It is an exciting new step you are about to take. However, it can also take you to delicate and emotional areas of yourself. Please don't rush the process of chakra awareness during meditation and don't worry if you find some chakras much too sensitive to look at. There is a good reason for this.

When a chakra feels difficult or over-sensitive or we feel we just can't work with it yet, it is usually because there is some deep-seated memory of something we have not yet let go of and it is causing us discomfort on some level. Through meditation, we have the opportunity to discover what that past hurt or upset might be and we can choose to gently release it. This doesn't necessarily happen immediately; it may take time and some nurturing before it heals. The more deep-seated and prolonged the issue, the more we have to work slowly and gently to help ourselves through it.

You can liken this to a physical injury. If you hurt yourself in a major way, such as breaking your arm, you don't immediately expect the break to heal, do you? You don't go out and try to play tennis straight away. Likewise, we can't expect a major imbalance in our aura to immediately heal itself just because we suddenly become aware of its presence.

Often our conscious minds don't understand where a particular upset or imbalance has come from. We might only know something doesn't feel right in an area of our life without being able to define it any more clearly than that. Through meditation, we can go deeper into the root cause of a situation and truly understand it on a spiritual level. That understanding alone is often enough to create positive change in our life.

Whilst we may not yet be completely free from the influence of that problem, just by understanding it fully, we are paving the way for healthy, productive shifts in our aura. This can then create a large chain reaction of positive changes. Once we understand why we have felt or behaved in a certain way, we feel the pressure, confusion or hurt of that situation beginning to slip away from us. When we feel less restricted, we are immediately releasing other energy blocks in our aura and allowing everything to flow through us in a wonderfully free and uninhibited way. Through being so much freer, we leave ourselves open to yet deeper and more inspirational meditations through which we can learn even more about ourselves and others. Encourage this to happen for you by being gentle with yourself at all times during these deeper meditations.

Whenever you come up against a blockage or resistance of some sort which feels impassable, breathe gently into it and see what is there for you. If nothing shifts, that is fine because you will return to it. Sometimes we have blocks in our lives because we are not yet ready to deal with certain major issues. Areas in your life will start to shift when it is right for you.

This ties in with our mini meditations when we practised awareness of life on an everyday level, being 'in the moment' (see Mini Meditations for Every Day). We discussed how we could only appreciate something by acknowledging it and understanding its present significance. Once we embraced something, no matter how mundane the task, we could truly appreciate it and we could start to enjoy the process.

Acknowledging blocks in your own life falls into this category. If, every time you come across a difficult area in your life which never seems to shift, you react in an angry manner, frustrated by your own lack of progress, how does that help you to embrace the situation and move forward?

The first step is to fully accept the blockage, to treat it lovingly and appreciatively. Know that this difficulty has come about because you have an important opportunity to grow ahead of you. Every 'problem' in our lives is simply a chance for us to learn something new. It's only if we embrace the so-called difficulty, and look forward to learning something new, that we give ourselves the chance for this blockage to start to clear.

Do remember this as you gradually work through the meditations with chakras. You might want to take this slowly and only do one chakra in a day – or even a week. Give yourself plenty of time to digest whatever information you receive from a meditation on a chakra. There is so much there for you to tap into and sometimes it takes a lot of gentle contemplation after the meditation before you can begin to understand it all. Also remember that meditation is meant to be an enjoyable journey of discovery, not a difficult challenge that you approach with anxiety. Whatever you don't want during your meditations, wash away. You are in control.

You may find that working consciously with your chakras enables you to pick up a lot of information on a variety of different levels, so it might be helpful to keep a Chakra Diary in which you monitor your responses. Every time you return to a chakra and meditate upon it, you will discover something new to help your learning process. Sometimes, conscious awareness of the information we receive in meditation can slip back into the unconscious and the learning is lost for a while. If you want to work actively with your meditations after you have finished, making notes will help you to remember and reflect on certain important issues.

Slowly work your way through each chakra exercise below, when you feel ready to do so.

Base chakra

Close your eyes and relax. Breathe deeply and go into your inner stillness. Rest there for a while. When you are ready, you can either go through and open up all your chakras, or you can choose just to focus on the base chakra and no other.

Bring your attention to the area at the base of your spine. Focus on the base chakra. How does that part of your body feel right now? Is it energetic and comfortable? Does it feel sluggish? Don't just concentrate on that area but feel your consciousness actually melt into the base of your spine. What information are you receiving now? Let yourself sit in the stillness for a while; notice the sensations that come and go.

Feel the grounding energy coming up through the opening of this base chakra. What does that make you feel about your own personal sense of being grounded? Do you go around each day being aware of what is physically around you? Do you enjoy food, all physical activities and your material possessions? How strong is your instinct for survival? Let your thoughts spiral on these different issues and see what information you receive. Remember to keep breathing deeply. Wash away whatever you don't want.

Now focus on the word 'survival', whilst keeping your physical focus on the base chakra. What does survival mean to you? Play with the word and see what happens. Do the same with the word 'root' and see what you can learn.

Bring the colour red into this awareness and see how it affects your perceptions. Notice if any animal images or other colours or associations come into your thoughts. Consider whether a sound or musical instrument would reflect this chakra well. Is there a scent that seems right here? Let yourself sit in the experience of the base chakra for as long as it feels comfortable.

When you are ready, withdraw slowly. Feel the base chakra slowing down and pulsing more gently. Gently bring your awareness back to the everyday. Sit quietly for a while before you get up.

Navel chakra

Relax and quietly prepare yourself for meditation. When you are ready, slowly take your focus to just below your belly button. Feel a little tickle or gentle pulsing as you focus on your navel chakra. This chakra opens both front and back, so remember to also focus on your back and feel the chakra opening there as well. This may be an especially sensitive area for you, so be very gentle as you explore.

Take your awareness into this area of your physical body. Does it feel soft and warm or unyielding and unfathomable? Slowly let yourself experience what is there for you. If it feels uncomfortable, withdraw and cleanse. Otherwise, continue.

How do you feel about yourself on an emotional level? Would you say you are an emotionally expressive person or quite self-contained? How does this affect the activity of your navel chakra? If you are happy to explore this area, ask yourself about your sexual relationships. How fulfilling are they to you? Can you relate to sex on a spiritual level? How is this reflected in your own relationships? Consider non-sexual relationships and ask yourself how important they are to you. Let your response to these questions come and go in an easy flow. Do not stop to question yourself too deeply. Enjoy the learning process without judging your own behaviour.

Take the word 'sex' into your meditation and let your thoughts spiral with it. See what you need to learn from this word. Then take the word 'emotion' and see where that leads you. Withdraw at any time if you find it uncomfortable. Remember to keep breathing.

Bring the colour orange into the meditation and see how you respond to it. Keep your focus on the navel chakra, front and back. Is there an animal or element that seems to approximate to these sensations? Do any relevant words or specific actions seem to be a part of this chakra? Is there a form of music or sound that would resonant well with this chakra? Think about a scent that would feel right.

Withdraw slowly and gently when you are ready to leave. Take time to close this chakra properly, both front and back. Use whatever image works for you and ensure the chakra is completely still before you finish. Wash away anything you don't want to take with you before you return to daily life.

Solar plexus chakra

Go into your meditative state and relax for a while. Breathe deeply right down into your stomach area. Now bring your awareness to your solar plexus. This is just below your ribcage, where your ribs end and you can feel the fleshier part of your upper stomach. The solar plexus chakra is just below the ribs and slightly to your left. There is also a chakra opening at the back, directly behind the front chakra. Tune in to both openings; feel them both coming alive.

Now take your consciousness into the area and see what you find. Does it make you feel comfortable or does there seem to be a lot of turbulent activity taking place? If going in feels hard, don't force it. Just let your awareness slowly drift in as far as it will go and if you meet resistance, pause and breathe deeply. See what you can accomplish as you let your breath do the work for you.

How would you describe your mental acuity? Do you spend a great deal of your time thinking and analysing everything? Would you say you are very logical? Do you have strong self-esteem? How determined are you to succeed in certain areas of your life?

Bring the word 'willpower' into your meditation. Play with the word and see what it tells you about your own solar plexus chakra. Still keeping your focus on the solar plexus chakra, meditate on the word 'mentality'. Wash away anything you don't want.

Become the colour yellow. Feel it pulsing through your solar plexus chakra and see what effect that has. Notice if any relevant images come up at this time, such as animals, objects or particular words. Meditate upon which musical instrument or type of sound would complement this chakra. Conjure up a scent that would belong here.

When you are ready, withdraw from the area. Close the chakra carefully front and back. Cleanse thoroughly if you have picked up anything uncomfortable. Sit quietly for a while before you get up.

Heart chakra

Close your eyes and let yourself slip into your meditative state. Breathe deeply and easily for a few minutes. Now bring your focus to your heart area, in the middle of your breast bone.

This is often a very active chakra so you may find it is already open. Notice if it feels too open. Does it feel as though it is pulsing quickly? Take a moment to tune in and control the activity of the chakra until it feels right for you. There are two openings, front and both, so remember to tune in to both.

Now move inside the heart area. Feel the activity there. How does it make you feel? Let yourself go deeper, if it feels comfortable. You may find this very powerful or possibly too emotional. Withdraw at any time. If you can, enjoy the velvety warmth of this area. Feel cushioned and protected by the gentle pulsing of your heart. Do you feel as though a lot of energy is also coming out of this chakra? Does it feel open and outward in sensation, rather than inward and receiving? Tune in to what is true for you. Notice what is happening without judging yourself, but allow yourself to understand your behaviour better through this awareness.

Now think about your attitude to loving yourself and others. How does love manifest itself in your life? Is it unconditional or very much based upon what others give you in return? Do you feel as though you give out a great deal of love but receive less in return – or is the opposite true for you? Where does spiritual love exist in your life? Can you feel love for universal truths and laws? Notice what happens to your heart chakra as you meditate upon these concepts.

Bring the word 'love' into the meditation. Notice how much more information you can glean from focusing on the heart chakra as you do this. Play with the word and see what it can teach you. Take the words 'self love' into your thoughts; then take the words 'universal love' and compare the two meanings. What does that tell you about yourself?

Bring in the colour green and feel it filling your heart chakra with pure, unconditional love. Sit in this joyful state for a little while. Feel any imbalances in your heart chakra being gently washed away and replaced by comfortable pulsing energy. Enjoy the healing sensation as your heart responds. Allow yourself to really feel the love and take it into your subtle energies. Realize you deserve it. Observe any images or words that come up during this time. Think about sounds or music that seem appropriate for this chakra. Decide which scent would be right for the heart area.

Now slowly withdraw. Gently close the heart chakra, front and back. This may be difficult for you to do if you naturally open your heart chakra easily and often leave it open during the day. Really focus on the heart chakra and ensure you can close it properly. Use the image that works for you and see it gently but firmly close.

Take a moment to pull some grounding energy up into your subtle body. As the energies start to change at the heart chakra and become lighter and brighter, it can leave you feeling light-headed. Make sure you ground yourself properly. You might feel quite vulnerable after working on this chakra, too. Perhaps you want to pull your cloak of protection around you before you get up. Keep it with you for the rest of the day if you want to.

Throat chakra

Go quietly into your meditative state. Enjoy the stillness for a moment before you focus on your throat area. Concentrate on the hollow of your throat and tune in to the gentle pulsing of the chakra there. If it feels less tangible or difficult to tune into, that is fine. As the energies become finer, so the chakras can be more difficult to detect initially. Know the chakra is there without trying too hard to feel it. This chakra opens front and back, so concentrate on both.

Take your consciousness into the throat area itself. See what it is waiting to tell you. Observe whether you feel comfortable in this part of your body. If not, ask yourself what you are feeling and why. Think about how much work your throat does each day. Notice whether it is pulsing comfortably or if it feels over- or under-used.

Now think about your ability to digest spiritual truths and how you work with higher awareness. Acknowledge how easy or difficult you may find this. How much do you speak with integrity and honesty; how often do you lie or refrain from speaking your truth? What do you feel about your professional life? How fulfilling is this to you? Notice, as you meditate upon these issues, how your throat chakra responds. Let the sensations come and go in an easy flow of energy. Wash away what you don't like.

Now bring the word 'truth' into your consciousness. Play with the word, keeping your focus on the throat chakra. Keep expanding your throat area as more information comes to you; let yourself become a limitless vessel for this teaching. Take the word 'integrity' into your meditation. It doesn't matter if you feel you don't know its true meaning; let your inner stillness and awareness teach you.

Introduce the colour sky blue into your conscious thought. Let it seep through into your subtle energies and fill your throat chakra front and back. Observe what happens when your energies fill with blue. Feel the expansion of this light vibration. Enjoy what it does to you. Notice what images come up for you; what possibilities do you see now in sound, images of animals, elements or scents?

Slowly withdraw from the throat chakra. Stop its activity as you do so and watch the chakra gently close, front and back. Make sure you wash away any uncomfortable sensations. Ground yourself and protect yourself. Make sure you feel well earthed before you get up.

Brow chakra

Close your eyes and go into a meditative state. Take a few extra minutes to relax and release tension. As you work at higher frequencies so you need more focus and deeper levels of understanding.

Bring your attention to the middle of your brow, above and between your eyes. Let your awareness flicker gently over your brow until you feel a very slight pulsing or tickle. Wait until you find this spot before you stop. Now focus on this area and feel the brow chakra very gently, very slowly unfolding and opening up. Let this happen both front and back as the brow chakra has two openings. You may feel a rather light-headed sensation as this happens, as though your energies are moving higher in your body and your aura is expanding and becoming finer and brighter. Enjoy the sensation.

Now feel your consciousness move into your forehead and notice how you feel. You may find this difficult initially, so move slowly with great awareness and sensitivity. If you feel you can't go any further, stop and breathe deeply. Breathe into your forehead. The chakra here is called your 'third eye', and often images and flashes of light can occur when it is opened. Whatever happens as you work with this chakra, just enjoy the experiences and let them come and go, washing over you in waves of awareness.

How open are you to receiving inspirational information? How much of your meditations are about spiritual truths and universal awareness, rather than focusing solely on your personal life? How much time do you spend meditating in higher awareness, trying to understand worldly and universal patterns of existence, rather than purely looking at the pattern of your own life? Can you see any correlation between your life and universal laws of existence?

Bring the word 'consciousness' into your meditation. Don't concentrate too hard but let the word dance in your mind's eye. Bring it up to the brow chakra and see it enter into it. What information are you receiving now? Try the words 'universal laws' and see what insights are given to you.

If you are struggling in this, let the wonderfully rich colour purple come into your consciousness and float into your brow chakra, front and back. This colour vibrates at a very high frequency, to help with shifts of consciousness. Feel the warm purple seeping everywhere throughout your subtle energies and let the colour teach you as it flows unhindered through your aura. Observe images, animals, scents and sounds that come to you as you concentrate on this seat of higher awareness.

Now withdraw very carefully. If you come away too quickly you may feel uncomfortable as your energies suddenly plummet. Slowly withdraw from the brow chakra. See it close front and back, using the method that works best for you. Wash away anything you don't need to keep with you.

As we move higher up the chakras, so you need extra time to let yourself come back to earth again. Use your grounding energy and feel it balance your energies again. Notice how heavy your body is feeling. Sip your water slowly and gradually reorient yourself.

Crown chakra

This is the highest, lightest and finest vibration of all the chakras, so give yourself plenty of time to settle and relax into your meditation. Make sure your breathing has slowed down and deepened. Sit quietly in your inner stillness. Take a moment to ask for spiritual guidance.

Now bring your attention to the top and middle of your head. Let your conscious thought move slowly around the area until you feel the sensation of the crown chakra. You may just have a very faint, very delicate perception of a different form of energy. Perhaps you will feel a little buzzing at the crown, or just know that something is there without quite being able to explain it. Tune in to this area. Remember the crown chakra is always open to receive energy, but now you want to open it further. This crown chakra personifies the lotus flower in all its glory and is represented by a million petals opening upwards to the sky. Feel all the beautiful petals opening out now, embracing all higher awareness.

Notice what sensations come to you as you do this. Let yourself sink into the crown chakra itself and enjoy the new feelings that you experience. As you are meditating on a higher energy now, you may find the insights are more elusive. Don't strain to try to understand more. Let yourself sit in this awareness without judging or needing more. Just enjoy the feeling.

Now let the word 'bliss' come into your meditation. See what it has to teach you. You may find there are no words to explain this; you may be immersed only in sensations at this chakra. Do the same with the word 'divine' and observe the effect this has on you. Let both words sink down into the crown chakra and be absorbed by your whole body.

Now bring down a beautiful, pure white light from above and let it pour in through your crown chakra and filter through all of your aura and chakras. Feel yourself merge with this pure white light and become one with it. You are nothing but pure white light, pulsing with total spiritual awareness. Welcome the insights that come into you as you do this. Don't worry if there are no words, no sounds, no images that can possibly relate to this experience. Just enjoy the sensation.

Now it is time for you to withdraw. Take your awareness out of your crown chakra and step away from it. Ensure the crown chakra slows down and becomes less active. It is always open to a certain extent, so you won't be able to close it completely, but make sure it is pulsing gently and comfortably. Notice how much easier it is now for you to identify with this chakra. Acknowledge how the crown chakra has gone from being a vague concept to an experience that is powerful and insightful. Give thanks for what you have learned.

Now come back into your physical body by focusing on your feet. Pull the grounding energy up through you. Wrap yourself in your protective cloak and keep it with you for a few hours so you aren't too open and vulnerable. Sit for as long as you can when you have finished, drinking your water and reflecting on what you have learned. Don't get up until you know you are ready to continue with your day.

You may have found some of those exercises very powerful whilst others may have left you feeling quite unsatisfied and uncertain as to whether you learned anything at all. This is the nature of working with our subtle energies, rather than purely using our physical bodies. Although our aura and chakras have always been a part of our spiritual body, because you are only beginning to discover their true existence and worth, it will take some time before you feel fully comfortable with these concepts. Meditation on all the chakras will help you enormously to understand yourself and others in a much larger context than you have considered before.

It is highly recommended that you keep your own personal Chakra Diary because it really will help you to chart your progress and to develop your personal relationship with your spiritual body. You may not fully appreciate how you are growing and progressing until you have a measuring stick against which you can keep comparing your movement. Once you are comfortable with your own chakras and can meditate on them freely, you will quickly forget that there was ever a time when you struggled or thought you couldn't feel them at all.

We are programmed to forget our accomplishments and to harp instead on our constant needs and unfulfilled areas. Be kind to yourself by constantly stopping to acknowledge your own success and progress. This acknowledgement will further speed your meditations and intensify their personal meaning and power for you.

You have been working extremely hard through this chapter and you may find as a result of all your focus that you feel some of the pleasure and relaxation has gone out of meditation. You are constantly being reminded to relax and enjoy yourself but you may find that some of the intense focus on the chakras, whilst it has been insightful in a way you haven't previously experienced, has been emotional and quite demanding. You will certainly understand now that meditation can work on so many different levels and that the more you are willing to put into it, the more you can get out of it.

However, there are times when we don't want to use meditation purely as a learning tool, we only want to enjoy relaxation at the deepest level. The final chapter in this part of the book is a kind of reward for all the work you have put in so far and consists of nurturing and comforting meditations that demand little or no personal input from you. Enjoy them!

FREEING MEDITATIONS

You have been asked to consider a lot of new concepts in this part of the book, and there are many more for you to look at later. But in this chapter I want you to take a break and give yourself time to appreciate what you have already accomplished. The meditations you will experience here are designed to free your mind and enable you to relax.

You can tackle these meditations in the same way as you have the others: by reading each one through first, then closing your eyes and running through them in your mind, remembering as much as you can. However, consider trying something different.

Do you have a good friend who has a soothing voice and is sympathetic to meditating and its benefits, and who would be willing to talk you through them? You could offer an exchange whereby you then talk them through the meditation afterwards so you can both benefit. If you are hesitant about involving anyone else, you can always record the meditations for yourself onto a computer or phone and then play them to yourself. It's possible you have a friend who would find recording them easier than talking them through with you in the room.

It is important to choose someone whose voice you really enjoy listening to, not someone whose accent or energy you find difficult or distracting. Your relaxation will come from the content of the meditation and the timbre of the voice of the person who is speaking. From your work with sound, you should now know what you find harmonious and what you find grating. The voice should be calm but not monotone, steady without being too slow, and warm without being syrupy.

You might want to practise out loud with one of the meditations and see how you sound. If you take the time to relax, focus your thoughts and concentrate on your breathing before you start speaking, you will probably be pleasantly surprised to discover that it isn't so difficult.

Although these are freeing meditations, you still want to take into account all the requirements on your Meditation check list (see page 60). You want to fully enjoy the meditations and obtain the maximum benefits from them. This is only possible through the discipline of the necessary rules being observed. If you want to test the theory, you might try meditating one day when you don't observe one of the rules. For instance, put on a tight pair of trousers and then try to relax into a meditation! There is nothing like experiencing something like this once to make you appreciate why you follow certain guidelines.

The first exercise is Opening Relaxation, which should be a preliminary to every subsequent meditation. It's important that you give yourself that initial time to sink into your inner stillness. When you move on to different meditations in this chapter, ensure that you always read out the Opening Relaxation first.

When you are ready, try some of the following exercises. You may naturally be drawn more to some exercies than to others. At some stage, you might want to go through them all, to see which you find most relaxing.

Opening relaxation

Close your eyes and relax. Settle your body comfortably; give a little wriggle or scratch your nose if you wish. Allow any tension to seep out. This is your time now, time just for you, to be alone and to relax and unwind. You are now going to release unwanted pressure from your body. You are going to feel any pressure or tension draining away slowly from your entire body. Feel it going from your head ... neck... shoulders ... arms and hands ... out through your fingers ... Now feel it draining away down your back, through all of your back, through every vertebra ... down through your buttocks and hips ... down your upper legs ... knees ... lower legs ... into your ankles and feet and out through your toes ... Feel that tension you have been carrying with you melting away deep into the ground, becoming nothing. Notice how much lighter and clearer you feel now. Go into your Cleansing Sanctuary and cleanse again. Make sure you release anything you might have missed just now. Wash it away. Let it go. You don't need it.

Now focus on your breathing. Watch it come and go through your body ... Feel as though each breath is being taken right down into your navel ... Feel each breath as it comes up and out through your nose ... Let your ribcage expand on each breath in; feel it contract as you breathe out. Sit in awareness of your breathing for a few minutes. Observe each breath in and each breath out ...

Whatever problems or anxieties come into your mind, now is the time to let them slip away. You can have them back again afterwards, if you wish, but for now they are not needed. You can be free of them. Feel them drift away from you ... Let them go in the white light, the pure water, the clear air or the roaring fire ... Say good-bye to them now ... See them disappear ... You don't need them ...

Feel yourself sink into your inner core, into the stillness inside of you. Take that journey inwards now, gently, slowly ... Let yourself go ... Relax ... Breathe into the silence, into the sacred stillness ... Now embrace this wonderful sensation of peace and safety ... Feel it running around and through you ... Feel yourself merging with the feeling, so that you and the feeling are one ... Nothing can harm you here ... You are safe ... peaceful ... still...

The garden

Now you find yourself in a garden. This is a beautiful place; it is the garden of your dreams. The grass is soft and warm under your bare feet, the sun is shining and it feels warm and comforting without being too hot. There is a soft, sweet breeze wafting gentle scents towards you. You can recognize various aromas of flowers and shrubs, all mingling together. You can hear bird song and the light rustle of the wind in the trees. You may hear a trickle of water and realize there is a pond in your garden or a river running through it. The colours everywhere are beautiful: the rich greens of the grass and plants, the blue of the sky, the plethora of colours from all the flowers and birds. Perhaps you see different wildlife: hedgehogs, squirrels, butterflies, a rabbit or fox.

Explore your garden. Walk around it. See how beautiful it is. Smell everything. Perhaps there is a wild strawberry patch or an apple from a tree that you want to taste. Enjoy the warm sun on your body. Hear nature around you: bird song, a bee buzzing on a distant flower, a squirrel cracking a nut. This is your space. Enjoy it.

You find somewhere to rest. Maybe there is a bench in your garden, or a comfy sun lounger or perhaps you just want to lie on the warm grass. You decide to rest for a while. You close your eyes and still feel the garden around you, smell its scents and hear its sounds. You can feel yourself merging with the beauty of the garden, appreciating everything from within.

You are wonderfully relaxed and at peace. Everything is right in your world. As you relax in your beautiful garden, a new insight comes to you, one that is uplifting and inspiring. You have not realized this particular thought before now. Relish this new truth. See how it is relevant to your life and how it can help you. Give thanks for receiving it.

Continue to rest in appreciation and awareness. Feel the nurturing strength and power of the garden around you, blessing all of you: physically, emotionally, mentally and spiritually ... Stay in this state for a few minutes longer ...

Now it is time for you to withdraw. You have to say good-bye to your garden, but you can return to it at any time in the future. You can resolve to return soon.

Remember that you are sitting/lying in your meditation room. Notice how heavy your physical body feels; realize how nicely relaxed it has become. Feel your energy coming back to earth again. Focus on your feet and the grounding energy. Open your eyes and focus on an object in the room. Drink some water. Appreciate the difference in how you feel now in comparison to how you felt when you started the meditation. Notice how differently you feel for the rest of the day.

Your garden may very possibly become a sanctuary where you want to return frequently. Each time you visit you will discover a new corner, or a new facet you hadn't noticed before. Your garden expands with your consciousness and always feels a totally safe environment in which you can completely relax.

This element of safety is very important. People might comment that surely walking through a real garden would relax you just as much if not more than meditating upon one in your mind. The truth is that when we are physically involved in an action and/or place, we carry all sorts of fears or concerns with us. We may not always stop to acknowledge them, but they are there. They could relate to the people you are with, to strangers who may be nearby or concerns about how long you have for your walk or whether the weather will stay pleasant. We constantly put conditions and concerns around our physical environment. There is no true space in which we can totally relax and let go of everything, other than through meditation. In meditation everything is as we create it and no one can interrupt or unbalance that. This is what makes meditation so powerful and unique.

Try the next exercise when you want to transport yourself to another location. Remember to do the Opening Relaxation first (see page 161).

The beach

You find yourself on a beautiful deserted beach. There is no one else there. This is your ideal beach. It is sandy or rocky, exactly as you want it. There may be palm trees waving on the beach or a straw hut. It is wonderfully warm and sunny, just the right temperature for you. There is a cool breeze blowing. The waves are lapping at the shore.

Take a walk and explore your beautiful beach. It is just for you. Walk barefoot and feel the warm sand or smooth rocks under your bare feet. Smell the ozone in the air. You can hear the waves as they fall upon the shore and the distant cry of sea birds. You can see the sunlight sparkling on the water. There are interesting pebbles and seashells you might want to examine. Maybe you want to dip your feet into the sea. The water feels cool and refreshing. You want to discover how large your beach is and what is waiting for you.

You find out that everything you could possibly need or want is here: a supply of large dry towels, sun lotion, drink, food, sun hat, large umbrella, spare clothes, perhaps a good book. Maybe there is a soft sun lounger or an inflatable bed to float on in the sea.

This is your time for you to enjoy as you wish. Perhaps you just want to lie down and let the warm sun soak into your body. Perhaps you want to take a refreshing dip, or lie on the inflatable bed in the sea and let the gentle rocking of the ocean waves relax you. Do whatever makes you feel good. Enjoy the activity that relaxes you most.

While you are enjoying yourself in your private paradise, you are also appreciating everything around you, acknowledging how beautiful and perfect everything in nature is. You become aware of the special power of the sea and its pull. You merge your energies with the energies of the sea and enjoy its strength.

At some time during your visit, you are also given an inspirational thought that hasn't been given to you before. It is so wonderful that you have to stop and fully reflect upon its profound truth. Give thanks for this new insight. Take it with you when you go.

Now it is time for you to leave. You must say good-bye to this wonderful beach, but you will be able to return whenever you wish. Know that you will indeed soon revisit this peaceful haven.

Now you are back in your meditation room. Your body feels heavy and relaxed. Focus on your feet and notice how heavy they seem. Open your eyes slowly and take a drink of water. Sit quietly, reflecting upon the insight you were given, before you continue with your day.

'The beach' can be a particularly lulling meditation and some people do fall asleep during it. Of course, you know that you are meant to stay awake during all meditations, but if you find yourself drifting off, this may be a sign that you need more sleep.

This can be a useful meditation even for people who in reality have a fear of the ocean. By tailoring it slightly, and imagining that the sea is in the distance, you can enjoy its presence without feeling threatened. The ocean has a unique and powerful effect upon our energies and it would be beneficial for you to appreciate it through meditation.

Try the next exercise when you are ready. Again, remember to start with the Opening Relaxation (see page 161).

The forest

You are walking in a beautiful forest. This is not a thick, dense forest; it is open and light with lots of sunshine. There are different beautiful trees around you and the sun is shining brightly through them, leaving dappled images on the soft ground beneath your feet. There is a gentle breeze blowing. This is your perfect forest: inviting, warm and very nurturing. You are alone here; no one will disturb you.

Walk slowly through this amazing place. You have never seen so many trees before, a variety of species, heights, colours and shapes. The scents coming from them are wonderful. Breathe in the intoxicating mixture and feel it circulating through your body, nurturing and rejuvenating you. You can hear the rustling of the leaves and the songs of various birds as they fly through this beautiful forest. There is a humming of different insects as they pass busily by. Perhaps you see a monkey or other wildlife in the distance, enjoying the bounty of the trees. The ground feels soft and warm under your bare feet.

You appreciate how every single leaf in the forest is individual; no two are exactly alike. You notice how many colours there are around you, not just green and brown but many rich hues of orange, yellow, ochre and tan. You may see vivid flashes of other bright colours as some trees burst into blossom around you.

You notice the bark on the trees, and how the textures differ. On some trees the texture of the bark is very rough or has knobbly sections, on others it is smooth, dark and velvety. The trunks have different shapes, too. You touch them to find out how they feel under your hand. They feel so beautiful that you reach out to hug the base of a tree. You feel the beauty and power of the tree coming into you and nurturing your energies. Move from tree to tree, exploring the different sensations, feeling your energies blend and merge with theirs. Some trees you want to hug for a long time.

After a while, you decide to sit down in a clearing in the sunshine. You rest in the middle of the forest, looking up at all the beautiful trees around you. As you sit there, you suddenly receive a flash of higher awareness, a greater understanding about some element of life that had previously eluded you. You wonder why you had not realized this before. You sit in the joy of discovering this new truth and give thanks for it having come forward into your conscious mind. You reflect upon its significance for you.

Now it is time for you to leave. You have to go from this wonderful forest, but you will return another day. You know that you will want to come back soon to continue exploring these inspirational trees.

Now you are back in your meditation room. You are aware that your body feels heavy and that your feet are resting solidly on the ground. Open your eyes and focus on an object. Remember what time of day it is and what day of the week. Have some water and wait a few minutes before getting up.

Some people are nervous initially of the forest because they think it will be dark and forbidding. It's important to stress that it is light and full of sunshine. Trees have amazing power that can be understood better through meditation. If you are ever alone and can hug a real tree, then do try it. It's a wonderful feeling.

These three relaxing meditations are good for you to enjoy at any fraught time in your life. The more you revisit them, the more the locations will come alive for you and the more benefit you will receive from them. You will find the locations expand and become more detailed and vibrant on each revisit as you yourself grow and expand. Different insights will come with each meditation, relevant to what is happening to you at that particular time in your life. However, first and foremost these remain the most relaxing and comforting of meditations: somewhere you will always feel safe and nurtured. It is important that we find that safe place within us.

Now it is time for us to move forward and to consider introducing another element into our meditations: spiritual guides.

PART TWO:

SPIRITUAL GUIDES

WHAT ARE SPIRITUAL GUIDES?

In the introduction in this book, we spent some time talking about whether you held spiritual beliefs regarding any form of higher consciousness. Irrespective of whether you did or not at that time, how do you feel about it now? After your experiences thus far with meditations, do you have the feeling there is something more out there, something that is not necessarily easy to explain but something that feels more spiritual than physical?

This can manifest itself in different ways for different people. Some may feel that by accessing some inner part of themselves, it is actually their own spirituality they are tapping into and unconnected with universal concepts. Others may feel as though they are not really doing the work during meditations but that other energies are coming into their field of awareness and helping to protect or guide them. Yet others may feel they are quite separate from all their experiences in meditation and they seem to observe what is happening, rather than feel a part of it. Some of you may still be struggling to feel much at all but still sense something more is out there, if only you could learn how to become connected to it.

Part Two is about learning how to tap into more of what is available to you on an energetic level during meditation. We have talked a lot about different energies: the energies of your aura and chakras; other people's energies and what they mean to you; the energies of elements of nature such as the ocean, flowers or trees; the grounding energies that we pull up through our feet and base chakra; the pure white energy that we bring down into our crown chakra, either for cleansing or for inspiration. You have been learning how to tap into all these on both conscious and unconscious levels and observing the effect they have on you. In other words, you have been doing a great deal of experimentation with different forms of energies. Spiritual guides are simply another form of energy, and you are now going to learn to interact with them.

So what are spiritual guides? To answer this, we are going to look at a few concepts, some of which you may already be familiar with, others which you may find more challenging.

Our starting point is to look at the great spiritual leaders in history. This can be God, Jesus Christ, Buddha, Allah, or any deity whom you wish to worship. It does not matter what name you give to your spiritual deity as long as you find their presence a comfort and they are an inspirational guide for you. There is an interesting consideration here: most of the deities people worship have at one time been considered to live in this world, in some form or another. To put it more concisely, at one time they had physical bodies but they have now been placed into the realm of higher spiritual awareness; therefore, they have gone from physical energy into spiritual energy. If you can accept that this can happen to a deity, is it not possible that it can also happen to other human beings: that they can transform from physical beings to energetic forms?

Thus we arrive at the notion of our physical body being an encasement for our spiritual one and it is only our physical body that we shed when we die. Our spiritual body continues in energetic form. Do you find this feasible as a concept or does your logical mind immediately say, 'Give me proof'? The theory about our spiritual body being separate from our physical body becomes even more complex when we look at the concept of reincarnation. Reincarnation is the belief that not only does our spiritual soul survive death, but that it is the part of us that is everlasting and eternal and we do in fact return to the earth for many different lives so that we may understand universal laws and truths.

In other words, our spiritual soul is the only constant and our physical bodies come and go in different times and different forms, as and when we need them. It is even said that our soul chooses which body it wishes to incarnate into, so that it can have the maximum opportunity for learning during that lifetime. The process of learning from each lifetime is to enable your soul to move closer and closer towards divine understanding and perfection. Following your soul's true path to accomplish this, and accepting responsibility for every single action you take, is called your karma. There is an excellent saying summarizing this belief:

We're not physical beings having a spiritual experience.
We're spiritual beings having an earthly experience.

You may immediately find this makes a great deal of sense; or perhaps you feel this is ridiculous. Whatever your initial thoughts, you need to accept this as a possibility if you want to learn how to work with your spiritual guides. You need to understand who they are, if you are going to forge any helpful links with them.

The best way to begin to embrace the idea of reincarnation is to learn more about it. It may help you to know that reincarnation is not a new, Western concept, although sometimes it may seem as though it is! In many cultures reincarnation is regarded as a natural part of evolution and many ancient teachings and religions are based upon it – Shamanism and Buddhism, to name but two.

It is also helpful to realize that down the centuries eminent, highly educated and also scientifically-minded individuals have embraced the notion of reincarnation: from Plato and Pythagoras right through to Walt Whitman and Carl Jung. Copious quantities of poetry make reference to reincarnation and its significance in our universe.

Perhaps most persuasively, especially for those sceptics among you, there are now some superb documented experiences of people who can remember their past lives. It is generally understood that cognizance of past lives is not handed down readily into the consciousness of each new physical body. The reasons for this are obvious. It is difficult enough for a person to handle the one life they are now living; can you imagine the repercussions of trying to constantly deal with a memory of a past life (or lives) and not being able to reconcile it with your present one? However, either through controlled conditions of hypnosis or through fragmented past memories, various people have remembered some of their past lives and spoken about them. Their stories make compelling study.

One of these is the story of Jenny Cockell, an Englishwoman who from a young age remembered fragments of a past life that was distressing. It took regression (the act of looking into past lives under hypnosis) and many difficult years of not accepting her present life and constantly being haunted by painful past memories, before Jenny was able to reach some peaceful resolution and let the trauma of her past life go. Only then was she able to move forward to some semblance of normality in her present life. Her story, *Yesterday's Children*, is a powerful testimony to reincarnation.

There are many other books available on reincarnation that you may find helpful. The story of Bridie Murphy makes fascinating reading;

an American woman, Mrs Virginia Tighe, reputedly had memories of having lived a past life as an Irish woman, Bridie Murphy. Her experiences were recorded in the 1950s in the USA. Local libraries and book shops will be able to advise you on these and other books on the subject. If you are struggling with reincarnation as a theory, you may benefit from stopping to read accounts of experiences of past lives to help you accept it. You can continue with the rest of this section when you are ready.

You may, though, be able to grasp the concept of reincarnation and move forward with it, even though you may find aspects of it confusing and difficult to understand on some levels. If you have reached the stage where you can believe there might be some positive energetic forces above and around us, let's look at exactly what this energy might be. Is it possible that spiritual guides are people who have lived a number of lives already and who have now become wise and enlightened souls, ready to guide and nurture us? What makes a good guide?

There is a popular myth that a spiritual guide always appears as a wise guru: a Native American, a Chinese sage or an Egyptian goddess. They always have beards or long, flowing hair. They wear antique robes, elaborate head-dresses or a multitude of colourful bird feathers. They are usually old. They smile benignly but have great inner power. What they say is always deeply profound and full of spiritual wisdom.

Without dismissing the above, let's now consider another possibility. What about a guide who had been a potato farmer? Let's say he was a cheerful Irish man who enjoyed tilling the land and having a beer down at the local inn. His language was perhaps quite colourful, he was poor, uneducated and didn't pretend to understand all that strange philosophy about after-life and karma. He enjoyed his communication with nature and his friends and family but that was the extent of his spiritual thoughts. He couldn't possibly be a guide, could he? Yes.

Spiritual guides are souls who have lived a variety of lives before. Guides can just as easily have been penniless farmers as all-knowing sages. The value of a spiritual guide lies not in its physical appearance, but in the individual path of its soul and what it can teach you in your present life to smooth your journey on Earth.

Many people don't ever 'see' their guides. They simply feel them around them; they might even get a certain scent in their nostrils (often of a flower or incense), they might feel a wonderful light breeze around them or just comforting warmth. Sometimes people feel or sense nothing, but their mind goes into another sphere and they are able to receive information through thought alone.

The physical appearance of a guide isn't really important, unless it matters to you. And if it matters to you, then your guide will understand this and will manifest itself to you in whatever guise it feels you can most identify with.

If you are passionate about Egyptian mythology and feel a deep affinity with the Pyramids, then a guide will be more likely to show itself to you as an Egyptian god. They offer themselves in a way that will make you feel more secure and comfortable. If you are feeling unsure about the whole existence of guides and uncertain whether you can handle this new discovery, your guides will come to you in the most gentle and unobtrusive of ways until you feel ready to deal with the guidance they want to give you. So what have they come to teach you?

The answer to this is individual to you and your own spiritual path. Therefore, each person's experience with his own guide is a deeply personal one. No two people have the same guides or the same lessons to learn. We are all unique. You don't need to compare your progress to anyone else's because it's irrelevant. People work at different levels and with different time scales. The only constant in this journey is that for everyone it is a very gentle, loving experience because guides communicate only to nurture, protect and guide you. They enable you to open up your mind to new possibilities and to embrace energy from a higher source that is not earthly. They give true, unconditional love that is infinitely enriching and uplifting.

We all have more than one guide; in fact, most of us have a whole host of guides who come and go during our lifetime, offering advice and comfort when it is most needed. Some will stay with us always. For instance, often guides who offer themselves to us in the form of constant protection remain with us throughout our lives. All of us have protective guides, but many of us never learn how to tune in to them. By forging links with them, you increase their ability to protect you. This is, of course, true of all guides; by learning how to acknowledge their presence and work more closely with their energies, you give yourself greater opportunity to learn and to grow spiritually. Other guides will come into your consciousness for shorter periods of your life and they will have a specific role to play in your development. When you have learnt what is needed from them, they will then move on to other people and continue their own cycle of assistance.

Many people talk about having their own guardian angel who protects and helps them. There has been a great resurgence of interest in Western society about learning how to tune in to angels. A lot of books have been published and various workshops and courses now exist on how to bring angels into your life. An angel is another word for a spiritual guide. If you find it powerful to envisage incandescent angels flying around you and sprinkling you with fairy dust, then that can be the way a guide will manifest itself to you. Images of angels can be so beautiful and very uplifting. Many people speak of seeing them at a time of great need in their lives, such as the occasion when a loved one passes over. However, they can appear for a wealth of reasons and provide guidance in so many areas of our life. Letting angels into your energy field is inviting spiritual guides to come and bless you with their wisdom.

Guides also appear in other guises. Everyone has animal guides, whether they are aware of them or not. Sometimes these animals come in silent forms of protection or wisdom; others may actually speak to you. This may sound strange, but when you are experiencing communication with spirit guides, normal convention ceases to be important. Often communication takes place on a telepathic level with spirit guides; you may not be aware of any actual dialogue flowing back and forth between you, but the exchange of information they have to give you occurs on a silent, profoundly deep level of understanding. Once you experience this for yourself, it feels natural and right.

If you have a close affinity with a certain species of animal, it is quite possible you may draw a guide to you in that form during your work with spiritual guides. Whilst some animals come into your energy field purely to protect and comfort you, others will come because their species has guidance relevant to an experience you are having. Let's take a theoretical example to clarify this point.

Perhaps you have reached a time in your life when everything around you seems to be plodding by at an interminably slow, unexciting pace. Perhaps you are desperate to speed up certain events and to move forward more quickly and are feeling deeply frustrated by the apparent lack of progress you are making. If you meditate with this in mind, it is possible you may find a large, gentle elephant or tortoise coming into your energies and inviting you to take a journey with them, to understand the benefit and beauty of moving slowly. By being able to blend with the energy of an animal during a meditation, you are given a unique opportunity to experience another dimension of life which leaves you better equipped to deal with what is happening to you. We explore this further in later chapters.

There is another important area to discuss with regard to spiritual guides once we grasp the concept that everyone is ultimately a spiritual energy and that our physical body is purely a casing that we inhabit for a short time to enable us to learn different lessons while we are on Earth. It can become very tempting for people who have lost loved ones to spend time and effort trying to contact them through meditation. Earthly attachments between people are naturally very strong and they are enormously powerful in shaping our spiritual growth.

However, when someone passes on, it is because the time is right for them to do so. This is intensely hard to accept in certain cases, particularly when someone has died young or in tragic circumstances. Even if someone passes on in old age, having lived a full and productive life, it is still usually very hard to say good-bye. There is a natural tendency in most people to want confirmation that the person who has gone is still 'alive' in some spiritual realm, or that part of them remains in an energetic sense to comfort you and keep you company here on Earth. Most people who have lost loved ones would acknowledge that letting go and moving on is one of the hardest experiences. Some people never quite manage it.

Therefore when, through meditation and communication with spiritual guides, you realize someone you have lost in a physical sense is not really 'gone' but exists in a spiritual energy form, you may have the urge to spend time trying to communicate with them. Whilst this is not a 'bad' thing, it isn't necessarily helpful either, for you or for them. People pass on because the time is right for them to do so, even if we can't understand that reason. That person has touched us on Earth and because we have both learned whatever we needed to learn from each other, that person has now moved on. We have to learn to progress without them, no matter how strong that attachment may have been and how hard it is for us to say good-bye. Part of our growth process is learning how to let go.

For the person who has passed over, their learning process will also continue in a spiritual sense. Whilst none of us can say for certain what that process is, what is clear is that they too have to follow their path. It can be argued, therefore, that if we spend a lot of time and energy trying to remain in contact with those departed loved ones, and constantly trying to call them back to us, we are not helping either their progress or our own.

This is not to say that loved ones who have passed over don't occasionally return to offer comfort and reassurance. Many people would say they have actually felt the presence of someone or something and found it profoundly healing and uplifting. It's important to draw a distinction between feeling the comforting presence of a departed loved one every so often and in a wonderfully nurturing way, and a situation whereby you are constantly seeking out the energy of a departed soul, through deep longing and sadness. Many people seek the assistance of a medium or clairvoyant to help them contact loved ones who have died. Certainly it's not wrong to want reassurance of their continued existence on a spiritual plane. Where the balance might tip into the unproductive and unhealthy is if that need for contact becomes something that the bereaved craves on a regular basis. Wanting proof of an after-life is a natural response for the newly bereaved, but letting it slip into a constant need for communication makes it into something else.

If, when you are meditating, you feel the presence of a loved one who has passed over, welcome and bless them for loving you so much that they want to return briefly to your consciousness, and then let them go again, lovingly and unconditionally, knowing that they too are working on their own spiritual path.

If you have exchanged whatever communication was necessary during your physical time together, it is unlikely that someone who has passed over will need to return to you regularly to offer specific guidance. Loved ones usually return for short periods as confirmation of the after-life, to offer protection and/or a moment of unconditional love and support. Welcome them but do not cling to their energy. It is interesting to note that whilst they can come into our energy fields when spiritually necessary, it is virtually impossible for anyone to call upon the energy of a departed loved one at will. Any medium will explain to you that they do not have control over which spirit will come through to them. It's a bit like picking up a ringing phone that says 'Unknown number'. Only they can call us; we don't even know who they are! This would seem to imply that their spiritual awareness allows them to make contact when the time is right and we have to learn to trust that higher awareness and work with them, rather than try to impose our own will.

A natural question that follows from this discussion is the issue of whether a spiritual guide is always someone who knew us at some time, whether it be in this life time or a previous one. Whilst this doesn't seem to be an important issue for spiritual guides themselves, it may matter to you. It seems that physical knowledge of someone in a past life isn't really necessary for different energies to be beneficial to one another. For instance, we may not properly understand the energies of certain matter, such as the rejuvenating power of sunshine or the joy of standing on a beach with the waves pounding upon the shore, yet we can still appreciate and benefit from these different energies. If we can understand that the disparate energies of souls are all part of a greater, collective consciousness, then we can acknowledge that we are, in fact, all part of each other and inter-connected and inter-related. In other words, all energies connect with all other energies.

We are not individuals living independently of one another but all part of a larger whole. Ultimately we all have to work together cohesively to be able to understand cosmic laws and consciousness. Connecting with a spiritual guide is about our ability to understand higher consciousness. We have to transcend earthly connections and attachments to do this.

However, it is possible that sometimes in very deep meditations you may have an insight that a guide with whom you are conversing is in fact someone you knew in a past life and you may have flashes of that past life come into your consciousness. This is because you are being reminded of a lesson in that past experience. The memory may fade from your consciousness quite quickly, because it is not necessarily the past life that is important but the lesson you draw from it. As we mentioned earlier, conscious memory of past lives can be confusing and unsettling and happen only rarely in meditations and when we are working with spiritual guides.

Some people confuse spiritual guides with ghosts. They are not the same energy and they do not have the same intention. Ghosts are indeed a form of energy but they are a disparate, disjointed fragment of energy that comes from a memory that has not quite managed to pass over into the spirit world. In other words, a ghost is a fragmented energy that has become detached from its true soul energy and is floating, lost. It is worth explaining this further so you don't mistake a guide for a ghost.

Spiritual guides make a conscious choice to offer you their energy and guidance and their presence stems from a state of integrity and a desire to nurture you. This is always the case.

Ghosts are a much more confused form of energy. Their inability to accept a certain situation on the earth plane, whether it be from trauma or the suddenness with which they passed over or the ties they still have with an earthly person or place, has prevented them from moving forward completely into the spiritual realm. A ghost has not made a conscious choice to come into your energies to help and nurture you; it is much more likely that it is a needy energy, seeking your help, solace or guidance. The energy of a ghost is usually sad and has a lost air about it. It has to be given gentle love and assistance to continue its onward journey, but this is not a function that you will probably be able to fulfil. Should you ever feel you are in the company of a ghost, always send it on its way with gentle love and compassion. Ghosts are hardly ever malicious, just lonely, but you are not the right companion for them.

Every single experience with a guide will leave you feeling uplifted and in a better frame of mind. There is no hidden agenda with a spiritual guide; they only ever appear to offer assistance in a manner that will help, not hinder, you. It is always inspirational guidance, free from earthly emotions such as being biased, conditional, jealous or ignorant.

It is this that makes a spiritual guide a uniquely positive and powerful influence in your life. How many earthly people can actually be totally unbiased? All humans have hidden agendas in some form or another. They might want to help you in every way possible, but each person has their own emotional baggage or hang-ups that may prevent them from being able to do so. This is why cultivating stronger links with your spiritual guides is a unique act with powerful repercussions. Spirit guides have the ability to help you in a way that no one and nothing else can quite achieve. As we are going to see, we can call upon relevant guides to help us with any difficult issues in our life.

This isn't to imply that once you learn how to communicate with your spiritual guides, your life will suddenly become very easy and you will have all the answers to your problems at your fingertips. You are here on Earth to learn and grow; there is not much progress involved if you are simply shown everything by a teacher and not allowed to experience things for yourself. However, guides will be able to ease your path, to steer you along the most helpful routes and to encourage you to discover truth and integrity for yourself. They are not going to live your life for you, but they are there en route to hold your hand when you stumble and to pick you up when you've fallen.

So you are now beginning to see that delving into the realm of finding your spiritual guides and working with them involves undertaking a complex and very personal journey that has to be embarked upon gently and with great sensitivity. The best place to start is with learning how to forge those first tenuous links. Initially you needn't worry about what a guide is coming to tell you; we'll just look at how you can draw them into your energy in the first place and then you can gradually learn how to deepen your connection with them.

If you feel you are now in a position to believe in and understand the relevance of spiritual guides, then you are ready to start this new journey. If you still feel uncertain or unsure of what a spiritual guide is, you might want to reread and absorb this chapter again. It's important you have some concept, no matter how tenuous, of the benefit and power of a spiritual guide before you continue.

FORGING A LINK

Many people worry that contacting spiritual guides is going to be a very difficult and lengthy process because it's about experiencing something intangible and somewhat mystic. They think they now have to deal with something completely new and rather elusive. In fact, you will almost certainly have had the experience of a guide being with you in previous meditations but simply not realized they were there.

Think back to the very first meditation you practised – The Camera exercise on page 11. Perhaps you felt an affinity with one of the animals you saw as you zoomed past them. You wouldn't have stopped to acknowledge this, but it may have felt very real at the time. Maybe when you were working with the Visual Image exercise you chose to use a picture with a figure in it and you felt drawn to the energy within it. It's possible that meditating on the yantra with the figure in it allowed you to feel as though someone was with you. Working with the chakras is also a powerful way of drawing upon spiritual energies who will help to guide you through different experiences. Perhaps when you were working with the freeing meditations at the end of Part One, you were comforted by the energies around you and almost felt that someone or something was there with you.

Given how many meditations you have experienced through reading this far, there are almost certainly occasions when a guide or guides will have been with you, although you may not have been aware of it. So you see, the issue is not about knowing whether a guide is around you or not. They are always there for you. Finding your spiritual guides is about learning how to tap into something that is already there for you and has always been there for you. In other words, you are being loved and protected at all times by nurturing energies. Now you just need to learn how to tap into them.

Isn't that an inspirational thought? Spiritual guides are always with us in different guises and in different levels of our energy fields: we are never alone. Taking that statement on board as a truth through which we can learn and grow is a valuable aid to forging links with our spiritual guides.

Some people would say they have felt the presence of other energies at different times in their life, not just when meditating. As we discussed earlier, in moments of great sadness, such as when someone passes over, so often people record feeling a deeply comforting presence that helped them through the pain. A private moment enjoying the beauty of nature can be a communication with spiritual energies. Some would say their religious experiences are akin to feeling the presence of a spiritual guide, although religion does not have to be part of the equation. Anybody of any denomination or faith can feel the presence of a divine spirit.

So how do we start this communication? As always, it begins with the techniques that we have learnt about. First and foremost, paying attention to our breathing and being mindful of each breath, is a vital ingredient. We have to be in a relaxed state before we are receptive to our spiritual guides. We cannot communicate with higher energies when we are tense, shallow-breathing and distracted. You have worked on so many different techniques for focusing your thoughts and deepening your breathing that by now you should be discovering the best methods that work for you. However, it is always worthwhile rereading the sections on breathing and using different tools for relaxation and concentration, so that you keep checking your progress and trying new ways of meditating. Do you always sit in a chair when meditating? Perhaps you might want to try lying down now as you work with your spiritual guides. If you favour certain music and incense when meditating, try changing them.

There are aids that you might find helpful for working with your spiritual guides. For instance, the stone celestine is said to help connection with your guardian angels. You could try holding a small piece of celestine or having a piece near you as you meditate. Essential oils such as sage and angelica are believed to help connection with spiritual guides. The colours of indigo and violet are also used to assist in accessing the higher realms of consciousness. You might choose to wear something in that colour or have an object in that shade near you as you meditate. There are also certain flower essences that are deemed beneficial for awakening spiritual guidance: St John's Wort and Violet are two of these. If you want to try some different music, you might consider instruments, such as harp, violin and viola. Wind chimes, too, can aid higher consciousness.

While all of the above might serve to help you to some degree, the best aid to contacting spiritual guides is a genuine and deep desire to want to progress along your spiritual path. A spiritual guide will work with you at a profound level in your life, truly allowing deep changes to take place inside you. If you are ready for this experience and want to embrace the possibilities that are out there for you, that attitude is the most effective tool at your disposal.

So let us now look at a simple exercise that will allow you to start forging this new link.

Tuning to a spiritual guide

Give yourself the time to focus on your breathing and let yourself sink into relaxation. Now focus on your own aura for a while and feel it gradually expanding outwards and upwards. Let this happen gradually and gently without pushing the process. Allow yourself to feel open and ready to embrace the positive energies that are waiting to come into your aura. Open all your chakras slowly, one by one. Cleanse through to release any unwanted tension or emotion.

Now feel your crown chakra opening even further and feel a beautiful white light pouring down from the sky above. You can call this divine light, pure energy, universal spirit, or use no words at all. Simply focus on radiant, pure, white light pouring down from above. Feel it become stronger and stronger as you focus upon it. Let it cascade over and through all of you. Feel bathed in its incandescent beauty. The more you focus on this light, the more powerful and radiant it becomes. Let it fill the room you are in. Sit in this state of awareness and appreciation for some time.

Now silently ask for a spiritual guide to come into your energy; ask that they make their presence known in the most appropriate way possible for you. Say that you are ready to acknowledge their existence and to be guided by them. Wait silently for someone to approach. This contact will be personal to you.

Some people feel their skin start to tingle gently as though a slight electrical current is passing through them. Sometimes it feels like a part of you is being softly tickled. It may feel just like a very gentle breeze blowing against your skin, or as though a soft piece of silk has lightly brushed across a part of your body. You may feel as though some energy is near you or at your shoulder although you can't see it. You might see gold or silver light or sense millions of tiny bright stars falling softly through your aura. Perhaps they might manifest themselves as rose petals or beautiful angels. Whatever the sensation you experience, welcome it and give thanks for it.

Some people see images through their third eye, the brow chakra. They see either a hazy outline or a clear image of their guide. Try focusing on your brow chakra; feel it opening to the beautiful white light above and around you. Ask your guide if it will manifest itself to you in some visual image. Allow time for this. If nothing materializes in your mind's eye, that is fine. Often it takes practice before this occurs.

When you know you are sitting in the presence of a spiritual guide, ask if they have a message for you. This may come in the form of words, an image, a feeling or sound. Quite possibly nothing may happen at this early stage, but ask and see what occurs.

Have a silent conversation with your guide and explain that you would like to work further with them. Make it clear that you are now ready for this new experience. Ask that they return again when you tune in to them. Thank them for coming to you.

Remember it is important for you to withdraw from this realm of higher consciousness or you will be left feeling disjointed and ungrounded. Give yourself time to cleanse and close down, paying particular attention to closing your crown and brow chakras, both of which will have opened a great deal during this meditation. Ground yourself properly when you have finished. Sit for a while and drink water before you get up and resume everyday activities.

Remember that whatever happened during this exercise, it was right for you. You may have felt a whole host of energies around you or you may have just felt the slightest tickle or breeze across your face. If immediately you saw an image and felt a strong connection with a guide, that is wonderful. However, it can often take a while before this happens.

We are going to work more and more with this beautiful white light from above as we continue our meditations. You may already have experienced it when you were focusing on opening your crown chakra in previous exercises. It is hard to explain this phenomenon of tuning in to universal energy because it is something you have to experience for yourself. Some people relate the feeling of this pure, white light as being a spiritual awakening or cleansing. Other people describe it as being infinitely comforting and uplifting. Some feel wonderfully safe and secure and want to bathe in its presence for as long as possible.

This pure white light is always available to us whenever we want to call upon it. The more frequently we tune in to its presence, the more powerful and beneficial it becomes to us. If you hold a particular religious faith or worship a particular deity, then you may choose to give this energy a name that is personal to you. If you hold no particular faith but wish to find a name for it, then tune in to the white light and ask what you should call it. As universal energy is infinite and constant, the name you give it cannot alter its power. It is simply to make it more real and accessible to you. The more you learn how to access universal energy, the easier it becomes to tune in to your spiritual guides.

You will need to repeat this exercise a number of times before you start to feel the benefit of it; as is the case with any new regime, you won't notice any improvement until you have been practising for a while. However, when the results do start to show, it can be so rewarding.

When you have spent some time working on the previous exercise, we are going to experiment further. You needn't rush to get to this stage. Wait until you have completed the exercise a number of times, and really focused on pulling down the white light into your aura and through all of you, before you continue.

When you're ready, we are going to look at how we can create stronger links with our guides. We are going to use a number of techniques to do this. Experiment with the following exercises over a period of time. Note which ones work best for you. Some may immediately feel powerful and right; others you may struggle to follow. Try all the meditations to discover for yourself which ones are appropriate for you.

The lift

Relax and open up in your usual way. Take your time. When you are comfortable and ready and resting in a state of awareness, check to make sure you are truly tuning in to the divine light above, around and through you. Focus purely on the white light.

You know that you would like to discover the source of this universal energy. As you concentrate on the beauty of the white light above you, you look up and realize that this light has now become a tall lift. It reaches up, through the clouds and into the universe beyond. The lift is a wonderful luminous white, emitting a radiant glow. You decide to step into it.

As you do so, you see two buttons inside, one marked 'Earth', which is flashing, and another one marked 'Spirit'. You press the second button, the door closes, and the lift moves quickly and quietly upwards. You travel for some time in this wonderful white space, feeling safe and secure. The lift then stops and the door opens.

You now see a glowing golden light shining into the lift. As you feel yourself being bathed by this beautiful healing warmth, you realize a heavenly figure has stepped into the lift and joined you. This is a spiritual guide, come to spend some time with you. Welcome the guide into your aura, ask if they have something to say to you. Often in the beginning, they come just to reassure you of their presence. They may not speak to you until another occasion. Enjoy their energy and thank them for manifesting themselves to you. Be content just to be in their presence without questioning or trying to understand more.

Now it is time for them to go. They walk slowly out through the door and melt into the golden ray of light. The door then closes and you find yourself being taken downwards again, back to the Earth. When the lift stops, the doors open and you step out.

Now you realize you are back in your room again, resting in your meditation pose. Bring yourself back to reality. Cleanse thoroughly, close down and ground yourself. Don't open your eyes quickly but rest for a few minutes, reflecting on what you learnt. Slowly open your eyes and focus on an object for a while before you get up.

This can be an extremely powerful exercise and the speed with which the lift moves can make you feel as though you are leaving your physical body behind. That is why it is particularly important to thoroughly ground yourself again when you finish this exercise. Don't get up until you feel properly re-orientated and ready to resume your everyday life.

If you dislike lifts and want to create the image of another vehicle that will take you into the sky, that is fine. This exercise works as well if you create a rocket, plane or an air balloon. You might even prefer to have a beautiful bird appear in the white light and feel yourself soar upwards on its back. It's fine to change the method through which you travel, provided it takes you effortlessly and quickly upwards and you feel safe and happy.

You may also find that when the guide appears, it is not clearly visible to you but is a disconcertingly hazy shape of indefinite matter. Guides do not always manifest themselves clearly from the beginning. It can take time and practice before you forge strong links. All that matters at this stage is that you are able to acknowledge their presence. Closer communication will come in time. Let's look at another technique now.

The crystal

For this you may want to have a real crystal or a picture of one in front of you, although this is purely for inspirational purposes. You do not actually need to have a physical object or representation, as you will be creating the image in your mind's eye.

As with the other meditations, relax and open up in your own way. When you are ready, bring your attention to the beautiful white light glowing above and around you. Focus on this white light. Feel the beauty of it entering you. As you concentrate, you become aware of a beautiful crystal lying in front of you. It is large and glows invitingly. Beautiful beams of light flow outwards from its centre. The pure white light from above is shining directly onto the crystal, making it shimmer.

As you study the crystal closely, you notice there is an entrance into the very heart of the crystal. You decide to walk into it. You find yourself entering deep into the centre of the crystal itself. It feels wonderfully comforting and uplifting. You are bathed in beautiful beams of light as you walk.

You find yourself in the middle of a beautiful large room, the crystal walls reflecting the wonderful white light and making it glow warmly. You stand in the centre of this crystal room, absorbing the powerful rays all around you.

Then you realize you are no longer alone. A heavenly figure has joined you in this space. It stands there, gentle, unobtrusive, comforting. Welcome its presence. See if it wishes to speak to you, but do not worry if it doesn't. It will communicate in time. Stay with your guide for a while. When the time is right, it will slowly blend back into the beautiful light around you.

Then you will know it is time for you to leave. You return to the entrance and find yourself leaving the crystal behind you. You close the door and slowly walk away. Now you realize you are back in your meditation room. You are back in reality. Think about the day, time and year you are in. Cleanse and close down. Protect yourself. Sip some water before you get up again.

There is something so beautiful about crystals, whatever their size or colour. They can be inspirational objects to have around you at any time. Start noticing the different crystals that are available in shops; you may know friends who have crystals. Study them; what does their energy make you feel? Learn to appreciate how beautiful they are and allow their energy to affect you positively.

If you found this a particularly helpful meditation, you may choose to spend some time learning more about crystals and learning to workwith their unique properties. Many people find having a crystal or two in their meditation room greatly assists both the power and depth of their meditations.

You may find as you repeat this exercise that the crystal in your meditation changes colour and shape on each visit. This is because the different crystals have different properties and uses. You may also find a different guide comes to you each time, depending upon what you need at a particular moment in your life. Again, don't worry if the guide isn't clearly visible. It will become clearer in time.

We are also going to use a technique to call upon a specific figure to come into your energy. Sometimes by requesting a definite image, this can strengthen our relationship with guides. In other words, being quite clear about what you would find helpful allows your guide to make a stronger link with you. As so many people find the image of an angel inspirational, we will start with this and then look at other physical images.

The angel

Close your eyes, relax and then open up. Spend some time pulling down the white light from above. Enjoy resting in its beauty and strength. Feel yourself strongly connected to this energy, feel as though you are melting into it and becoming one with it. There is no distinction between your energy and the pure white energy; you are all one. When you feel in tune with this universal energy and can see how inter-connected you are with everyone and everything, ask silently that this relationship be allowed to deepen further.

Ask that a beautiful angel manifest itself to you, to show the level of energy and purity in this realm of togetherness and understanding. There are no barriers where true consciousness exists.

You sit quietly and wait, trusting, knowing all is well. Then you see in your mind's eye a shape beginning to form. Your own angel is slowly manifesting itself in front of you, in a shape and guise that is personal to you. This is happening gradually and effortlessly. Notice if your angel wants to move and fly around you or if it remains still, silent and beautiful. Its presence is beautiful, far beyond normal words of explanation. Quietly soak in its wonderful energy. Thank it for showing itself to you. When the time is right, it will slowly fade away into the white light again, perhaps leaving a faint iridescent glow behind.

> You know it is time for you to return to reality again. Take your time to readjust. Cleanse and close down. Ground yourself. Wait a while before you open your eyes and continue your day.

You may have been surprised that an angel showed itself to you! We sometimes have preconceived ideas of what we believe angels should look like. When they do reveal themselves, they look quite different. There is no guarantee your image and theirs will match. You may discover that different shapes, colours and sizes of angels will appear at different times.

Since angels are such a light and very beautiful form of delicate energy, it is sometimes possible to see them when you least expect it. You might be sitting enjoying a quiet moment in a deserted garden and suddenly realize one has presented itself to you. You may close your eyes as you drift off to sleep and one will manifest itself in your mind's eye for a brief moment before slipping away again. These are precious moments of being blessed by gentle spiritual love; welcome them but do not expect them. When we don't demand or expect, but simply 'be', we naturally open ourselves to all sorts of wonderful spiritual guidance and love.

The same is true of animals or any creatures as spiritual guides. The next exercise is to help you forge a relationship with an animal guide.

The creature

> Allow yourself to sink into your inner stillness and relax. Now focus on the white light coming down and surrounding you. Let it slowly infiltrate every part of you, through your aura, through your chakras, through your very muscles and bones. Sit in this state of awareness for a while. Feel yourself merging into the universal energy.
>
> When you are ready, silently communicate that you feel able to receive an animal guide into your energy field. Ask that the divine spirit choose a suitable animal to manifest itself. Explain that you are now ready for this to happen and that you would welcome the teaching that comes from this creature.
>
> Sit quietly and wait, resting in a state of stillness and trust. Try not to focus on any particular animal or creature. Know that what comes

will be right for you. You feel the energy change as the creature starts to appear in front of you. You realize that an animal's aura is a very different sensation from that of an angel or another kind of guide. Welcome this new energy. Ask that the creature be shown to you as clearly as possible. Enjoy the creature's presence as it becomes more vivid in front of you. Acknowledge its unique power and ability to add a new dimension to your level of universal understanding. You may find the creature wants to communicate telepathically with you; this is a natural and comfortable process. It may want to say nothing but just imbue you with its comforting presence. Soak in the energy being offered to you and thank it for manifesting itself. Now it slowly fades back into the white light, leaving behind a gentle memory of its beautiful energy.

As it melts back into the ether, you realize you are back in your meditation room. Cleanse, close down, protect yourself. You may find the residue of this different energy remains intangibly in the room. Enjoy its healing, nurturing presence. Appreciate the fact that this was a different experience and a wonderfully enriching one. Sip your water and sit quietly as you reflect upon this. Consider how each creature will have its own unique energy, and that this is only the beginning of a new dimension of understanding. Ground yourself again before you stand up and continue your normal routine.

Animals or creatures of any description have an energy very unlike that of a human or angel spiritual guide. Whilst it can be hard to explain how it differs, once you feel it for yourself, it is very easy to identify. This means that in the future when you close your eyes and call a spiritual guide into your energy, you will learn to tell if a guide is a creature, angel or human before they actually manifest themselves. The energy that precedes their presence will be unique to them.

In fact, each spiritual guide has its own energy and you will gradually be able to tell the difference. Once that feeling is specific to a guide, it no longer seems so important for them to manifest themselves physically to you. The sensation of their energy is enough for you to be able to work with them and absorb their guidance. The individual feeling of a guide can also be accompanied by other extraneous phenomena. For instance, a certain guide may come with a particular essence or scent. There may be a distinct sound such as a bell or flute relating to that guide. You may even hear an animal sound relating to a particular creature. A specific colour may be relevant or even a special taste in your mouth. These factors are not especially important, except in so far as they strengthen your relationship with a particular guide. They are simply helping you to use physical, earthly experiences to intensify the spiritual experience. As by nature we are programmed to feel more reassured with physical sensations, this can be a very useful stepping stone to greater spiritual awareness.

Whatever physical sensations accompany your meditations with spiritual guides, you might want to make notes. Once you open the doors into the world of spiritual guides, you will realize just how many there are out there, willing and able to assist you along your personal path of growth. Once you begin to forge links with them, and learn how to identify their different energies, you can start to work at a deeper level and communicate in a much more profound way.

However, just before we delve into that experience, it's important to mention one point. With all your work so far with spiritual guides, every single experience should have been uplifting and nurturing. If by any chance you have had an experience that was not comfortable, you need to wash it away immediately. The cleansing techniques you learnt earlier come into play with all communication of a spiritual nature. Provided you were focusing purely on the universal energy and immersed in its strength, there is no reason why you should have picked up anything unpleasant.

However, it is just possible that in your inexperience you lost your focus on the pure white light for a short time and delved into other areas without realizing it. If you did encounter anything with which you weren't happy, it's essential that you reiterate that you are in control at all times. You can clear an energy from your field at will because you have power over your own energy. If at any time an energy should come towards you which is not a guide but some form of lost or confused energy, remember to cleanse it away immediately. If a presence makes you feel uncomfortable, it is not a spiritual guide. Wash it away. You don't need it.

Occasionally you may feel that the energy of one of your spiritual guides is over-powering. This isn't likely to happen often and it won't necessarily be an unpleasant sensation, but the energy may still feel too strong. You could liken it to being outside on a very windy day and deciding you would rather be indoors! It is fine to let your spiritual guide go, if this is the case.

Let it know you would welcome its return on another occasion, but now is not the right time. Spirit guides will always leave at your request. Remember, you are in control at all times.

Now let us progress into deeper and deeper communication with our spiritual guides.

COMMUNICATING ON A DEEPER LEVEL

You may already feel that you are progressing well with your guides. It is a wonderful sensation when you start to feel and/or see them around you and realize how much spiritual help and love is available for you to tap into. It can be quite an emotional experience. You may also have had some silent verbal communication with them already, or conversations on a telepathic level which you found powerful and helpful. If you still feel that links with your spirit guides are tenuous, the exercises in this chapter should help you to improve communication with them.

What we are going to look at now is how we can call upon specific spiritual guides to help us in particular areas of our life. To do so, we have to learn how to focus on one area and then call the most appropriate spiritual guide into our energy fields.

As a first step, it might be most helpful to start by calling upon a spiritual guide whose primary purpose is to offer you protection. Protective guides come in all shapes and guises, so don't be surprised if yours come to you in forms you aren't expecting.

Getting to know who your protective guides are also strengthens your innate ability to protect and defend yourself. We open up a great deal during meditation and although you have learnt how to cleanse and close down thoroughly, it is very easy for us to keep opening ourselves up again without realizing it. The more meditation we do, the easier we tend to find opening up, although unfortunately we don't remember the closing down process as often.

Working with the chakras and universal energy also leaves you quite vulnerable. The more you tap into your own spirituality, the more you become aware of other people's energies and you can easily find yourself unconsciously tapping into them. Of course this has the great benefit of making you more aware and compassionate of others, but it also has the downside of making you more vulnerable sometimes. Hopefully, you have been remembering to use your Cloak of Protection exercise whenever you need it. If you have forgotten about this exercise, it would be a good idea to return to page 145 and refresh your memory. Finding your protective spiritual guide is another effective awareness tool that will render you less vulnerable.

So it is important that you don't rush the following exercise. Don't try to find your protective spiritual guide in a quick five-minute meditation. Wait until you have a chance to really relax and give yourself plenty of time to sink into a deep, meditative state.

Your guide to protection

Go through your usual opening up process, remembering to spend time pulling the universal energy down into your aura and through all of you. Enjoy the process; don't rush it.

Really allow yourself to sink into a deep state of relaxation. As you do so, bring the word 'protection' into your consciousness and let it float around your energy field. Meditate on the word for a while. Play with the word and see what you can learn; see what insights come to you. Give thanks for whatever you are given.

Now pull your protective cloak around you. Relish the sense of comfort and security this gives you. Sit quietly for a while, your eyes closed, feeling the nurturing sensation of the cloak.

As you appreciate its protection, start to think about where the cloak came from. You were aware it was handed to you in some fashion in the very beginning, but you probably didn't stop to think about its origin. Start to think about this now. This very spiritual cloak of energy and protection that you appreciate and use regularly does have a source somewhere in the realms of higher consciousness. Who decided it was the right cloak for you? You may feel you pulled it from the depths of your subconscious, but who helped you to make this spiritual decision? Your cloak is your gift from a spiritual guide who loves and wants to protect you.

Reflect upon this statement for a while. Realize that you would like to thank the guide who has given you this wonderful gift. You would like to meet them. Still with your cloak around you, ask silently that you be allowed to meet the guide who has given you your cloak. Feel your brow and crown chakras opening more fully as ask. Let the beautiful white light come down into your crown chakra and float through both openings of your brow chakra. Remember to breathe comfortably and deeply. Wait quietly, without apprehension, trusting they will make themselves known to you.

After some time, or perhaps quite quickly, someone will show themself to you. If their image is hazy and indistinct, ask that they make themselves more visible to you. Communicate with them and explain that you cannot see them clearly yet. If you ask gently, they will listen and try to help. Sometimes it is because your brow chakra is not fully open and you are not allowing the white light to flow unhindered through you.

When the image comes, if it is not as you anticipated, that is fine. Do not wash it away, unless you feel uncomfortable with its presence. Let yourself explore this new image. It may be a creature you cannot recognize. It may be a human form or an angel. It will come in the shape that is right for you to handle, even if you do not necessarily understand it at first. However it manifests itself to you, you want to welcome it and thank it for coming into your energy.

Now you need to explain that you would like to get to know it better. Ask if there is a name that you may call this new guide. A name will help create a stronger contact. It is also helpful if you have a name that you can call upon if you need your protective guide at any given time. Explain why you want to have a name; some guides have not been on Earth for a long time and they may need to be reminded of the strength of earthly ties and needs.

This process of having a silent conversation, a sort of telepathic communion, soon feels natural and normal. Remember it is also fine just to be silent and to let information be given to you. It is powerful to sit in that deep silence for a while and to let your guide speak when the time is right. This is why you cannot rush a meditation with your spiritual guide. They do not work on the same 'earth time' as we do, so what we feel may be a long pause is simply a natural energy flow for them.

During your work with your guide, it is important that you try to melt into their energy so that you can gain the most possible from this contact. They do not need to benefit from our physical energy; they are there for our benefit and to help us as much as possible. It's important always to appreciate that and to acknowledge the time they give you.

You might want to start your conversation simply by expressing your appreciation that they have chosen to protect you. There are many humans they might have picked and they have decided to help you. Thank them for this gesture. Ask your guide how they can best protect you and when and how you should call upon them. Ask them if they have noted occasions when you were unprotected and vulnerable and you neglected to protect yourself properly.

Your protective guide is not just there to literally protect you, but also to teach you how to protect yourself and what protection truly means. They may tell you about certain physical items that may increase your sense of protection, such as specific crystals, incense or a talisman. Let them know you want to learn. Closely listen to what they are saying. Spiritual teachings are not necessarily simple and easy to grasp; they are intended for us to take as a concept and then expand further, using our conscious thought to formulate our personal understanding of them.

Ask that they remain in your consciousness as you meditate again upon the word 'protection'. See if they have any more insights to offer as you work on the true meaning of this word.

When the time is right, they will withdraw from your consciousness and fade back into the white light. Remember to thank them as they go. Remember what they have said and that you can call them back into your consciousness when you need them.

Now it is time for you to withdraw from your meditation, to cleanse and close down. Make sure you use your cloak of protection. If it has slipped from you, remember to call it back again and draw it closely around you. Resolve to use your cloak and call upon your guide of protection whenever you need it in the future. Sit quietly for a while before you get up.

You may find this whole exercise much more powerful than you expected. If it had little effect, then it is very important that you return and meditate upon this protective guide again soon. It is so important for us to have protection and to know how to look after ourselves, particularly when we are in the realm of heightened awareness.

If you can remember any particular teaching that your guide offered you, remember to act upon it. If they recommended that you use a particular sign as a symbol of protection, ensure that you go out and find it and have it with you. It doesn't matter if this takes the form of a talisman that you wear around your neck or a small picture of the symbol that you keep by your bed or in your pocket. If they recommended a particular incense or essence, acquire some and keep it with you at work as well as in your home environment. Spiritual guides do not recommend action lightly; if they give you specific advice, take it and give thanks for what you have been offered.

You can repeat this exercise and find that a different guide may come through. We don't have just one protective guide, we have a number of them and can call upon them on different occasions. For instance, you might find a large, powerful beast comes into your energy on an occasion when you are physically vulnerable, perhaps walking alone at night somewhere or in the company of people whose energy feels threatening. You may find you have a very light, delicate angel who comes to you when you are feeling emotional and tearful. There might be a spirit who guards your home, one who looks after your car or protects you when you're travelling, a guide you may want to send off with your children or loved ones when they leave the house.

The act of feeling and being protected comes in different guises and at different times in our life. For instance, we all know we feel much more vulnerable if a loved one has just died or we have split up after a long relationship or lost our job suddenly. However, these three instances have very different expressions of vulnerability attached to them, and at each of these times our spiritual guides will come to us in the way that helps us most. Therefore, the more open and receptive we are to their different energies, the more they can positively affect us.

The more deeply we delve into spiritual realms, the more important protection becomes, in every way. Keep renewing your contact with your protective guides. Don't just do the previous exercise once and then forget about it. You deserve and need the most effective, nurturing protection possible at all times in your life.

Let us now look at how we can draw other guides to us and what we may learn from them. The best way to start this process is for you to acknowledge an area in your life in which you know you need some guidance. So you are now going to choose an element of your life which you feel you need to do some work on and see if you can draw an appropriate guide to you, who can help you in this task.

This is very personal to you and it can really encompass any scenario or concern. However, it's no good just deciding you are unhappy at work and taking that as the situation you want to look at. You need to be more precise.

In other words, if you decide you are dissatisfied with your career at present, you need to identify what is causing the dissatisfaction. Is it that you feel you are in the wrong job entirely or that you are struggling with the particular position you hold? Is the difficulty the people around you at work or the work itself? Does the dissatisfaction relate to you not feeling valued in your work or is it about not having enough money?

If it is the last of these, you would therefore take the question 'Why am I not earning enough money at present?' into your meditation. You wouldn't ask 'Why am I not happy at work?' The clearer you can be about what you want to look at, the more help you will receive with your meditation.

So now is the time for you to take an honest look at your life and choose an issue you would like to understand more. Remember, the more specific you are, the more help you will get. Really take your time to decide what you want to work on. You also have to choose a situation that you are willing to understand more about. You have already discovered meditation can be profound and deeply touching. Therefore you need to have an open attitude to whatever you are going to meditate upon. If some issues are far too painful, leave them until a later stage.

When you have chosen an area, make sure you can be specific about the issue. Try to express it in one simple question. If you are stuck, here are a few examples of powerful opening questions:

- Why am I always angry with my mother/father/partner?
- Why do I feel a failure as a parent?
- How can I change my job?
- Why do I feel nervous about going abroad on holiday?
- Why do I feel so tired all the time?
- Why do I never have enough money?
- Why can't I find the right partner?
- Why do I often get headaches?

These might spark off further thoughts that enable you to choose an issue that really matters to you. Remember, you want to be ready to face this area in your life openly, honestly and without fear.

When you have chosen your issue and know that you feel happy about working with the real reasons behind this problem, then you are ready to work through the exercise below.

Finding a specific guide

Start off by relaxing in your usual way and letting yourself sink into a comfortable, meditative state. Take time to really focus on your breathing and feel it deepen and lengthen. Focus on the white light above and feel it become stronger. Trust in its power and beauty. Let it cascade around and through you. Open your chakras and feel the white energy flowing through them all. Sit in this state for a while.

Now let your focus go inward to that quiet, sacred space inside you. Go into this place with pleasure, feeling safe and secure. Breathe deeply and feel yourself relax. When you are ready, remember the question you want to ask. Bring the question into your conscious thought and say it silently, first of all to yourself, without seeking any outside help. Let the question float around and through you. Notice what insights you can glean by taking this question into your meditation.

If you notice different parts of your body being affected by the question, observe the responses without trying to alter them in any way. You may find a certain chakra pulsing more powerfully than normal. Wash away what you don't want, using your cleansing technique. When you know you have understood all you are capable of on your own, call upon a spiritual guide to help you further your knowledge and understanding.

Remember the white light that is still flowing through and around you. Focus on the light above you and call upon a guide to come and help you. Ask that you be given a guide who will be the most useful to you at this time. Repeat the question silently as you ask them to help you. Then sit quietly and wait. You may sit for some time in this state, waiting patiently. Keep focused on the issue you want to understand more about.

During this stage, you may find yourself drifting into a scenario which you were not consciously creating. Sometimes this is a very powerful way of learning more with our spiritual guides. They may gently lead your conscious thought onto another level. As you sit quietly, you may realize you are being transported into another setting, or taken into an unexpected realm of thought.

If your issue is with your mother, you may find yourself being taken back to an incident you had when you were a child. This may be a conscious memory or something you had forgotten. If your issue is about work, you may find yourself in a new setting, giving you an indication of what you might want in your career. If you are trying to understand where your headaches are coming from, you may be shown an image of something that clarifies this for you.

Your spiritual guide will gently show you these images, as though you are taking part in a film whose script you haven't read, so you don't know what is going to happen next. If you are not naturally visual and normally don't see much, your guidance may come in the form of sensations or sounds. They will be personal to you.

Whatever scenario you find yourself in, accept you are being shown what is appropriate for you. This isn't always clear at first. You may find your trust wavering, wondering if what you are experiencing is simply your imagination. Keep your focus on the scene unfolding in front of you without questioning it. You may find it is not until the end of the 'film' that you understand.

Sometimes this can be an emotional journey. Many past hurts can reveal themselves during work with our spiritual guides. However, they are showing them to us purely so that we can heal and learn from what has happened. We have to learn that those past events need have no control over us now. By our guides showing them to us clearly, we can relive something and then know it is time to let it go. Our guides can also help us in the letting go process.

Guides never show anything to you to upset you; they are motivated purely by unconditional love. Therefore if you are being shown a particular scenario, it is because they know you are now ready to face the issue and to let it go. Most of the issues concerning our present life have at their roots some incident in our past. Through working with our spiritual guides, we may be shown a number of flashbacks, some of which we don't even remember. We are shown them so that we can release the emotion from that event and thus release the block that is preventing us from moving forward in our lives.

During these flashbacks, your guide will sometimes appear in a particular guise. Sometimes they don't appear physically but you are given a strong sense of them being there, watching, almost as though a member of an audience. Sometimes they are one of the characters.

> When your 'film' is finished and you have taken the insights you have been given into your energy field and digested their impact, your guide may stay with you for a while if they feel you still need them, or they may silently disappear into the white light again. You may only feel them there and then sense they are gone. When you work with spiritual energy, it doesn't equate with earthly behaviour and using earthly words to describe spiritual activity doesn't help.
>
> Whatever happens during your meditation on this personal issue, it will be very private experience. If you feel emotional, that is fine. Make sure you take time to wash away whatever you don't want and protect yourself thoroughly when you finish. If you are feeling vulnerable, ask your Protective Guide to come down and stay with you for a while. Make sure when you finish your meditation that you bring your cloak of protection securely around you. Close all your chakras slowly and carefully. Keep your cloak with you for a while, even after you get up and continue with your day.

This meditation may have taken you into a different realm, a new world of understanding. This is because we are now beginning to work with spiritual guides on a much deeper level.

You are now understanding that spiritual guides don't operate like a teacher who stands up in front of a class and lectures on one particular subject. The spiritual world is much more complex and subtle than that. Your guides are working with your energy on all levels, trying to help you to help yourself.

We are allowing spiritual energy to come into our own energy and make positive changes within us. By experiencing these 'films' we are in effect letting our spiritual guides manipulate our own spiritual energy field. This is very sensitive work. It may leave you feeling more vulnerable and emotional for a while. However, the wonderful aspect of this experience is that it affords us a unique opportunity of letting go of old, unwanted blockages and stale energy that have been preventing us from living our life in a truly 'whole' sense. The more we work with guides in this deeper sense, the more profound this experience becomes.

As we have been dealing with more sensitive issues, now seems a beneficial time to look at calling upon another specific guide who we will want to have around us on certain occasions.

You may have felt during the previous exercise that there are emotions not quite healed, or unsettled feelings, somewhere within your body or energy field. This is quite understandable, given that you are dealing with deeper realms of spiritual energy and are therefore touching raw areas of yourself that you have not gone into before. Who might help us in this new field? Your Healing Guide. Unlike your Protective Guide this entity is not covering you up to shield you from outside influences, but is there to help heal the delicate areas of your energy field. This following exercise is particularly important if you have recently finished the previous exercise and are still feeling the residual effects of it.

Your healing guide

Open up in your usual fashion, giving yourself time to relax and focus on breathing. Open your chakras, one by one. Concentrate on the white light and feel it coming down, around and through all of you.

Now retreat into your quiet inner space, but as you do so allow the beautiful white light to come into it with you. Sit in your sacred space, with the beautiful white light washing over you. Feel comforted by its presence.

Focus on the pleasure of the colour white. Think about what a pure, healing colour white can be. It is associated with healing in so many practical ways, being used in hospitals, by doctors and nurses, in bed linen. Bathrooms and kitchens are often white, symbolizing cleanliness and purity. Angels are often depicted in white. Ask yourself what white means to you. Let the colour white wash over and through you. See the word in front of you and let it dance around. See what white has to say to you. If you find it a difficult colour, ask yourself why. See what insights come to you.

Now ask yourself what the word 'healing' means to you. This word conjures up different images for different people. To some people it may be a scent: a beautiful delicate rose or the smell of a fresh lemon. It might be a sound such as the peal of church bells, the chirrup of bird song or the pitter-patter of rainfall. Others may have images: perhaps a hot bubble bath or white cotton sheets or even a white figure. Some might know it just as a feeling: cleansed, whole, pure. Whatever it means for you is personal; the power of healing lies in your own individual relationship with it.

What would you describe as 'healing'? It can be the touch of a loved one when you're ill, or being able to drift into a deep sleep when you're tired. Perhaps a walk by the sea is your kind of healing. Maybe music is all you need to release stress after a hard day. Stroking an animal can also be healing. Maybe you find an activity such as swimming, yoga or gardening therapeutic. Meditate on the types of healing you can think of and see what each means to you.

Acknowledge there are occasions when you need another type of healing, especially when working with meditation and your spiritual guides. Acknowledge that the deeper you work on yourself and your own personal spiritual path, the more you need to understand healing on a deeper level. The more you acknowledge that you are a spiritual energy as well as a physical being, the more you have to look at other means through which you can heal yourself.

As you are meditating upon this truth, let yourself soak in the white light and ask your healing guide to make themselves known to you. Wait quietly until they manifest themselves to you in some fashion. It may not be what you were expecting. We are so conditioned to think of healers as doctors in white coats that it can be surprising if something totally different shows itself to us. Your healer may not be a human figure; it may be a creature you don't recognize or an angelic form. It may even be a feeling that you suddenly have of being cleansed and rejuvenated; you may not see anything. Perhaps you receive a waft of beautiful scent or you hear a particular sound.

Your healing guide will be whatever is most powerful for you, although you may not recognize it as such immediately. Spiritual guides constantly test our sense of what is normal and beneficial. Whatever has manifested itself to you, thank it for coming and ask what you may call it for future reference.

If there is a part of you that feels it needs healing, whether it be on an emotional, mental, spiritual or physical level, ask if they will help you with this. Explain what it is you are feeling and what you would like help with.

You may again find yourself taking another journey to somewhere you have not been before. This can happen in a number of ways. If your discomfort is physical, you may be taken on a ride into the physical area on which you are focusing and be shown the true cause of your discomfort. If you are struggling with some emotional issue, your 'film' may show you the cause behind this.

It is also possible that your healing guide may not think it is appropriate for you to understand further at this stage and that you may simply need gentle love and nurturing to heal the area that is uncomfortable. Then it is quite likely you will experience some physical sensation that will indicate gentle healing is taking place. This might be the cooling of an inflamed area or a calm feeling descending in an area of you that has felt agitated. Perhaps a part of you felt it was blocked and stagnant and you feel a gentle tingle as energy starts to flow again.

Remember you must ask for this help; your guides will not immediately barge into your energy field and start working on you. Guides cannot come in unless asked. The more receptive you are to their presence and the more you actively express your desire to work with and learn from them, the more powerful they can be.

Really invite this divine spirit into your energy. Let them know you want to enjoy this experience. Thank them for their time with you. When they melt away again into the white light, always send them on their way with blessings of love and appreciation.

When they do go, you may be left feeling quite altered energy-wise. It may take you a little time to adjust. The energy differences may be subtle but they are usually noticeable. You might feel a little light-headed, as though your feet aren't quite on the ground.

It is particularly important that you cleanse and ground yourself thoroughly. Closing down is also important, and in whatever area you have received healing, remember to cover it with some extra protection. You might do this in the form of a spiritual gauze or bandage. You might just want to protect it with the white light or your cloak of protection. If you have been given a protective talisman or crystal from your protective guide, cover this area with that. Be gentle with the area you have received healing on.

Make sure you drink a glass of water when you finish. Water is a natural cleanser and helps to rid the body of toxins. It is a physical adjunct to the spiritual experience you have just undergone. If you feel light-headed when you rise, sit down again and repeat the grounding energy exercise. Don't continue with your day until you feel that you are thoroughly back on this earth.

Your healing guide in particular is a very gentle and sensitive energy. It is also true to say you may have more than one healing guide and you may encounter more of them as you continue along your meditative path. Some healing guides will also feel much more powerful than others, and you will have to adjust to their different energies.

They are there to be called upon for whatever areas in your life need healing. Of course, there is a word of warning here, and this applies in all work with your spiritual guides. They are not there to be called upon for the smallest event in your life. If you cut your finger or feel slighted by a thoughtless remark someone has made, you do not necessarily need your spiritual guides to come and sort that out for you! Remember that your guides are a complement to your life and you do not want to feel tempted to use them at every opportunity.

First and foremost, you want to learn how to handle your own spirituality and work with it on a level that is insightful for you. Spiritual guides are not a crutch upon whom you lean so that you never learn to walk unaided; spiritual guides are friends who come and walk beside you for a while before leaving you to continue your journey on your own. It's important to understand the distinction.

If you ever try to use your spiritual guides as a means of doing your spiritual work for you, you will notice that they will not easily manifest themselves to you. All spiritual guides operate from a level of pure integrity which we humans have yet to attain – and won't unless we try to fulfil our purpose on this Earth and try to gain greater wisdom and compassion.

This brings us to a yet deeper level of work with our guides and the next chapter, in which we are going to look at how we might delve into the realm of understanding our own personal karmic path through working with our spiritual guides. This is not an easy realm to enter, and you might benefit from rereading this chapter and working through more of your personal issues before you continue.

UNDERSTANDING KARMA

You may remember our earlier discussion about karma and what it means: the concept that whatever you give out in life is what you will receive back. In other words, every action we take has a cause and that creates an effect. By accepting this sense of responsibility for our own actions, we learn how to follow our own karma and thereby discover our own spiritual self and our own individual spiritual path. Whether we choose to walk down that personal path, when we find it, is another decision that we make.

Following karmic law and understanding where we fit into the universe is a pretty tall order. You may feel that you could never manage this enormous task. In fact, you have already taken a number of large steps towards doing just that.

You see, every meditation you experience takes you just that bit closer towards understanding who you really are. You have already progressed from seeing yourself as a purely physical being (if that was indeed how you viewed yourself before starting to read this book) and developed a sense of your own spirituality, simply by accessing that inner stillness deep within your own energy field. Working with your spiritual guides has taken you yet deeper into this complex issue of who you really are and why you are here. Now we are simply going to explore this further so that you can gain a better understanding of life as a whole.

You really do need to spend some time on the exercises in this chapter. The deeper you work, the more time you need to allow yourself to truly relax. This process can't be rushed. You may also find yourself discovering yet more emotional aspects of you which you haven't tapped into before. If you don't feel quite ready for this journey, that's fine – leave it for now, and return to this chapter later.

As always, you need to have your cleansing techniques ready for these exercises. You have to remain responsible at all times and remember you are in control. If you get half-way through one of the karmic meditations and don't feel prepared for what you are being shown, then it is your responsibility to take control: wash away the imagery and return to reality, remembering to thoroughly close down and protect yourself.

You may find working with your spiritual guides is more complex in this realm. Everything may seem lighter and brighter and the form of your guides may not be as visible as before. This is because in the higher realms of consciousness the energy we tap into is finer and less earthly. We have therefore to concentrate much more and intensify our awareness towards whatever we are meditating upon. You really have to let go of extraneous sounds and images. To remain completely alert and yet utterly relaxed is an ideal state in meditation, but it is not easily accomplished. Hopefully you are now getting closer to attaining this state.

In our earlier discussion about karma, we touched on the possibility that each soul actually chooses which body it will reincarnate into, dependent upon what it wants to learn during that lifetime on Earth. This can be an emotional area. We all have different childhood experiences, some pleasant, some not so pleasant.

Going Back

We are going to start this journey towards understanding our own soul path by meditating on our childhood and, in particular, our relationship with our parents. If your parents are no longer alive or you are not in contact with them, still go back through the childhood process and see what you can learn. You may choose to switch your focus to whomsoever was there for you during this time. It may be an adopted parent, guardian or simply someone who was there during your childhood years.

If just thinking about this scenario upsets you and you don't feel ready to tackle it, that is fine. You can return at any time when you feel ready. Some of you may be looking forward to this journey, aware that there is much you want to understand about your relationship with your parents/guardians. When you are ready, begin with the following exercise. Remember to stop at any time if you are not happy with what you are uncovering, then cleanse thoroughly, close down and protect yourself.

Parental karma

Start with your usual relaxation process, remembering to open up all your chakras and focus on the white light above. Pull it down into and around you and then let yourself sit in your inner stillness for a while. When you are deeply relaxed and ready, continue.

Focus on your earliest childhood memory. Take yourself back to that time and remember what you felt. Let yourself experience it on all levels; feel it, sense it, smell it, hear it, touch it. Let yourself be taken back in time through your memory bank and relive it all. Remember all of it. If it was unpleasant, acknowledge that it is now in the past and cannot hurt you. Let the pain go. Wash it away.

Now you are going back further in time, much further back. You are going back to when you were just a toddler. Feel what it was like when you could barely walk, remember your first few unsteady steps. Go back further, to when you were sitting up and watching the world, unable to walk yet, just learning to feed yourself. All these memories are in your subconscious; now let them float up to the surface. Remember them. Now you are young and helpless, dependent on others for everything. You are very tiny and vulnerable and your world is very small. You sleep a great deal.

Now you are going back still further. You are taking a journey downwards into deep, silent stillness. It becomes dark and warm and comforting. Let yourself sink lower and lower. Enjoy this lovely rich velvety darkness. You are going deeper and deeper into nothingness. Sink down further. Relax into it. Feel yourself become empty. Nothing. Breathe into the dark nothingness. Sit in the beauty of being nothing, feeling nothing. Relax. Rest in this soft, velvet blackness. Stay here for a while. Enjoy being nothing.

Now become aware of a golden light far in the distance. Although it is a great distance away, it is coming towards you. Sit quietly and wait as this wonderful golden light gradually approaches. When it is near you, let the golden light enter into your solar plexus area. Take it deep into your energy. As you do this, feel it become part of you and feel yourself melt into the golden light. You become one.

As this happens, you are shown an image of your mother and father. You now watch a film unfolding. It is showing your mother and father in a way you have never seen them before. It is showing them as they really are. You follow their life. As you do so, you see why you chose to be their child. You understand why you have come into their life and also what you have to teach them. You let this profound realization sink through all of you, through all the layers of your being and acknowledge its significance.

The film continues. You watch your mother through her pregnancy with you. You become aware of what your presence means in her life. You observe your father and see what this means in his life, too. You watch what happens after you are born and how it affects them. As you absorb all this information, you realize how complex the relationship is between all of you. You can acknowledge for the first time that whatever happened in your childhood, you are not in any way to blame or to be held responsible for it. You realize that all of you are simply following your own spiritual paths and that they are crossing at certain points along the way.

You follow your early childhood and see how all the people around you interact with each other. You see where you fit into the complex puzzle and what you have learnt and also what you have helped others to learn. You are shown different moments in your life and why they happened. Your earliest childhood memory is also played back to you during this time and now you are able to understand it in its true context and see how others were also affected. You are slowly brought up to the present day and your current relationship with your parents/guardians.

Sit quietly for a while in stillness and peace, assessing the insights you have received as a result of this journey. Stay here for some time. As you finish digesting everything, you feel the golden light withdrawing from your solar plexus. It gently moves out of your energy field and then hovers a short distance away. You become aware that the golden light is manifesting itself as a spiritual guide to you. You may see this guide or relate to it simply as thought forms and light.

Have a conversation with this guide. Ask its name if you have not met it before. Ask if it has further information to impart to you. Realize that it was taking you through this film and allowing you to experience everything for yourself. Thank it for its teachings. Appreciate any more insights you are offered and let them be absorbed into your consciousness.

When the time is right, your guide will melt back into nothingness and you will remember what room you are in and what time of the day it is. Ensure that you properly cleanse and close down. Ground yourself. You will probably feel light-headed after your long journey into higher realms. Sit quietly and drink your water. Focus on an object in the room for a moment before you get up.

Ask yourself a few practical questions that will help earth you again. These can be trite questions such as 'How much tea/coffee do I have left in the cupboard?' or 'What colour underwear am I wearing?' Ensure you are well grounded before you continue with your day.

If this was an emotional journey for you, that is understandable. The majority of us have issues surrounding our childhood and our relationship with parents/guardians and siblings. You may want to repeat this exercise on a number of occasions before you feel you can really understand why you chose your parents. If you feel stuck during this exercise, remember always to take the time to breathe deeply and to release tension.

Make sure you really enjoy the relaxation process during this meditation. Especially enjoy the beauty of sinking down into that velvety stillness and that wonderful sense of nothingness that comes when you loosen all ties with earthly connections. It is only by letting go completely that we give ourselves the opportunity to see everything in a much wider context. When we are busy going through the minutiae of everyday life, we so rarely stop to consider where we really are and what we are really doing. The going into nothingness aspect of the exercise is an extremely important part. If you don't achieve it, you are probably going to be receiving insights coming from your own energy, rather than working with higher spiritual energy. The less you feel at that stage, the more effective and insightful the meditation will be for you.

If you still feel emotional for a while after finishing the exercise, you should probably take some time to have a meditation with your healing guide. As we discussed, we are now working with much deeper levels of your energy field and you may want the extra help of your spiritual guides.

Looking at where you have come from and why is a powerful basis for looking honestly at where you are right now in your life. The more you appreciate your past, the more it makes you question where you are right now. Of course, it may take some time before you feel able to really explore your past, and that is fine. You might take months meditating before you feel you have gained any real insight into your past and why you chose your parents.

The issues surrounding karma are not purely black and white. They are complex and multi-layered; sometimes it takes a long time to work through all those layers and to reach the real truth. You can take your time during this process. When you get stuck, why not give yourself a 'breather' and go back to the deeply relaxing exercises in Freeing Meditations? You can return to this deeper level of meditating when you feel refreshed and ready to do so.

When you do feel you have gained a real understanding of your past and you can see it as a valuable learning process that has allowed you to get to where you are now, continue with this chapter.

Assessing Our Present

We are now going to look at how to make an honest assessment of your life. This will involve all areas of it: your friends and family and your relationships with them; how you feel about your work and home environment; where you feel you stand as far as integrity and a clear conscience are concerned. We are going to look at how you feel about your life right now and where you can acknowledge that you are following your spiritual path or deviating from it. There are a lot of issues in this section, so don't worry if you feel you can't yet look at them all. Read through the next exercise first and decide which area you would like to deal with.

Your present karma

Take up a comfortable meditating position, close your eyes and relax. Open up when you are ready, going through the chakras one by one. Pull the beautiful white light down into your room and let it cascade over and through you. Then feel yourself sink into your wonderfully relaxed state. Really sink down into the luxurious sensation of being unfettered, unrestricted by earthly limitations. Feel the stillness and peace engulf you. Sit in this state for a while.

Now consciously ask your thoughts to focus on one aspect of your present life. Whatever comes into your mind first, that is your chosen subject to meditate upon. It can be tempting to go on and think about another subject, perhaps one that is less complicated or less emotionally demanding, but accept the first thought you were given.

First, let your thoughts float freely on this aspect of your life. Let images come and go, try not to hold on to anything but let them ebb and flow naturally. You may find yourself drawn into different scenarios relating to this issue; observe them but do not become involved. Relax into what you are being shown.

Now feel yourself sink deeper into your meditation. Let yourself fall into your soft velvety blackness. Feel empty. Feel nothingness. Take your time to sink into this state. When you are compleely empty, stay in this state for a while.

Then notice that the beautiful golden light is coming towards you. Let it approach and enter into you through your solar plexus area. Feel yourself filled with golden light. Feel it seep through all of you and become one with it.

Now focus on the chosen issue again. Consciously ask that you be shown the way forward that is harmonious with your own spiritual path. Observe what is now shown to you. It may not be clear or obvious at first. Watch closely without questioning what you are seeing. It may seem to be unrelated to the issue you have chosen;

this may be because the issue you are dealing with has repercussions in another area of your life and you didn't know this until now. You may be shown how this area cannot be sorted until you deal with something else first. Trust you are being shown what is relevant to you. You will notice how all areas of your life are affected by each other; this becomes more clear as you delve into your present life. You may see that an issue in your life now has been caused by something you did a long time ago and you may have to still sort out past issues before you can move forward.

If your issue concerns another person, observe how much detail you are given from their point of view. Realize that you had not properly considered their feelings and position up until now. Ask your guide for more information about them, so you may fully understand the situation. Embrace this knowledge and take it into all levels of your aura, to digest it through all of you.

Notice as you are shown how to move forward with this issue that guidance comes from a state of pure integrity and truth. Resolve that you will deal with all issues of your life this way in future. Realize that your karmic path is not one of good and bad but about learning and progressing. If you did something in the past that you need to sort out, it is not because you are 'bad', it is because you had something to learn. You are now learning and being taught how you can progress, both for yourself and others.

If you are learning a great deal from this issue and feel there is so much to understand, that you cannot grasp it all, ask your spiritual guide that you be left with one clear vision with which you can move forward in a practical way. Remember, your guides may not be at all 'earthed' and sometimes you need to ask them to give you clear directives that you can use in an earthly way. If you have an issue with someone that you need to sort out, it isn't enough that you have the purely spiritual angle. You need to know what to do to progress on Earth, too. Sometimes this insight comes from you alone; sometimes spirit guides need to assist you.

The golden light will recede from your solar plexus when you are ready to finish. Your guide may manifest itself within the golden light or it may quietly fade back into the ether, dependent upon how much you have already worked with them.

Give yourself time to return to reality. Cleanse, close down and protect yourself. Cover yourself with your protective cloak. Sip your water and remember to ask yourself a very practical question before you get up and continue with your day.

This exercise can be helpful in so many different areas of your life, but particularly if you are having difficulty with somebody in a work relationship and you want to understand what you can possibly learn from what is happening to you. We can be rendered especially powerless when we feel trapped and not able to get away. The frustration and anger that stem from this can prevent us from seeing things clearly. Of course, an inability to see things clearly can also be true of relationships with family and friends, but often we understand them better because we interact more frequently with these people. Also, we often have the feeling with work colleagues that they have been thrust upon us without our consent. This exercise can really help us to move forward.

When you repeat this exercise, you discover that different issues come forward into your consciousness each time. It is a good idea not to be too determined that you will deal with a specific issue before you start the meditation. Sometimes the issues we think are most pressing actually stem from other areas of our life that we need to deal with at another time. We have to work our way through the issues that are holding us back in a chronological order. As I have already said, karma is a complex issue.

Continue working with this meditation, each time looking at a different aspect of your life. Remember to intersperse your revisits with deeply relaxing and undemanding meditations that allow you to simply 'be' and to recharge your energy field. Understanding your karmic path is a slow, gentle process.

Let's look at one further area before we leave our journey into karma. We have looked at why you might have chosen to be born to your particular parents. You have progressed to looking at your life now and the significance of the people around you. You have taken a close look at what is really going on with you and what you are or are not accomplishing in your life right now.

Of course, going through these meditations is taking considerable time, and that is just as it should be. But we can only take in so much information before our brain hits overload. We have to assimilate the different insights we receive and sometimes they can take a while to sink in. It is quite common for a meditation you did a year ago to suddenly come back to you and only at that point are you able to understand its meaning! For this reason you might want to leave the following exercise for a while and look at it after you've repeated the ones above a number of times.

What's Ahead

The next part of this chapter deals with understanding how you might want to progress next in your karmic path. It seems obvious to state that unless you are very clear about how you have got to where you are today, it's going to be difficult to look further ahead. In other words, you need to understand where you've come from and where you are now, before you proceed to what is coming up in your future.

It's also important to realize that guidance about your future does not involve having to drastically change large areas of your life. This is not about seeing into the future and learning how to follow a preordained path. Nothing is mapped out absolutely ahead of you because you are free to think and do as you wish at all times. The next exercise is purely about understanding what is out there for you to benefit from and to enable you to keep your eyes open for possibilities in your future.

It is difficult to accurately predict anyone else's future, let alone your own. Your individual karmic path is just that – individual. You may have a number of paths open to you and you can be pointed in various directions, but ultimately you decide for yourself which route you will take. Even how much you choose to be swayed by others comes down to you. You decide if you want to listen to them or not. Others can't influence you unless you want to be influenced by them.

However, as we have already seen, spiritual guides are operating from the highest realms of integrity and unconditional love. It would seem to make sense, therefore, to seek their guidance about our future, on the basis that they may be just about the wisest and most powerful teachers we could wish to have.

So when you feel that you have fully explored your karmic roots through the exercises above and that you have gained a real understanding of your past and your present, then you may be ready to delve into the possibilities for your future. If you decide to move forward to this exercise and little results from it, that may be simply because you aren't ready. So, move on when you feel the time is right and don't worry if it isn't.

Your future karma

Settle comfortably and close your eyes. Open up through your usual channels. As you open your chakras, pay particular attention to your brow and crown chakras. Focus on them fully and when you feel the white light above you, pay particular attention to pulling it down and through those chakras. Really feel the white light flooding in through your crown and seeping slowly through every part of you, every muscle and fibre, right through into your bones. Notice how wonderful it makes you feel, how safe and secure and yet deeply empowered at the same time.

Sink down into your velvety blackness. Take your time. Go slowly down the layers of your consciousness into the depths of your subconscious mind. Let the sensation of emptiness and nothingness descend upon you. Relax into it. Stay here for some time.

Then see the familiar golden light approaching. Welcome it into your solar plexus. Also feel it coming in through your crown and brow chakras. Feel the wonderful tingling sensation that comes over you as this happens. Feel truly blessed and enriched by this light. Let it fill you until you become the golden light itself, leaving earthly connections behind.

Now take time to reflect upon all you have learnt recently about your past and present life. Let the film of your past and present be shown to you, noticing the areas in which you have learnt. Observe areas that still seem unclear to you; resolve to work further with them. Enjoy this process. Fully appreciate for the first time how every area of your life is inter-connected, how nothing has happened 'by chance' or been a negative experience, because everything has been profoundly meaningful and right for you; realize that you are grateful for everything you have been through. Acknowledge that situations that you once might have called dreadful or unfair were simply the greatest opportunity for learning and growing.

Now ask that you continue to be given the opportunity to grow and follow your karmic path. Ask if there is anything further you can do to help this process. Make this request silently with deep sincerity and willingness. Sit quietly and observe what is shown to you next. You may be given brief glimpses into possibilities for your future. You may see that what you are doing is going to change in the future; this may be your attitude to something or your physical circumstances. You will not necessarily be shown any time frame for these scenarios and some may seem very faint and hazy. Others will seem obvious and natural to you. You may feel sometimes as though you know what is going to be shown before it actually appears in front of you. Know that whatever is shown to you can never be bad or unpleasant; every experience is a good experience. Every opportunity to learn and grow is a privilege and can be embraced.

Also know that nothing shown to you is an absolute. These are opportunities awaiting you and they probably await you on different paths. You have to decide which path to take; therefore some of these incidents may not occur during your present lifetime. You will choose for yourself.

Watch the situations as they are shown to you. Observe if you feel drawn to a particular scenario and then ask yourself if you are drawn through selfish, earthly motives or if it is attached to a deeper spiritual significance. Notice if you react from a position of true integrity or through human desires. It is not wrong for you to respond humanly, but ask yourself what the lesson is for you if you do. You may find a great deal is shown to you or it may be a frustratingly brief glimpse of something indistinguishable. If the latter occurs, you may not yet be ready to face your karmic future and have more work to do on your past and present.

When the time is right, the film will cease, you will find the golden light withdrawing, and you will find yourself remembering that you are back in your meditation room again, surrounded by earthly reality. Go through your process of cleansing and closing down. Protect yourself. Sit quietly for a while, reflecting on what you have been shown. Ask your conscious thought how well you can relate this to your life now, and whether you can see a possible, different way forward in some aspect of your life. It is fine if you don't yet see any insights for your future. This will come in time. Make sure you then cleanse and protect yourself again before you get up and continue with your day.

The insights from a meditation as deep and profound as this are not usually black and white. You are normally left with a sense of something important being imparted to you but are unsure as to how you should proceed. This is because spiritual changes in our lives happen very gently and gradually, to prepare us for the enormous energy changes that occur within our aura as a result. We cannot change quickly without making ourselves ill, so the more we meditate and reflect upon our life, the more insights we receive and the more slowly we have to act upon them. Don't be surprised if the effect of your meditations is felt months and even years afterwards. This is just as it should be.

The meditations in this chapter are all basically exercises through which we can learn how to create empathy in our life and, by so doing, discover our true spiritual path. Unless we truly appreciate and understand other people, we cannot move forward.

Do you now feel you are making some progress in this complex business of understanding and sorting out your own personal life? The changes you may want to implement will take time.

Once we start to follow our true karmic path, it doesn't automatically make life easier. Often, it makes earthly life more difficult for a while as we try to readjust, but spiritual awareness and a deep, abiding sense of peace and calm are our rewards. These benefits are immeasurable.

As we have now worked through to a very deep level of meditation, it seems a suitable point at which we can stop to look at some trouble spots we may have encountered along our journey. Being stuck in some way can occur at any time during meditation, whether it is through feeling physically uncomfortable or thinking that we have lost the power to relax completely. We are now going to look at these trouble spots and what we can do to overcome them, before we move on to Part Three and delve into our dream world.

TROUBLE SPOTS AND HOW TO CLEAR THEM

You will no doubt have discovered some blockages along your meditation path; you wouldn't be human if you hadn't. Difficulties during meditation are common and there are various solutions that may help you. During this chapter, we are going to concentrate on a number of the most frequent problems and practise applying a few techniques to overcome them. These problems might be:

- Feeling physically uncomfortable during meditation and wanting to move around
- Being unable to remove troubled, earthly thoughts from your mind
- Not being able to find inner peace
- Not visualizing anything at all during meditations
- Feeling as though you have no personal spiritual guide
- Not grounding and closing down properly when you finish
- Not finding time to meditate

There may be other problems you can think of, but these are some of the most common.

Discomfort

Let's start with the physical issue of being uncomfortable and wanting to wriggle about. This is extremely common and affects almost everyone when they first start meditating. You may have devised your own solution by now but, if you are still struggling, here are a few suggestions.

You may simply not be letting yourself relax enough first. The tendency is to want to rush into the deeper level of meditation and not bother too much about the breathing and relaxation section. This means you are denying yourself the very tool through which you reach deeper levels of meditation! It is natural during the beginning of every meditation to want to move around, to scratch your nose, to readjust your clothing, to stretch your arms and shoulders or roll your neck gently to one side and then the other. You might want to undo an article of restrictive clothing. It's not important that you stop all movement when you sit down. It is important that you give yourself time to settle and make yourself comfortable.

Once you stop moving and sink into your regular deep breathing, you may still find you want to move. This could be for a number of reasons. It may be that you are feeling you don't really have the time to meditate properly right now and you are trying to fit it in between other activities. It may be that your mind is still on those other matters and you are being distracted. It may be that you are uncomfortable about the meditation you are about to embark upon and not sure if you will like what you uncover. It may be that you simply aren't breathing properly.

If any of the above fit your scenario, then stop to breathe! Simply ask yourself if you want to continue with the meditation. If you don't, that is fine. You can meditate on another occasion. As has been stressed often enough, meditation should be a joy not a chore.

If you are sinking into your relaxed state and you suddenly develop an itch, then you might choose to respond in a number of ways. You might want to simply scratch it and then go back into your relaxation. You could also try another technique: instead of ignoring the itch and hoping it will go away, you can actually bring all your focus onto the part of you that is itching. This may sound odd but it can achieve exactly the opposite of what you might expect. Instead of finding the itch intolerable, it simply fades away. Try this yourself and see how you respond. Some people repeat the word 'itching' several times. Acknowledging the itch seems to make it fade without having to do anything else.

If you feel restless during the meditation or you feel your leg going to sleep or your neck aching, you might want to try stretching the uncomfortable part. This isn't an ideal solution because it will distract you from your meditation. However, if you do it very slowly and mindfully, appreciating each tendon and muscle as it is stretched, it is possible that this very movement becomes a sort of moving meditation. In other words, you don't just move suddenly and shift all your energy into another area but instead incorporate a slow movement and stretch as part of your awareness of your body.

The most common reason for wanting to move during meditation is not because physically we need to do so, but because we are unconsciously seeking distraction from whatever we are meditating upon. It is usually only when we feel uncomfortable in some way that we focus our awareness back on our physical body. You might want to stop and ask yourself what it is about the particular meditation that is making you feel as though you have to move.

The last point to mention is that perhaps you have not chosen a meditating position that is good for you or you may not be sitting or lying correctly. Look back over the positions shown on pages 65 and 66. These positions are important because they allow the body the maximum opportunity to relax, without putting strain on any part of it. If you are hunched forward in your chair, with a curved back, you are going to put strain on different parts of your body and you will feel uncomfortable. You will also not be able to breathe deeply. Check your posture in a mirror to observe the shape of your body when you start to meditate.

Difficulty Clearing the Mind

Let us move on to the issue of not being able to remove troubled thoughts; again, this is such a common problem and one that almost everyone who meditates has to address. Stilling the mind is perhaps one of the hardest disciplines of meditation to master, but it is crucial if we are to progress. Unfortunately, the mind very rarely seems to want to co-operate in this matter!

Sometimes looking at this problem in a very logical, cool manner can help. Try thinking of it this way. What possible benefit can these worries be to you during your meditation? None at all. Will you be able to solve anything by letting these issues run permanently through your brain? No. If you let them go, simply for the purposes of the meditation, will that be of any benefit to you? Yes. You know that if you let them go and sink into your meditation, you may even find the solution to some of them during your meditation. In other words, you have everything to gain by letting them go and everything to lose by holding on to them. Start each meditation by knowing this is your special time during which you let go of your worries. Really stop to acknowledge the benefits of this. Remember, you can have them back again afterwards, if you insist!

This stage is really all about you learning how to take control of your thoughts. Often we tend to behave as though our thoughts rule us, which is simply ridiculous. We can change thoughts, get rid of them, create new ones, do whatever we like with our minds. The first rule is to learn that we are in charge of our thoughts, not the other way around. If the worrying thoughts persist, keep reminding yourself of the benefits of letting them go for a certain period of time. Tell yourself you deserve this reprieve, treat it as though you are giving yourself a little holiday. After all, that is what meditation really is: an enjoyable mini break.

It may also be useful for you to devise new images to help you let go of your thoughts. When developing our own individual cleansing technique, we talked about different images that might help this process, such as washing something unpleasant away or putting it in a balloon. What technique are you using now? Is it really the most powerful one for you? Next time you struggle with emptying your head of unwanted thoughts, create a new image to get rid of them. Our techniques can get stale through repeated use and lose their effectiveness.

Wanted – Private Space

This leads us on to not being able to find our private world of inner peace within. This issue is all about trust. If we lack belief in something, it is not going to come into our lives. For instance, if we believe we don't deserve a loving relationship, we will not experience one. If we think we're not good enough to get that job promotion, we won't get it. It relates to our working with karma: whatever we give out, we will receive back. If we don't trust that we have this inner peace within us, we won't find it. Trust is an enormous influence in all areas of our life and the older we become, the more we realize that unless we trust, we can't enjoy life.

Each of us has this core of inner peace and stillness within. It is impossible to be without it, because it is actually the very core of who we are. Sometimes we do a very good job of covering up this inner realm. We put all sorts of camouflages and thick coverings on top of it, which then makes it more difficult for us to find. However, this doesn't mean it isn't there. It simply means we have to learn how to peel away the layers to reveal the true person underneath. The joy of doing this through meditation is that it is a completely personal experience. No one else needs to know what you are doing or to see the real 'you' if you don't choose to show them. What is important is that you find it for yourself.

You might want to ask yourself if there is something about uncovering the real 'you' that you find threatening. Is it because you have a fear that you aren't really a nice person underneath it all? Is it because you are afraid of being too vulnerable? Is it because you aren't certain who you really are and you are apprehensive about finding out the truth? Is it that peace and silence make you feel uncomfortable because you prefer a lot of noise and action around you all the time? Going into silence is about hearing the truth. Are you afraid of the truth?

If any of this touches a nerve with you, all you have to do is to stop and think about your fears. They are groundless. They have no basis in reality. If you think about the laws of spirituality as we have discussed them, there is no such thing as being 'bad'. There is simply a state of being enlightened and a state of being unenlightened. By not allowing yourself to discover your world of inner peace and stillness, you are denying yourself the opportunity of becoming enlightened. You are opting to stay in a hazy world of undefined fear, rather than experiencing the joy and understanding that comes with finding out who you really are.

You might find it helpful to meditate upon the word 'trust' if you are still struggling to find this inner core of silence and peace. Trust is a good word for releasing blockages, particularly blockages created by needless fears. Once you understand the true meaning of the word 'trust', you will be able to move forward in your meditations.

Seeing Difficulties

Some people are blessed with the ability to create clear and colourful images of a variety of phenomena during meditations, but it is extremely common not to see anything at all. If when you meditate you are unable to visualize and it is as though you are sitting there with a blank screen in front of you, don't be upset. This does not mean you are doing something wrong or that you are missing some vital ingredient. Some people simply aren't visual by nature. They may hear, feel or even taste something, but not literally see it.

There has been a lot of research into this area of human behaviour, particularly with neuro-linguistic programming (NLP), which is popular as a training tool in many large corporations. One part of this training package is the concept that people can broadly fall into three categories: visual, aural or sensory and that by understanding which category a prospective client falls into, a company can successfully determine the best method of conducting business with them. Most people fit broadly into one of these three categories.

If you are a predominantly aural person, this means you tend to listen much more than see. If this is so for you, then you will find that you may not see your spiritual guides or indeed any image at all. However, it does mean you may hear very clearly, so your guides will be able to talk to you directly and give you guidance that way.

A person who is predominantly visual will probably have more trouble hearing what a guide may say to them. They may see the guide clearly in front of them but to actually hold a conversation with them will be hard work.

If you are mainly a sensory person, this means you go on your feelings much more than on what you see or hear, so your guides would make use of this means of communication and let you use your innate sense of feeling to understand a scenario. It means you might actually touch, smell or taste during your meditations, too. This all takes place on a much more emotional, sensory level and allows you unique insights into a situation.

If you want to know which category you fall into, there is a simple exercise to help you determine the attitude you naturally adopt. You will need a friend to help you in this exercise, because you can't do it by yourself. To work without preconditional thought, it is best if both of you do the following exercise first, *without reading the results that follow it*. This will allow your responses to be spontaneous. This is a very simple, quick test and will take you and your friend only a few minutes.

NLP exercise

Sit opposite each other, a few feet apart. One person asks the questions, the other replies. Then you swap over. Decide how you want to work. Whoever does the questioning has to keep their eyes fixed on the eyes of the person giving the replies. This is essential.

The person who questions asks a question that requires the other person to think for a moment before answering. It can be a simple question such as 'What did you do last weekend?' or 'How did you celebrate last New Year's Eve?' As the person thinks and then replies, notice which way their eyes move. They will do one of the following:

a. look up and from side to side or look straight ahead
b. look directly side to side
c. look down and side to side

Make a note. If you are unsure, ask another question that will require them to think for a moment. Check what happens to their eyes.

Now swap over. The other person questions and notes the eye movement of the person who replies. When you are sure what your responses are, check below to see which category you fall into.

Tests have shown that if you responded in the 'a' way, as in looking up and side to side or looking straight ahead, that you are predominantly a visual person. You tend to react more powerfully to things you can see rather than you can hear or feel.

If you had a 'b' response, that is you looked directly side to side as you answered, this would indicate you are naturally an aural person. So you can listen to things and absorb them more powerfully that way, rather than watching or feeling something.

If you had the 'c' reaction – you looked down and side to side – then you come under the category of kinaesthetic, which is just a long word for someone who responds very much in the feeling sense. You tend to act on and respond powerfully to your own feelings, as opposed to having to see or hear something.

There are occasions when, depending upon the question we have been asked, we might respond in different ways. However, if you question someone several times with routine questions, it is impossible for them not to give a fairly uniform response with their eye movements. They are natural, involuntary responses. It is actually very difficult to change how we behave. If you want to prove this for yourself, have your friend ask you a question and then try to respond with your eyes in a manner that is not naturally you. It is surprisingly difficult to do!

This exercise is simply to open up a possibility that may not have occurred to you before: that your meditations may reflect how you naturally react. So whether you see, hear or simply sense things in your meditations, there is nothing wrong with you!

Whatever category you fall into, there are advantages and disadvantages to each. Being one type is not better or more powerful than another. The categories are simply different. It is also true to say that, over time, you may develop in the other areas as well and may end up seeing, hearing and sensing your guides. The more we practise our communication with spiritual guides, the more powerful our connection becomes. It is therefore natural that we would end up improving our skills in areas in which we initially didn't have a strong affiliation. If you are mainly visual, it doesn't mean you can't develop your aural and sensory responses. You simply may take a little time to do so because it isn't a natural state for you.

Once we stop worrying about whether we see, hear or sense our guides and simply get on with the process of communicating, many of our blocks about relating to them disappear. As soon as you know it is not necessary to actually see your spiritual guide, that is likely to be the time when they suddenly manifest themselves in front of you! This is not because your guides are doing anything different; it is because you have released your own blocks and opened yourself up further to allow them in. So do try to let go of this concept that you have to experience spiritual guides in one particular fashion. What happens is right for you and you don't need to compare your experience of meditation with anybody else's.

The same is true of all meditation, of course, not just relating to communication with spiritual advisors. When you walk through your garden or along your beach or into your forest, you may not be seeing much at all. However, you may hear all the glorious bird song, the lapping of the sea and the whispering of the trees. You will gain your peace from that. You may simply feel the presence of the garden and its surroundings, feel as though you are sitting on a beach or walking through a forest and that sense of feeling you are there is enough for you to benefit from it.

The Absence of Spiritual Guides

Having looked at the issue above quite closely, it may help you with the problem of feeling you have no personal spiritual guide at all. You may have been thinking that if you don't see a guide, you haven't got one. You can now see that that isn't true at all. Worrying about not having any guides may also be connected to our earlier discussion about trust.

Every single person alive on this Earth has not just one but a whole host of spiritual guides. You are not alone. You have your own guides.

Everyone does. If you are not yet communicating with them, it is not because they aren't there for you, it is because you are putting up some barrier within your energy field that is preventing them from manifesting themselves to you. Your spiritual guides are always there for you but they can only come through if you release your earthly emotions of doubt, fear, cynicism and anxiety.

You can do this through focusing on the breath and breathing into the emotions until you dispel them into the ether and get them out of your energy field. Once you have done this, don't be hesitant about calling your guides to you. Let them know you are there and want to enjoy their presence. You must ask for spiritual guidance and not expect them automatically to be there. Keep remembering they are all there for you and it simply takes trust and asking for them to appear for it to happen.

Incomplete Grounding

The problem of not grounding yourself and not closing down properly affects you, whether you realize it or not. We are all guilty of not taking enough time to immerse ourselves back in reality when we finish meditating. Often this is because the benefits of meditation are so great and so pleasant that we feel we want to continue with the wonderful sense of well-being when we get up. It can sometimes feel as though the world of meditation is preferable to the pressures and reality of life on Earth. You might feel the process of grounding yourself and closing down is not a problem because you don't particularly want to do it anyway.

However, there is a serious danger attached to not grounding yourself and closing down thoroughly when you finish. You have spent a lot of time looking at how powerful meditation and work with spiritual guides can be, because you are allowing your own aura to be affected by different positive forces. You are letting other energies interact with your own personal energy, and this is a very vulnerable position to be in. You are in a heightened state of awareness during meditation and are ultra-sensitive to what is happening around and through you. You observe everything that is happening to your body and your aura as you meditate, and you have learned how to cleanse away anything you do not want.

When you finish meditating it is another matter. You are back in the real world again where not all influences are positive and helpful. There are people out there who will drain you of your energy, given the chance to do so. There are also a lot of needy people, particularly in crowded urban environments, whose own energy state is confused, unhealthy and negative in the extreme. Out in the 'real world', you are also not as focused on what is happening with your own aura, because you are distracted by earthly pressures and responsibilities.

Can you see the danger in this scenario? You are not aware of when you are open, closed or protected and yet you are surrounded by a wealth of different energies bombarding you from all angles. It is not a healthy situation to be in.

Always, always remember to close down, ground and protect yourself. Before you step outside your home, take a minute to put some protection around yourself. Pay special attention when you are in crowded environments to give yourself proper protection. On no account allow yourself to wander out into the midst of society and still be in that euphoric state of heightened awareness. It is too dangerous and will only leave you open to all sorts of negative energies.

It is worth talking here about some extra forms of protection that you might want to use when you are out and about in crowds. You know how effective your cloak of protection can be and how useful your different cleansing techniques are. You may have formed a close alliance with your guide of protection and know you can call on them when you want to. They may have shown you some talisman, symbol or object that represents protection and safety for you. Perhaps you have found useful the protective properties of certain flowers and crystals we discussed earlier and you have these around you. Everything you have discovered so far will help you. However, there are also some extra thought processes you can use to give you extra protection on occasions when you might need them.

The first thing you can do if you find yourself in a vulnerable environment and you don't feel protected enough is simply to create an extra form of protection for yourself. Use your thought processes to do this. For instance, imagine yourself wearing an impenetrable form of body armour. All of you is covered in this shiny metal which renders you completely safe. You might choose to imagine a beautiful crystal completely encasing you. Maybe you prefer to be resting behind a filter screen which will trap anything unpleasant. You could pop yourself inside a bright new dustbin if you like, and pull the lid over you! Perhaps the divine white light from above shining all around you is more powerful as an image. Create something that feels right. Do this at any time, but particularly when you are in a crowded place that makes you feel claustrophobic or uncomfortable. When you feel vulnerable is also a good time to use one of these visualizations.

There is a useful technique you can employ if you are being bombarded by someone's energy and you wish that person would either stop it or go away. Simply imagine that you are holding up a mirror in front of them. All you have to do is visualize a big mirror between you and this other person and make sure the mirror side is facing them. This is an extraordinarily powerful tool that can bring amazing results. Try it next time you find yourself in a confrontational situation. You don't have to say or do anything, just create this big mirror in front of them and watch what happens. It may take a moment or two but their attitude will change. They will either run out of steam, turn away or change in some manner.

Do you know what you are doing in this instance? You are turning their energy back on them. This is a karmic form of self-defence. You are not using your own energy to be judgmental or do them harm: you are simply giving them the opportunity to subconsciously experience receiving back what they have been giving out. Try it one day and prove to yourself how effective it can be.

You can also increase protection around your home and work environments too. We have already looked at how certain essences, crystals and flowers can be a form of protection. If you have found a symbol that also means protection and safety to you, then you might wish to have it around you, either as a drawing or as a small object in your drawer or bag. You might want to wear a talisman around your neck. If you find a particular animal powerful as a protective image, then have a model or picture of it somewhere in your living space. If a certain colour is synonymous with you feeling protected, then have it around you. It might be something small such as a cushion you sit on or an item of clothing, or you might even choose to paint a room in that colour.

Feeling grounded is also part of the protection process. Certain spaces have a more earthly feel to them than others. Generally darker colours such as red, brown and orange are very good for feeling earthed and grounded. Of course you may not want to paint a room in those colours, but you might wear brown on a day when you need to steep yourself in reality. (Conversely, when you meditate you may choose very different shades such as lilac and white for inspiration.) Certain scents are also good for grounding, such as patchouli and vetiver.

You can ground yourself by pausing to think about the roots coming out of your feet and going deep into the ground, anchoring you to earthly ties. This is one of the quickest and most effective ways of returning to your physical body after a meditation. It's good to do any time when you feel ungrounded, such as when you come out of the cinema after seeing a film and being transported into another realm. The same is true after reading a book or listening to music. Always ground yourself again.

Lack of Time

The last issue on our list is about finding the time to meditate. This is another common difficulty. We tend to fill our lives with so many earthly responsibilities that anything extra such as meditation can feel like an indulgence. If you do regard it as a treat, rather than an essential part of your life, then you are missing out on the true benefits of meditating.

Meditation is not about escaping from the reality of our earthly existence; it is about helping us to live more harmoniously within it. This means finding out how to improve every facet of our lives on an emotional, mental, physical and spiritual level. When you meditate, you are not being indulgent and spoiling yourself, you are actually facilitating the very process of living.

If you are struggling with trying to find enough time to meditate on a regular basis, when you do next have the opportunity, try meditating on the word 'meditation'. This will give you the chance to rediscover what meditation really means and to strengthen your relationship with it.

The Breath

Lastly, there is one tool that will help you solve or find your way through any difficulty you have with meditation: the breath. No matter how often you have had the importance of breathing stressed to you, no matter how often you have been told to breathe, it cannot be enough. We all keep forgetting to stop and breathe deeply and yet, when we do, the results are immediately apparent.

Whatever trouble spot you hit at any time before, during and after meditation, the secret to unlocking the difficulty will always be to breathe into it.

An exercise you may not have been remembering to do on a regular basis is the Alternate Nostril Breathing (see page 117). This is such a powerful means of balancing energy within the body and once you have practised it even a few times, you will find it easy to get into the rhythm of it. In fact, return now to this exercise and spend a few minutes doing it, before you consider delving into our next section, which takes us into the world of dreams and their spiritual significance.

PART THREE:

DREAMWORK

WHAT ARE DREAMS?

Working with dreams is very different from meditation and requires quite a different approach. For this reason, it is suggested that initially you treat your meditating as a separate activity from your dreamwork. Later, we will see how we can effectively merge the two and learn from both. This part of the book is about looking at the true power and hidden meaning of dreams and how gaining a true understanding of their significance can impact positively in all areas of your life.

First of all, let us get one fact very clear. Everyone dreams. Everyone. This has been demonstrated scientifically. If you did not dream, you would be severely disturbed and unable to function as a 'normal' human being. Dreams are essential to maintain our sanity. We will discuss this more in a moment, but for now it is important for you to realize you do dream. Each night. Always.

If you are someone who does not remember dreams (and this is quite common for a number of people) do not feel this section is irrelevant for you. You can learn how to start remembering your dreams through a few simple techniques that will be explained shortly. Do not feel you are alone or unusual because you don't remember your dreams. Just as every single one of us dreams, so every single one of us can learn how to remember and to work with our dreams, provided we want to learn how to do so.

If the reverse is true and you seem to dream copiously each night, and your dreams are disturbing, exhausting and nonsensical, there is also no need for you to be concerned. You are not dreaming constantly through every sleeping moment (as will be demonstrated to you shortly), but because your dreams are so vivid, you are being left with that impression. You can learn how to control and work with your dreams so that they become a comfort and inspirational as opposed to worrying and tiring.

Many people feel that the majority of their dreams are inconsequential and boring and therefore not worthy of analysis. If you feel this way, you are simply missing the opportunity to discover the true meaning behind your dreams. You can liken it to walking around an art gallery and glancing at wonderful paintings. However, because you don't understand what so many of them really mean, their significance will be largely lost on you. You may appreciate them for what they are, but their hidden power will be denied to you. It is not until you have a guide to interpret their meaning that the paintings come alive and have a vibrancy and energy of their own.

Your dreams are at present probably like those paintings before they have been explained to you. The beauty of working with your own dreams is that you can learn how to become your own interpreter, so that your dreams become a rich, beneficial adjunct to your life and one from which you can learn and grow.

It is important to realize that your dreams do have power. Your task now is to learn how to read them accurately and effectively.

So what exactly are dreams? This requires a multi-faceted answer because we need to look at dreams from a physical, emotional, mental and spiritual perspective in order to understand their value in a holistic way. Some people might say that dreams are purely a mishmash of everyday events, replayed in a usually distorted and chaotic jumble through your mind while you are in an unconscious state. These people might also believe that dreams are purely to act as a filter for your mental clarity, that dreaming during the night is necessary to empty your head before preparing for the onslaught of the next day's activities. There may be an element of truth in that. However, we are going to look at dreams in a much wider context than that, in an attempt to understand more fully what is really happening when we dream.

The Physical Aspect

If we look at the physical interpretation of dreaming, this is not as detailed or as well understood, scientifically, as one might expect. Physical analysis of dreams became more identifiable through the invention of the electroencephalogram (EEG) in the 1930s. This measures electrical impulses given off by the brain. (There is also the electrocardiogram (ECG), which measures impulses from the heart.) Although research from the early 1900s revealed that nerves and muscles gave off electrical impulses, it was not until the inventions of the ECG and EEG that scientists had quantifiable means of measuring what was taking place. By the 1950s, two distinct sleeping states had been identified by EEG monitoring, that of dreaming and non-dreaming.

These states are determined by the activities of certain waves of electrical impulses, defined as alpha, beta, theta, delta and gamma. There are other waves involved whose significance is still being studied. We are not going to spend a lot of time going into the differences between these waves. However, it may be helpful for you to have a quick run-down of the activity associated with the five types of brain waves mentioned above.

Alpha activity occurs as the body enters into a deeply relaxed state. This can be monitored in people who are meditating at a deep level, such as yogis. Beta waves are noted when there is intense mental focus or concentration. It is also found in states of anxiety. Theta waves are linked to creative and inspirational states. Delta waves are connected with a state of deep sleep, when one retreats from conscious activity. Gamma waves are not completely understood and are still under investigation. It is known they are similar to Beta waves. If you want to understand more about these electrical waves and how they affect us, try your local library or spend some time delving into recently published medical journals.

Researchers identified what has become widely known as the REM and NREM states of sleep. REM stands for Rapid Eye Movement; NREM means Non Rapid Eye Movement. In REM states, one can see the person's eyelids fluttering and the eye itself is moving within the eye socket. If you have ever observed a cat or dog sleeping, you will probably have seen their eyes, whiskers and often paws twitch madly. Humans have often assumed it is because they are dreaming of chasing mice or rabbits.

Initially, it was believed that we only dream during REM states and that no dreaming occurs in the NREM phase. More recently, though, it has been discovered this is not quite accurate. The NREM phase does produce dreams but they have been shown to be quite routine and everyday in content and often are not easily remembered by dreamers. Dreams during the REM state are much more vivid and often there is a great deal of activity in them. Their content may seem quite strange when we analyse them later, while during the dream process it seems quite acceptable to us. One theory is that NREM dreams are about sorting out mundane daily matters and REM dreams are concerned with much deeper, intrinsically spiritual aspects of our lives.

Research shows that during sleep we humans go through a series of NREM and REM states. Our first REM state occurs approximately an hour or so after we first drift off to sleep. This is a particularly deep state and is the hardest from which to wake someone. We may remain in this state for about 90 minutes and then we go into lighter, NREM sleep for a further 90 minutes or so. We alternate between these states five, six or seven times each night, depending upon how long we sleep. A longer period of REM sleep occurs shortly before we wake; it is generally the dreams we have during this period that we remember best. It is intriguing to realize that we have also had a series of other dreams right through the night, even though we may not be able to remember their details.

So you now have a brief version of what is occurring physically during your sleeping and dreaming states. What has also been proved through scientific research is that when people are deprived of their deeper REM state of dreaming, they become seriously disorientated and mentally distressed. Sleep is, of course, essential for physical rejuvenation but the theory that it is also necessary to allow the brain to rest and recharge its batteries can no longer be accepted as true.

EEGs have shown conclusively that far from resting when asleep and dreaming, the brain is engaged in constant activity. It is fair to say that the brain activity alters significantly, from a fast, low amplitude to a slow, high amplitude, but it certainly doesn't lie still and 'rest'. At this point let's look more deeply at the possible true benefits of dreaming.

The Mental Aspect

As mentioned, if deprived of dreams, we become mentally unwell. So therefore we now know with certainty that dreaming is synonymous with mental health. So why are dreams so important in this sphere of our lives? We would all acknowledge that each of us processes an enormous amount mentally on a daily basis: through our work, through our personal lives, through striving to be the best we can, through striving to live up to what we feel we should be. We put ourselves under a lot of mental pressure all the time. We know we can't shut off mentally during our sleeping and dreaming states, because our brain refuses to shut down, so what is happening during this time that makes it so crucial for our well-being?

Earlier, we discussed the commonly held notion of dreams being a process of clearing out our minds to prepare us for the next day's activities. That seems to make some sense. No doubt you can think of an occasion when you went to bed anxious and upset and then woke up the next day feeling calmer and less stressed. The old saying, 'sleep on it', refers to the process of making any important decision. Perhaps you have drifted off to sleep mulling over a particular problem and then, upon waking the next morning, suddenly felt better or seen a way forward that hadn't occurred to you before. This can happen whether you remember dreaming or not. Often a situation that seemed so bleak and desperate at night can appear in a very different light in the morning. Whilst the physical rest is no doubt a welcome part of this improvement in our state, we also know that some mental processes have been taking place while we were unconscious.

No one can prove what those processes are, apart from monitoring brain wave patterns and observing that they are changing. Our own proof comes in the fact that we feel better mentally after sleep. One theory is that the dreaming state is actually offering our subconscious mind some solutions to the mental turmoil we are experiencing. In other words, whether we remember it consciously or not, our dreams are actually guiding and nurturing us. You could say that they are like a healing doctor, offering some prescriptions along the way to ease our stress. The reason we often experience repeat dreams on a regular basis is simply because we are not taking the 'prescription' being offered.

Some people can wake up feeling stressed after a night's sleep, feeling as if they have had many experiences throughout the night; some of these experiences they may remember, while others may be elusive. They wonder if the sleep did them good, because they actually feel as though they have gone through so much, certainly mentally, even if not physically. It may be that they are being shown repeat dreams because this is a time in their life when they have a particular lesson to learn and they are not heeding the guidance offered to them. If you wake up feeling tired, it is possibly because you are being shown how to make a breakthrough in your life, but you are not letting the information seep from your unconscious, through your sub-conscious, to your conscious thought. (We shall look at how to encourage this process in the next chapter.)

The Emotional Aspect

We know our emotions are very closely tied up with our mental thoughts. We also know we can become very emotionally involved in our dreams and the after-effect can be felt long after we wake up. As children we often had very powerful, emotional dreams. These could take various forms, such as nightmares where monsters chased us or wish-fulfilment dreams where we suddenly found a lot of money or were given our dream toy. On waking we were so pleased to find the former was a dream and so disappointed to find the latter wasn't real! No doubt you can remember the strong emotions you felt on such occasions. (Remember, if you are someone who has never recalled your dreams, it doesn't matter. You can change this, given time and new techniques.)

We can also have dreams that make us very emotional, such as dreaming of losing a loved one or being reunited with someone who has passed over. Perhaps you have had frustrating dreams where you are about to experience something wonderful and the dream suddenly fades or drifts into another scenario. Maybe you have been very angry in a dream and then woken up still feeling very cross and had this sensation stay with you for some time afterwards.

Dreams can tap into powerful feelings. Perhaps you have woken up feeling deeply depressed or particularly good without knowing why. What may have happened during a dream cycle which has not manifested itself in your conscious thought? How helpful might it be for you to be able to pull it forward into your consciousness and to learn from it?

Dreams can also be the reverse of what we have been discussing and seem very impersonal. We can feel as though we are observers in a scenario, as opposed to being personally involved. So what aspect of our life would benefit from our taking a step back and seeing something in a more dispassionate manner? Deep emotions and the absence of emotions can both be valuable teachers in our learning process.

The Spiritual Aspect

Let us turn now to the last aspect of what dreams actually are or might be and look at their possible spiritual significance. How much is your own deeply personal and unique spirituality connected to what you dream? The best way to move into this complex and revealing area might be to take a look back through history and see how dreams have been regarded. When you really start to delve into the perceived power of dreams from ancient times to the modern day, it is quite revealing to discover how much importance has been attached to them. Dream interpretation has a very long history, much of which seems to have been conveniently forgotten by us in the West.

Some of you have no doubt heard of the Freudian or Jungian analysis of dreams. However, both Freud and Jung are modern interpreters and the real history of dream analysis goes back many thousands of years.

The Egyptians were deeply interested in dream interpretation, certainly from at least 4000BC to 2000BC, although the effects of their study of the subject were felt for much longer. Many of the ancient monuments and statues around Egypt bear hieroglyphics concerning fragments of dreams, including statements such as 'A bed on fire means your partner is unfaithful to you'! Many such inscriptions are found around the shrine of Asclepius-Imhotep, a famous Egyptian physician and healer.

Most ancient civilizations took dream interpretation further than the mundane and regarded it as a valuable means of ascertaining higher consciousness and spiritual truths. We can go back to 25BC where Philo Judas's 'Book of Giants and Civil Life' refers to Abraham as the first dream interpreter. The earliest surviving book on dreams is Artemidorus's 'Oneirocriticia', dating to the 4th century and the only major book on dreams that was published right up until the 19th century. It was translated from the Greek into English and reprinted more than thirty times. Artemidorus's book was a collection of Assyrian, Babylonian and Egyptian folk-lore and talks on 'cosmic' dreams whereby messages were passed on from the gods above. Their god of dreams was An-Za-Oar, who presided in an underworld called The Great Land.

The ancient Greeks, of course, had Zeus, father of the gods, and his son, Morpheus, god of dreams. At many of the Greek shrines you found dream oracles, where people went to have dreams interpreted. Even then, classical scholars tried to find physical explanations for dreams. References to dreams and their significance can be found in the writings of many scholars, including Plato, Galen, Cicero, Aristotle, Pliny and Hippocrates. Hippocrates stated, 'Some dreams are divinely inspired but others are the direct result of the physical body.' Could we not take this in a modern context as a reference to the REM and NREM states of dreaming?

The ancient Chinese were also deeply committed to dream interpretation. They believed it was vital to look beyond the material and delve into the spiritual realm, an attitude reflected by Taoism, the philosophy and religion of China. In Chinese folklore, the butterfly is reminiscent of the soul. In one of his imaginative writings the fourth century BC philosopher, Chuang Chou, expressed a beautiful dream as a conundrum:

Chou sleeps and dreams that he is a butterfly. He wakes, and then wonders if he is in fact but a figment of the butterfly's dream.

The Chinese believe you decide your own reality. While we are awake the dream state is unreal but while we sleep the dream state becomes reality. A Chinese sage sums this up rather well:

While men are dreaming, they do not perceive that it is a dream.
Some will even have a dream within a dream.
And so when the great awakening comes upon us, shall we know this life to be a great dream.
Fools believe themselves to be awake now.

(You could also relate this saying to the concept of life and reincarnation and the path of a soul's journey. In other words, you could interpret this as meaning our time on Earth is but a dream and our real life is our soul's complete journey, of which reincarnation just a small part.)

It is also important to point out that many other ancient records from around the world – such as Celtic, Arab, Indian, Japanese, French and Russian – all make reference to the importance of dreams and to the necessity of analysing them accurately. If this aspect of dreamwork interests you, there are many good books available on the historical significance of dreams. You may find it fascinating reading.

One of the richest sources of dream interpretation is the Bible. Both the Old and New Testaments make numerous references to the significance and power of dreams, such as this one:

For God speaketh once, yea twice, yet man perceiveth it not.
In a dream, in a vision of the night when deep sleep falleth upon men slumbering upon their bed, then He openeth their ears and sealeth their instructions.
(Job 33:14–16)

Also well known are Jacob's famous dream, involving the ladder, and the Pharaoh's vivid dreams, but countless others can also be found. It is an interesting fact that the Hebrew word for 'vision' and 'dream' is the same as 'to see'.

Other ancient religious writings also contain references to dreams and their significance: the Hindu *Bhagavad-Gita* and Upanishads, the Taoist *I Ching*, the Islamic *Koran*, the Egyptian *Book of the Dead*, the Judaic *Torah* and the Buddhist *Tripitakas*, to name but a few.

We can trace dream interpretation through the early Christian fathers with people such as Gregory of Nyssar in the 4th century who, in his book 'On Making Man', decreed that the visions in his dreams were divine messages through which one could better understand and value one's self. It is known that St Augustine regarded his dreams as communication with God and his angels. Thomas Aquinas also wrote about how dreams could be used as prophecies.

In the Middle Ages the word 'dream' took an another meaning, when the Church authorities decreed that dreams and their interpretations were messages from the Devil. From this point on people began to use 'dream' in the sense of a lost hope, as in 'I wouldn't dream of it'. No overt interpretation of dreams was accepted during this period.

It wasn't until the 19th century with the advent of Sigmund Freud (1856–1939) and his work that dreams started to be re-established in the Western world as a valuable means of analysis. Freud is largely known for his acknowledgement of the 'collective unconscious', which he decreed it was possible to tap into during dream states. To put one of his theories in simplistic terms, he believed we had conscious and unconscious memories and that accurate interpretation of our dreams would allow us access to our unconscious mind.

To do this, he developed what has become known as the 'free association of ideas', where people use a seemingly unrelated string of words or phrases which ultimately leads them into true awareness of a particular state of mind. The idea behind this is that we all have memories locked away inside us and through letting the brain flow unhampered from one thought to another, we will eventually find ourselves at the root cause of any situation. It is fair to say that many people today still find Freud's 'free association' a useful tool in analysis.

Freud also saw man as a being composed of three parts: ego, id and super-id. These bear some relation to what we might now call mind, body and spirit. Freud's assertion that all dreams represented wish fulfilment, and his insistence on relating most dreams to a sexual nature, led to disagreement from many quarters and some people are very dismissive of what Freud uncovered through his work. However, unarguably, his work enabled a much more detailed and intense investigation into the power of dreams.

Carl Gustav Jung (1875–1961), a pupil of Freud's, disagreed with his teacher's theories on sexual repression in dreams. He also believed that it was more valuable to work with the dream itself and its significance than with free association. Jung spent a great deal of time researching ancient dream analysis and gradually came to acknowledge what he called the spiritual element of dreaming. He also became interested in the duality of life, not just in humans, but also in nature. He coined the words 'anima' and 'animus', which refer, respectively, to the feminine and masculine elements within each of us.

Jung strongly believed in archetypes in dreams which he described as being ancestral or primordial images, the significance of which may have been forgotten through time, but whose true meaning can be rediscovered through dream analysis. Jung split human minds into the unconscious, the conscious and the collective unconscious. The last mentioned he described as '... the foundation of what the ancients called the sympathy of all things.' Jung's delving into the spiritual unconscious did much to reintroduce us to long-forgotten ancient concepts.

In addition to the works of Freud and Jung you may find interesting the ideas and/or research of other respected professionals who have investigated dream analysis: Alfred Adler, Delage, Calvin S. Hall, Keith Hearne, Maury, Fritz Perls (creator of Gestalt therapy), Radestock, Scherner, Stricker, Strupell and van Eeden.

Dreamwork is also part of the cultural tradition of various Native American and Australian Aboriginal tribes, who use interpretation to help them attain spiritual fulfilment and to live peacefully together. The Huron and Iroquois tribes of North America hold actual dream festivals where they meet and discuss their various dreams and use the collective information as a means of determining their future direction in society.

Similar respect for the power and usefulness of dreams is shown by other peoples, too, such as the Maoris in New Zealand, Zulus in South Africa, the Temiar-Senois and Patani people in Malaysia and Inuits living in Hudson Bay. In fact, it is quite difficult to find any significant area of the world where dream interpretation is not valued.

Before we leave the historical aspect of dream significance, we'll take a quick trip through history and look at some events where dream interpretation had a bearing on the outcome. We'll also look at some literature and observe where dreams have been referred to or have had a major influence on world events.

Alexander the Great was known to have had a dream when the city of Tyros was under siege. Through analysis of his dream, which involved a spirit called Satyros dancing on his sword, Alexander determined he was meant to renew his attack on that city. This he did and the city surrendered quickly. The fact that the word 'tyros' was contained within the word 'satyros' formed part of the interpretation of the dream.

Julius Caesar had vivid dreams and he accepted their guidance with great diligence. Ironically, he is known to have completely disregarded a dream had by his wife Calpurnia in which it was predicted there would be danger for him on the Ides of March. Had he not ignored the message in that dream, history might have been very different.

Napoleon Bonaparte is known to have had dreams about military manoeuvres. Upon waking, he is said to have followed through on his dreams, using toy soldiers in a sand box to further plan each campaign.

The following story may be familiar. A soldier was sleeping in a bunker during the battle of the Somme in 1917. He dreamt the bunker had collapsed on him and he was suffocating. This nightmare woke him and, badly shaken, he dashed outside for some much-needed fresh air. Within seconds, a French shell landed on the bunker, killing all the occupants. The grateful corporal thanked God and realized he had been saved because he was meant to progress onwards to much greater things. The man's name? Adolf Hitler. We can only speculate how, if Hitler had refused to act upon his dream, the history of Europe would have been altered.

There are countless references through literature that make fascinating comments upon dreams and their relevance. If you read books by any of the following people you will find somewhere within them ideas and reflections that may make you think about dreams in a different way: John Bunyan (called the Immortal Dreamer and the Mad Dreamer), Lewis Carroll, Samuel Coleridge, Graham Greene, Victor Hugo, John Keats, Walter de la Mare (called a visionary poet), Edgar Allen Poe, Robert Louis Stevenson, William Shakespeare, Percy Bysshe Shelley, Leo Tolstoy and Alfred, Lord Tennyson. There are also many others you may find inspiring. Take a book of collected poems out of the library and spend some time leafing through the pages. You will probably be surprised to discover how frequently there is some reference to dreams that speaks of their power, mystery or benefits. Shakespeare's plays are filled with references to dreams. Take, for instance, this comment by Prospero in *The Tempest*:

We are such stuff as dreams are made on
and our little life is rounded with a sleep.

At the conclusion of *A Midsummer Night's Dream*, Shakespeare suggests the observer can treat the whole play as though it were but a dream as Puck's last speech encourages:

If we shadows have offended,
Think but this – and all is mended –
That you have but slumbered here
Whilst these visions did appear.
And this weak and idle theme,
No more yielding but a dream...

(One can take this in a much wider context and think that perhaps Shakespeare is drawing an analogy between the play and a human being's time on Earth. There is so much rich imagery in Shakespeare's words if one delves below the surface of them, which is why he has delighted and mystified us through the centuries and will no doubt continue to do so.)

The eminent Russian writer Count Leo Tolstoy also put it beautifully when he said:

... now our whole life, from birth unto death, with all its dreams,
is it not in its turn also a dream, which we take as the real life,

the reality of which we do not doubt,
only because we do not know of the other more real life?

Many inventors, musicians and painters have also drawn inspiration from their dreams. Elias Howe said his invention of the sewing machine came through a dream, as did Friedrich von Kekule, who discovered the closed chain or ring theory. James Watt had a dream that led to his invention of ball bearings. Many musicians claim to have heard music in their dreams and then awoken to consciously compose the piece.

Painters have also drawn inspiration from the imagery in their dreams. Leonardo da Vinci was an extraordinary man, not just a painter, sculptor and architect but also a composer, writer and inventor. He was known not just as a dreamer but also a visionary, which could be another word for genius. The difference between someone such as da Vinci and others is that whilst we all might have inspirational or visionary dreams not everyone has the capability to carry them through into the real world and create something beautiful from them.

Surrealism, an art movement founded in France in 1924, did much to bring visionary dreams onto canvas. In the work of Goya, Dali and Max Ernst there are examples of extraordinary dreamlike images brought to life. They may not always make comfortable, cosy viewing, but they are certainly deeply powerful and very thought-provoking images.

So after all this discussion, have you been encouraged to rethink your concept of dreams and how powerful they might be? The danger with reading about great historical figures and their visions is that it is tempting to then think that they deserve to have amazing dreams because they were truly extraordinary people but that you can't possibly claim to be so interesting in contrast!

Yet remember, every one of us is unique and important and has a personal destiny to fulfil. We have spent considerable time discussing this in many ways through our work so far with meditation and communication with spiritual guides. We have been trying to understand more about ourselves and those around us and how we fit into the world as a whole.

Now we are going to look at how remembering and understanding our dreams is another tool we can use to help our personal progress. If, as you work through the chapters coming up, you feel discouraged or believe that you don't really have the ability to understand what your dreams are about, remember that our history is full of people who treated dreams as a normal and wonderful part of their personal progression. The interpretation of dreams was a natural part of everyday living. As we would go to the shops and buy bread and milk, so an ancient Greek or Egyptian would go to see their dream advisor and discuss what their previous night's dream meant as far as their personal life was concerned. In many parts of the world today, that behaviour continues as a healthy and essential part of life.

Come back to this chapter sometimes and reread it, especially whenever you feel as though you are not managing to remember your dreams very much or you feel lost as to how to interpret them. Reread it to remember your roots. Practice will enable you to discover your true inner self.

YOUR DREAM DIARY

The first task ahead of you, as you delve into your new world of dream analysis, is to learn how to remember your dreams, accurately and vividly. This isn't as difficult or as daunting as it sounds. For those of you who remember your dreams reasonably well, it is still advised that you create your own Dream Diary as described during this section, because whatever you are remembering now is probably not as strong or detailed as it might be. No matter how efficient you are as far as dream recall is concerned, there is always scope for improving your memory.

It's important to acknowledge that there are a number of reasons why you might find dream recall difficult initially. It may not be because you haven't bothered to focus or because your brain is lazy or because the dreams simply aren't interesting enough to remember. You may not recall them because part of you doesn't want to look at them and what they mean. This is why you have been encouraged to look at different aspects of your life through earlier work in meditation and spiritual guide communication. As you enter the world of dreams you are dealing with the subconscious and higher consciousness on a much more complex level. The more work you have put in already as far as trying to understand yourself and your soul's path, the easier you will find it to embrace dreamwork.

It is also all right if you start working through this Dreamwork section and then discover you don't feel quite ready to look at this area yet. Dreams and their analysis can be very powerful and although the insights you are offered may be deeply profound and affect you deeply, it is fine to decide you are not yet ready for their messages. You can continue to work with your meditations until you feel ready.

It is fair to say that you are more likely to find your initiation into dreamwork to be a very gentle and gradual process. Your unconscious is programmed to naturally be quite sympathetic to your issues, however great or small they may be. Therefore it is most unlikely that you will find yourself being bombarded with sudden, powerful dreams, because your inner self will know it is not ready to receive anything too challenging at this stage. It is more likely you will find your progression with dreamwork is slow but sure. This is particularly true of the early stages. It is only later that you may feel you have periods of standing still for a while and then suddenly leaping ahead with your understanding of yourself on a much deeper level. We progress at the rate that is right for us.

Constructing the Diary

So let us now move on to look at how we can construct a helpful Dream Diary. There are several important elements. First and foremost is your commitment to this new area of exploration. The clearer you are about this being something you want to do and from which you are confident you will reap benefits, the more likely you are to gain good results.

The first task is to go out and buy yourself a book specifically in which you are going to record your dreams. Choose something you really like and feel drawn to, whether it's the colour, size or even the shop from which you purchase it. It doesn't have to be expensive, but it is suggested that it's a decent size, even up to A4, as you will soon discover there may be a lot you want to write in it. You might prefer a binder with separate sheets that you can move about as you wish. Decide whether you want to use a pen or pencil and make sure it has a decent nib and is easy to use. If it's a pencil, keep it sharpened. Again, choose the colour and shape you like. You want to feel comfortable with the tools you are using.

You may prefer to use your phone or your computer instead of paper and pen/pencil to record your diary. That is fine. Simply ensure that whatever you use is readily available and file the recordings properly. Have it in your room ready to use each night. If you have someone who sleeps in the same room with you, you might want to have a torch available to save disturbing them. Make sure that whatever you are using to record your diary is easy to find, even in the dark. These are small but important points, because you want to make recording your dreams as easy and hassle-free as possible.

It is essential you make a note of your dreams as soon as you wake up. Our thoughts and handwriting can be very messy and jumbled at this time of the day, so you might prefer to have a piece of scrap paper onto which you make your first notes and to then transfer these to your Dream

Diary. It depends upon how naturally tidy and ordered a person you are! Likewise, you might want to make written notes from the comments you record on your machine.

If you do transcribe them, make sure you write down exactly what you have said. Don't be tempted to rearrange or alter what you said because you think it will sound better. This is not about you looking good or supposedly saying or thinking the right thing about your dreams. It is all about you being 100 percent honest and recording exactly what you dreamt without embellishment. This is crucial for you to be able to really work with and ultimately understand your dreams.

Whatever method you choose, speaking or writing, there are a few basics you always want to include. One is to put the date of each dream. Decide whether you want to use the date of the night you go to bed or the morning on which you wake up, but be consistent to avoid confusion. It is helpful also to record the approximate time. If you wake up at 3am and want to scribble a few quick thoughts, try to remember to put 3am. Dates are extremely important because they can refer to anniversaries, birthdays and/or deaths. Frequently, the relevance of dates and numbers may only be apparent much later. If you have accurately recorded the date of your dream, it is always there for you to return to at any time.

Apart from the date, there are certain other elements we always want to include about each dream. Obviously there is the dream itself. You want to describe this immediately upon waking. It is no good deciding you'll get up and clean your teeth and have a drink before you write it all down. The dream memory fades almost immediately upon waking. The speed with which you write your thoughts down is absolutely crucial. Once you have experienced this a few times for yourself, you will realize how important it is. Grab that pen or start recording as soon as you regain consciousness. It will become a habit if you allow it to.

When you write down or record the dream, first of all describe the clearest memory of the dream and the general gist of what occurred. Then go back and fill in details. Make sure you do not embellish it with any untrue elements. It can be so tempting to want to make it seem more exciting or more profound. Often the most wonderful dreams are the most simple, once they have been analysed. Do not try to make your dream into some sort of appealing filmic adventure. Be honest.

Once you have recorded the dream itself, then immediately go on to how it made you feel. Be specific about your emotion. Notice if a particular element of the dream was important, emotionally. Again, don't embroider anything. Don't try to make something feel better than it did. If you were upset or frightened, say so.

Make a note of your immediate thoughts about what it meant. Don't spend a long time analysing it, just use your first, gut reaction to what you can remember about the dream. Does it feel relevant to any aspect of your life now? Make a note of any key symbols or items within the dream that feel important. Also note any people who came into your dream and how they made you feel. Do this quickly, without any deep soul searching.

Now you want to make a note about influences in your life at present. For instance, were you watching a television programme or reading a book before you drifted off to sleep? What was it about? Did you have a heavy meal or did you go to bed hungry? Perhaps you had had a fair amount of alcohol or were on some form of drugs or medication. Make a note. If there was a significant event at work or home during that day, comment on that as well. Perhaps it was a particularly hot, cold or stormy night weather-wise. Maybe there was a full moon or a new moon. All these aspects could affect you, but you won't be able to judge until you keep a record.

Lastly, give a brief summary at the end and say what you think the dream meant overall. Then we're going to leave a blank space for you to return and comment on that dream at any time in the future, when it seems appropriate to do so.

If all this seems very detailed and feels as though it is going to take a long time, remember that you are being encouraged to do this as quickly as possible. It is not about you taking a long time but about you being as fast and spontaneous as possible. That is why some people find it so much easier just to record it by speaking into their phone or computer because it is quicker and the thoughts can sometimes flow more easily.

So this is how it is suggested you lay out your Dream Diary. You may add other elements if it helps you:

DATE:

TIME:

DREAM:

FIRST THOUGHTS:

INFLUENCING FACTORS:

SUMMARY OF MY INTERPRETATION:

SPACE FOR LATER THOUGHTS:

Depending upon how involved or powerful your dream was, you may need a fair amount of space. You can see why an A4 size book was recommended. It is also suggested that you leave an entire page blank for the section marked 'Space for Later Thoughts'. This is because, as your work through your dream analysis and become more and more proficient at interpreting what has gone on, you will be able to glean so much more information from even a simple dream. You will discover you have a great many more thoughts about it than you first expected.

If you record your dreams, it is more difficult to access them, as you will have to keep replaying the recording to remember the details. For that reason it may be more helpful to transcribe them after you have made the recording. You might find it easier to scribble on a piece of scrap paper and transfer this to your Dream Diary later. You will know what works best for you once you have experimented a little.

If, in the early stages, you have hardly anything to record because you cannot remember much, that is fine but always record something. This is to establish a pattern in your subconscious that you are not about to give up, that you are making a determined commitment to doing something on a regular basis and making it into a daily routine. You know we all dream, even if we can't remember what we've dreamt. We simply have to encourage the mind to work in a different way. It can be likened to taking up some form of physical exercise. Initially it can seem hard work and our muscles respond grudgingly and without enthusiasm. Once we are fitter, those muscles start to feel easier and we enjoy the process more. Remembering your dreams is like this; the more we practise, the more natural it feels.

If you can't remember your dream at all then just start to put down how you are feeling when you wake in the morning. Find an adjective to describe your state of mind. Still make a note of surrounding influences in your life. You can even make a note of which position you were in when you woke up – side, back etc. Once you create a commitment to your Dream Diary, you are allowing the energy to flow and creating the possibility for dream recall to come flooding towards your conscious state.

It is also helpful for you to say a clear affirmation before you go to sleep at night. Affirmations are short, positive sentences which you repeat several times to help introduce a new thought process into your mind. The concept is that we have a lot of negative thoughts running around our heads all the time about what we can't do or are no good at and that it is extremely helpful to programme some constructive, encouraging statements which will aid us in retraining our thoughts.

Affirmations are always short and always phrased in the present. For instance 'I will remember my dreams' isn't a particularly powerful statement because it doesn't state clearly when – it could be next week, next year, next lifetime! Also, you want to avoid any negative sense. To say 'I don't forget my dreams' isn't very helpful either, because your brain will only hear the word 'forget' and 'dream' and not listen to the whole sentence. 'I remember all my dreams' is clear and positive.

Try saying 'I remember all my dreams' three times, slowly, clearly and out loud. Initially, saying something like that can feel rather strange and your mind may immediately take over and say 'Oh, no, you don't!' The power lies in the repetition of the phrase and the refusal to listen to the old thoughts going around your head which try to negate the new powerful statement. It takes time, of course, but it can be an excellent tool to help you expand your thinking process and create new possibilities.

Of course, affirmations can be used in all areas of your life, not just for dream recall. Try making up your own affirmation for an area of your life in which you would like to make changes, but remember the affirmation needs to be short, positive and always phrased in the present.

Relaxation is also a big element not just in falling asleep but also in the quality of your sleep and your consequent ability to remember your dreams. We have discussed various means of relaxing already in earlier sections and it is a good idea for you to go back and renew your association with some of these exercises, such as the Relaxing the Muscles exercise on page 74. This is particularly helpful for encouraging your body to sink comfortably into your bed. You can also do this exercise without tensing each part of the body but by simply allowing your focus to rest on an area and to feel it melting into the bed. This variation is explained below.

Going to sleep

Let yourself sink back comfortably into your bed. Lie on your back and let your legs and arms spread outwards from your body. Let your feet flop outwards and have your hands resting palm upwards. Ensure your chin is tucked comfortably down into your throat and there is no tension in the back of your neck. Wriggle your body to make sure it is comfortable. Close your eyes.

Now begin to observe your breathing, but don't try to alter it in any way. Let some breaths be shallow and others be slower and deeper. You aren't trying to be in control. Just observe without judging yourself. Continue observing your breath for a few minutes.

Now bring your focus to your right foot. Tell yourself it is heavy and relaxed. Feel it melt into the bed as you say this silently to yourself. Take your time. Actually feel the muscles in the foot relax and feel the foot become heavier. Enjoy the sensation of release. Now tell yourself your lower right leg is also heavy and relaxed. Feel it melt into the bed. Again, remember to take your time. The joy with this exercise is savouring each part of your body as it relaxes. Continue this process, working up through the right upper leg, right hip, right side, right shoulder, right upper arm, right lower arm, right hand. You will probably notice now that the right side of your body feels as though it is sinking into the bed but your left side feels lighter.

> Now work through the left side with all those parts of the body: left foot, left lower leg, left upper leg, left hip, left side, left shoulder, left upper arm, left lower arm, left hand. Remember to focus only on one part of your body at a time. You will realize you are now feeling more balanced between the right and left sides of your body.
>
> Now move your focus to your torso and continue saying 'heavy and relaxed' to each of the following areas: the buttocks, lower back, middle back, upper back, neck, back of the head, top of the head, the face, upper chest, chest, stomach. Take your time.
>
> Linger over any areas that remain tense and won't sink into the bed. Divide your body into smaller sections if it feels right for you. The face, in particular, can hold great tension. Try working through separate areas such as forehead, eyes, cheeks, mouth, chin, ears. Remember, you can do this exercise as slowly as you like. The slower you are, the more you will relax. There is no rush; you have all night.
>
> When you have gone over each part of your body separately, tell yourself that your entire body is heavy and relaxed. Repeat this three times as an affirmation, silently to yourself: 'My entire body is heavy and relaxed.'
>
> As you sink yet further into the bed, drifting gently off to sleep, remind yourself that you remember all your dreams.

Many people don't manage to continue the whole process of relaxing each part of their body because they drift off somewhere during the middle of it. If you find this happens to you, then you might want to say your affirmation about remembering all your dreams at the beginning of the exercise, so it is already in your subconscious as you drift off to sleep. A lot of people can't sleep on their back, so it is fine for you to want to turn over onto your side at some point during the process. Whatever helps to send you into a comfortable, deep sleep is to be encouraged.

Encouraging Sleep

There are other reasons why people may not get to sleep as easily as they would like, and it is believed that some of these factors may influence dreams and their quality. For instance, if you were to eat a heavy meal just before going to sleep, your physical body would be working so hard to digest all the food you had consumed that it would render relaxation impossible. Certain foods, such as tea, coffee, alcohol, dairy produce and chocolate, act as stimulants, and thus prevent sleep. However, as everyone's metabolism is unique, it is quite possible you may discover through time that it is some other substance that adversely affects the quality of your sleep and dreams. For instance, you may love having a warm, milky drink each night as you get ready for bed. That is fine, but just one night try going without and see how it affects your sleep and your dreams. That is where your Dream Diary becomes so useful, because you are keeping close tabs on possible influencing factors. You will soon notice a pattern if a specific food or drink is affecting you.

Conversely, some substances are said to be extremely beneficial for sleep and relaxation, one of the best known being camomile tea, which is a herbal remedy. It's likely you will either love it or hate it, as it has a distinctive taste. Sweetened with honey, it can be very pleasant. The herb valerian is available packaged as a tea and is good for tension. It also comes in capsule form. There are many gentle herb remedies available from health food shops which may help you drift off to sleep. Any form of hard drugs is liable to severely disrupt your sleeping pattern and affect your dreams in a negative way. If it is at all possible to avoid sleeping pills, please do so, but obviously if you are on medication you must consult your doctor before stopping your dosage or altering it in any way.

If you don't want to consume anything before sleep, then another alternative is to encourage a relaxed state by using incense or essential oils. Lavender oil is highly effective for promoting sleep. If you don't have an incense burner, then simply put a few drops of the oil onto a cotton wool ball and place it near your head. If you opt for this technique, make sure you buy a proper, pure essential lavender oil from a reputable dealer. If you buy a cheaper synthetic alternative, it will probably have little or no effect. We discussed the importance of this earlier, in Part One (pages 96–101), when we talked about scents during meditation. Frankincense, jasmine and rose essential oils are also helpful for sleep and dreams, but they will cost considerably more than lavender oil, so it is suggested you start with lavender and see what effect it produces in you.

Taking a long, deep, relaxing bath before bedtime is also suggested. If you add a few drops of lavender oil to the water, you are also doubling the possibility of your drifting off into a comfortable sleep.

There are also practical steps you can take to reduce stress. Are you someone who goes to sleep thinking and worrying about the thousand and one things they haven't done or need to do? Then keep paper by your bed and simply write down what you know you want to accomplish the next day. A simple act such as putting your concerns down onto paper may be all it takes to stop you from lying there and worrying about them.

Also try to establish a regular pattern of sleep. Routine breeds better sleep. Disruption is not easy for our physical and mental bodies to handle. Whenever possible, try to go to bed at about the same time each night and get up at approximately the same time each morning. Of course, our lives are not always that orderly and perfect, but it is something to which you can aspire. Notice how well your body responds when you do follow a routine. This may be an element you want to include in your Dream Diary: details of your sleeping patterns.

Whether you follow any orthodox religion or not, saying a small prayer can also help to relax you. You do not have to pray to a specific deity, although if you follow a particular religion obviously this may be a comfort for you. You can try saying something quite short and simple, such as 'I place my trust in your great wisdom and ask that you help guide me through my life.' You might try an affirmation such as 'I am at peace' or 'I sleep wonderfully well every night.'

Some people also find it a comfort to have a particular object around them. Most of us probably remember when we went to sleep as a child clutching a favourite soft toy. As adults, our tastes may have changed. Perhaps you want to have a protective symbol around you to help you relax, such as an inspirational painting or a carved animal or deity. Colours may be important to you. Do certain colours make you feel more restful and release stress? Wear night attire or have a pillowcase in that colour.

Perhaps you are drawn to stones and crystals. It is said that certain stones produce better sleep and more prophetic dreams. Try having a small piece of celestine, jade, jasper, lapis lazuli, opal or sodalite either near your head or even under your pillow at night. See if any of these affect your dream process.

Music can also be a helpful bridge from consciousness to the realms of sleep. Choose something personal. Anything with a soft, slow rhythm is likely to help. It may be classical music that suits you. You may find some of the New Age music such as waterfalls, bird song or light tinkling piano music comforting. Try to avoid the spoken word, or, if you do opt for this, then make a note in your Dream Diary which tracks you used. Observe whether it has influenced your dreams in any way.

All these suggestions are good for you to try, so that you form a closer understanding of your personal sleep patterns and also your dream recall. Remember, everyone is unique. If you compare notes with someone else who is exploring their own dream and sleep processes, you will no doubt discover that they respond to completely different elements around them, don't worry about this as it is particularly normal.

Make sure you make a note in your Dream Diary about the different experiments you conduct. Anything new that you try can go under the heading of 'Influencing Factors.'

Remember, first and foremost, the most powerful kick start you can have to dream recall is your own pure intention that you wish to remember your dreams. Your own commitment is the first and most important stage. Everything else will follow in due course.

Once you have started your Dream Diary and begun the process, firstly of being aware that you really are dreaming and then being able to recall your dreams, you may find yourself becoming slightly frustrated. You know you are dreaming different things and you may even notice a pattern where certain dreams or elements of a dream keep reappearing. However, becoming aware of your dreams does not automatically make you a good interpreter of your dreams!

So we now need to progress to a further stage where we look at our dreams in greater detail and with a more personal approach. You are not going to be encouraged to see particular objects or events as being related to some specific, generic meaning. You are going to be encouraged to look at every one of your dreams in your own personal way, using your own inner wisdom and knowledge to unravel their intricate meaning.

Your Dream Diary should be filling up by now with remembered fragments of dreams. If you are still struggling, spend some more time on your meditations and ask to be shown why it is that you are not remembering your dreams as you would wish. A spiritual guide may assist you in this process. Try calling upon the name Morpheus, the god of dreams and sleep, for guidance.

If, after trying the various suggestions in the preceding chapter, you are still struggling to remember anything, it is simply because you are creating blockages that are preventing the information from getting through. There is a reason for this blockage and it doesn't mean there is anything wrong with you. It does mean you need to understand the reason for it before you will be able to progress. Work with your meditations and spiritual guides to help you understand what is happening.

Understanding Deeper Meanings

So how do you start to understand the deeper meaning behind your dreams? You may have found certain patterns and been able to identify recurring emotional responses to some of your dreams. You may even understand what you think some of them are about and also be able to dismiss others as purely influenced by an event or experience of that particular day.

What is important is for us always to personalize our dreams. This means that although often in dreams we can appear to be the observer and to watch certain events unfold, it is more powerful for us to assume that what we are watching is a part of ourselves being shown to us. In other words, higher awareness is allowing a certain part of us to become detached in a dream and to be shown to us in a particular way for us to be able to understand it more clearly.

This is a very powerful distinction to make and it allows the dream to become much more significant. It also means we start to delve into deeper parts of ourselves, of course, so you need to know that you are ready for this stage. As you have already been looking at your dreams for a while through creating your Dream Diary, you will probably welcome moving into this area of more intense dreamwork. If you still are not ready, then just keep adding to your Dream Diary and leaving the more detailed analysis until a later stage.

If you are sure you are ready, then make a conscious commitment now to interpreting every part of your dream as being a part of you. So if you see someone else or something in a dream, ask yourself first of all how it might relate to you. Do not immediately assume it is another energy come to show you something. Assume that you are being shown a part of you in a separate way, to allow you to really understand how this part of you is functioning or not functioning and that the behaviour or action you are observing is what you do or could do. This is a powerful stage to move onto in dreamwork. It can be emotional but it can also be wonderfully rewarding, deeply revealing and profoundly insightful.

Do not worry, as you continue working through the sections coming up, if you find stages where you feel utterly lost and uncertain about how something relates to you. Remember, higher awareness is a gentle, unconditionally loving force; it could even be described as being a part of you. It will not throw at you information you are not yet ready to handle. You will be shown breakthroughs as and when they are ready for you to deal with them. Continue working at your own pace.

If you find certain areas really difficult to grasp, know you can return to them at a later stage. Sometimes it takes a dream being shown to you in a particular way for its signficance to register. That is often why we have recurring dreams. Our subconscious is trying to show us ways of interpreting something but we don't always understand the 'code'. We have the breakthroughs when we are ready to deal with them.

There are certain common factors that tend to crop up in dreams, things such as buildings, modes of transport, bodies of water, animals/creatures/ monsters and other people. You may find most of your dreams have elements of these in them. It may be helpful for you to see these objects in a more psychological approach, although we are not going to accept this will always be the case for you. We will start off with generalizations and learn how to be more individual as we progress.

Remember, there are no hard and fast rules with dream analysis. What follows are rough overviews that will allow us the opportunity to begin our interpretation and then encourage us to progress and learn how to work more deeply at our own personal level. Make up your own mind as you continue reading. You are going to be encouraged to see everything in a much more personal way now.

Dream analyses: Buildings

These are often described as different parts of your mind. What do you think the different levels within a house might therefore mean? Think about what the loft/attic, first floor, ground floor and basement/cellar of a house might represent. Reflect on this first, before you continue reading. Did you think of any of the following? A general interpretation could be: the loft or attic is your higher consciousness, the first floor your higher ideals, the ground floor your everyday life, and the lower ground or basement your subconscious fears or desires. You may have thought something quite different, and that is fine.

You want to be encouraged to be unique in your dream analysis, not to follow the crowd. Keep reading and acknowledge that some of this may be very useful to you and some notions you may want to discard. Simply remain open to the possibility of it all but also be content to have your own opinions.

The size of the building is also relevant. What does an enormous building suggest to you? What about a tiny dwelling? The size of the building can relate to your self-esteem; an enormous building might indicate an enlarged ego or supreme confidence; a tiny dwelling might suggest lack of confidence and self-worth. Perhaps you think something different. The windows in the property and the appearance of the building are also relevant. The number of windows could relate to how open and receptive you are to others. The condition of the building itself may refer to how well you look after yourself. The front might represent the 'face' you show the world and the back might indicate your own private world. What else do these aspects of a building mean to you?

The location of the building is also important. If it is perched precariously on the edge of a cliff, what would that make you think? It could indicate you are feeling very vulnerable and frightened of being 'tipped over the edge' or it could indicate you love living your life on a knife edge. If it is in a deep, dark forest it may show you have a great need to withdraw from others and to seal yourself away in a safe cocoon. It might also show that you love meditation and seeking that wonderfully dark, deep inner awareness which is a part of us all. A building on top of a mountain might show that you are seeking higher awareness and ideals or simply a need to lift yourself out of the mundane, everyday world. It might show you running away from reality.

The type of building is also significant: is it a church, hotel, lighthouse or igloo? There are many different types of dwelling and they all mean different things. Take a moment to think about what these different types of buildings might mean to you before you continue reading. Close your eyes and think. Have you thought of any of the following? A church might mean sanctity, higher consciousness, safety or withdrawal; a hotel could mean changes in life or a need to get away; a lighthouse might refer to gaining a higher, clearer perspective of some aspect of your life or retreating to observe the sea; an igloo might refer to being cosy despite the cold of someone or something near you; perhaps it represents someone with a cold exterior but a warm interior. Did you think of any of these aspects for yourself? Perhaps you thought something different again.

Think about various elements within a building, such as the chimneys or guttering. What about the individual rooms such as a bathroom or kitchen? What would an elevator mean for you? Think about different internal furnishings that you might find in a building and what they might represent to you.

Can you see how one building can have many meanings to different people? You might find it interesting to ask someone else what a building means to them and note their response. This is all to show you how personal dream analysis can be. No matter what you may be told that an object means, or however many books tell you it should mean this or that, the ultimate aim is for you to have enough tools to decide for yourself what your own dream means to you.

You might find it helpful to make notes in the back of your Dream Diary about what various objects mean to you. This doesn't imply that your attitude won't change or it won't mean something else on another occasion, but it gives you a little 'security blanket' of thoughts to which you can return, whenever you feel lost over a particular dream interpretation. Often whatever you feel initially, particularly if it is a strong response, is a good starting point for you to work from. More in-depth analysis will come later, as and when you are ready to deal with the complexity of the issue involved in your dream.

So perhaps you will want to keep your Dream Diary handy as you run through the following sections. Do let your imagination run riot as you continue reading. No thought you have is right or wrong, it is simply unique to you. Enjoy the freedom!

Transport

Think about the different sorts of transport you know or use. Let us start with the **car**. What does a car mean to you? It might mean freedom or escape. It might mean feeling very earth-bound and tied up with family duties and work responsibilities. Most transport would seem to indicate a journey of some kind, although the vehicle itself might represent you or your fears or wishes. What does an old car that is falling apart say to you? What about a Rolls Royce; a Land Rover; a Ferrari; a people carrier? If the car is empty or full, what does that mean? Perhaps you feel very alone or weighed down with enormous responsibility to others. Any part of the car could be saying something about you. It could be a symbolic representation of you. What does a shiny exterior but a dirty interior signify; a worn-out engine; a car with no mirrors; a flat battery; a dirty exhaust? As you consider the importance of these details, so you will be training your subconscious to think about all these aspects and to notice them more in your dreams. It will help you to dream in more detail.

Consider a **bicycle** now and what it means to you. Perhaps it is about being environmentally friendly and having a slower pace of life. It might represent your youth when you used to tear around on one. Perhaps it therefore means no responsibility and great freedom, or it may remind you of delivering local newspapers and your first experience of earning your own money. Perhaps it symbolizes feeling held back because you would prefer a car but can't afford one at present. What does it mean to you? If there is someone riding the bicycle, observe who it is. Do not be quick to assume it isn't you. Perhaps it is an aspect of you being shown.

Boats are another consideration. As water is typically tied up with emotional issues, a trip on a boat may mean taking some emotional journey. The vessel itself is important, of course. What would a fast speedboat say to you? How does a small rowboat make you feel? Think about a canoe, a luxury yacht, a ferry, a large freight ship and a cruise liner. Notice how the different boats make you feel and the issues they bring up for you. Remember, there is no right or wrong answer. This is not a quiz! This is for you to explore what intrinsically feels true for you. Think about what happens on a vessel, cruising along slowly, going through storms, running aground, docking and casting off. What might these represent in a dream?

Now move on to thinking about **planes**, the only mode of transport that whisks us above the ground at great speed. How does this make you feel? It might be said that plane journeys are about travelling somewhere, either physically or mentally, at great speed. Perhaps you are frightened of flying; what other fears are present in your life as a result? Perhaps planes signify a powerful means of running far away from a situation, or perhaps they demonstrate being able to raise yourself above the everyday and move towards greater spiritual awareness. Think about a two-seater plane and having someone with you on a journey; what would that mean to you? Think about travelling in a crowded jumbo jet or doing flying stunts alone in a small plane. Allow yourself to develop a relationship with planes and flying and see how it makes you feel. Jot a few notes in your Dream Diary.

Let your thoughts drift on to **motorbikes** and how they make you feel. Don't worry if this creates a strong reaction in you. Many people find the image of a motorcycle to be inextricably linked with masculinity and aggression. If you have this response, that is fine. Ask yourself what a female on a motorbike would mean to you. If you own a motorbike or are passionate about them, consider their significance for you. It may be that you enjoy the unique freedom of being your own person and not answering to anyone, or you may fear personal closeness and the ties of family commitment. Let yourself explore how you feel without judging yourself or others. If you have never been on a motorbike, imagine yourself driving along on one and see what emotions that creates in you.

Consider a **lorry**. If you drive one for a living, your reaction will be different from someone who has never stepped into one. Ask yourself what you think a large lorry means to you. Perhaps this is an irritating symbol if you find yourself being stuck behind them on motorways all the time; perhaps you find them powerful, even sexual images and quite exciting. Maybe they seem associated with work and drudgery. Think about the different cargo that lorries carry and what that might mean to you. How do you feel about carrying a tanker of oil; live animals for export; containers of sweets; boxes of firearms?

Now let your focus rest on a **bus**. Think of it being crowded and then completely empty. How does that make you feel? Imagine driving the bus; imagine being a passenger. What is the difference to you? What does being the driver of a bus that is full represent to you? Think about the bus itself being a part of you. Think about the bus breaking down; getting on a bus but not having enough money; missing the bus; getting on the bus and discovering it's going in the wrong direction. What might these scenarios symbolize in your own life? A journey with a bus often means other people being with you on your journey. What would certain people on the bus with you mean to you?

Let us move on to a **train**. How do you feel about this mode of transport? What might an old steam train indicate, as opposed to a new intercity high-speed train? Many people would say the former indicates outmoded attitudes and the latter new, innovative ideas, but it is also possible you might feel it means traditional values versus the dangers of modern technology. Neither attitude is right or wrong. Think about an underground train. What does travelling underground mean to you? You might think it shows dark, unresolved areas of concern, or perhaps it means deep, profound meditation. Perhaps it feels powerful to you because it is a step nearer to the power contained within the Earth's core. Perhaps it makes you feel claustrophobic and not in control. Think about whether you would like your train to be crowded or empty or somewhere in between. Would you like someone sitting next to you on this train? Who? What meaning would that give to the journey? Where would you like the journey to end? What would it mean if you got off before the journey ended? What would a stowaway on the train mean to you? Perhaps you feel as though you could be a stowaway.

Lastly, think about a **space-craft** and what that would mean to you. Is it frightening or exciting or both? Think about different types of space-craft you have seen, either in science fiction material or in photographs of supposed UFOs. What would it mean if you dreamt you were travelling inside one? Where might you go? Ask yourself about your personal relationship with outer space and what one might find out there. Question your own belief in energies from other planets and galaxies being able to communicate with us. Perhaps you don't believe in this aspect of existence but feel that space travel may be taken on a spiritual level, relating to higher consciousness and to taking figurative journeys into new areas of awareness. How might higher consciousness manifest itself to you in a physical or emotional sense? Remember to make notes on your initial thoughts about all these spheres. Your conscious mind may not remember them all again so easily.

If you dream about other modes of transport such as a hot air balloon or trams or even that your journey is always on foot, then use the same process to question yourself and what it might mean.

Let your imagination come into play and enjoy the process. Don't limit yourself to what you think it ought to mean or what you have been told by others that it means.

Whilst transport almost always signifies a journey being taken in some area of your life, whether it is literal or symbolic, it is important that you can learn how to interpret the details of such a dream in which it occurs. That is why the more you question what a form of transport means to you and how it looks, feels, smells and behaves, the more you will learn how to dream in detail. You may find that certain transport comes to signify certain areas of your life. For instance, being on a bicycle may always refer to a part of your everyday, physical life, whereas boat trips may be about helping you resolve emotional issues. This will be different for everyone. Remember, the appearance of the form of transport in each dream will always be important; sometimes it may appear as clean and bright, other times as malfunctioning, sometimes as fast and efficient, other times as sluggish or non-operational. All this is significant. You determine what it means for you.

Now let us turn to bodies of water. As we mentioned earlier, water in dreams is very much about our emotional body. You may not know that the chakras within our etheric bodies are often related to an element. The navel chakra, which is very much about our emotions, is represented by the element of water.

Water

With water, it is important to look at different aspects of what you are experiencing. Let us start with the size of the water. Are you dreaming about an enormous ocean or a tiny whirlpool of water? Water could be represented by a puddle or a deep, hot bath. Think about different bodies of water and how they make you feel. Imagine yourself beside or in a huge expanse of sea. How are you feeling? For some of you this will be frightening; others will find it exhilarating. What does this immediate response say about your emotions?

What does an enormous expanse of water say about you? Are your emotions very well contained or are you openly expressive about how you feel? What happens when you are suddenly encouraged to become the opposite of what you intrinsically feel is you? Put yourself now into a tiny enclosed space of water. How do you feel now? Safe or claustrophobic?

Think about the state of the water itself. Imagine the ocean raging with high whitecaps, the waves pounding furiously upon the shore. Notice how you respond to this. Now create the image of a still, calm sea, the waves gently lapping at the shore. Decide if you would want to go into this body of water or not.

Let your thoughts drift on to a narrow brook babbling swiftly over stones, turning and twisting as it runs away into the distance. How does this make you feel? What aspect of your emotions is represented by this stream of water? Make the brook much wider, have the water slow to a more leisurely speed, perhaps have it become a thin, delicate trickle. Have the brook dry up altogether. Notice how you respond to each change.

Alter the image to a big, circular lake; make it a completely enclosed body of water. Notice what this means to you. Is there a boat anywhere on this lake? Take a trip on it if you wish and see how you feel. Notice if the lake's water feels deep and mysterious or shallow and clear. Is it calm or is the surface rippled by a stiff breeze?

Let your mind move on to other areas of water. Imagine a hot bath. Fill it with bubbles. Put oils into it. Imagine yourself stepping out of it and seeing that it is now dirty. Observe it cold and empty. Notice if there is anything else in the bath. What sort of bath is it? Realize that it all matters: the kind of taps, the colour of the bath, its shape, its size. Does it have an overflow? What sort of plug does it have? Everything means something in a dream and often the smallest detail can have great significance.

Imagine yourself splashing through puddles outdoors. What sort of puddles are they? What footwear do you have on, if any? How does it make you feel? Are the puddles dirty or clean? Is anyone else with you?

Ask yourself if you are someone who prefers to be on or by water but not to immerse yourself in it. What does this imply about your relationship to your emotional body? If you love diving deep into the water, think about what this says about you. If your dreams have floods in them, what does this show about your emotional state? Think about dreaming of dams, bridges or objects floating in the water.

Water is also symbolic of the act of cleansing and purifying. Think about what being cleansed means to you. You will have developed your own method of cleansing through earlier work in this book, but now think about cleansing specifically in relation to water. Create different forms of cleansing. Think about standing under a waterfall, being in a jacuzzi, running into the sea, getting into a bath. Notice which really feels cleansing and rejuvenating. Ask yourself what this shows you about your emotional preferences.

Dreaming about canals is said to refer to the process of birth. This could be a symbolic birth or your actual birth. Ask yourself what a canal in your dream might mean to you. If you receive a different interpretation, make a note of it in your Dream Diary.

If through all these images, you were left feeling that water represented more for you than purely emotions, and that different bodies of water make you think about certain aspects of your life, that is wonderful. Just make sure you are clear about what you felt initially with the various images and then make a note of them for future reference.

If you are feeling confused and uncertain over what you are feeling, if perhaps you have already read a number of books on dreams or been told what certain things mean and you feel stuck with those interpretations, then simply remember to keep cleansing away the old thoughts. Try saying a new affirmation to yourself, such as 'I trust my own instinct with all my dream interpretations'. Decide you will not be bound by old recordings in your mind, but allow yourself the joy of new, fresh experiences and encourage your own thought processes to expand into as yet unknown areas.

Although initially it can be difficult to make everything we dream into a personal reference, once you start to do this and eventually get into the habit of it, it becomes easier and easier and allows your mind to expand rapidly. Through practice, for instance, you will quickly be able to see how a building in your dream is completely representational of a part of your life and understand whether it is about your past, present or future. With further practice, you will also know when you need to interpret your dream on an even deeper level and learn when small details take on a big significance.

Let us look now at how other people might manifest themselves in our dreams. There will probably be a wealth of different people coming and going in your dreams, both those you know and those you have never met before. We will look at a few possibilities regarding their significance and then it is up to you to determine for yourself what their appearance means to you on a deeply personal level.

People

There are firstly the people you already recognize who may come into your dream world. This can apply to people both living and dead. If they have passed over, you might immediately just think they have come to greet you or to pass on a message, but it may be something more than this. Their own personality may be reminding you of an element of yourself that you are either ignoring or abusing. They may be showing themselves to you simply to show you part of yourself. Again, remember your commitment to personalizing your dreams as much as possible. Try not to assume a person you know is there because they need to make themselves known to you. Energies who have passed on do not usually return to satisfy their own ego; they are not that selfish.

It's also important to ask yourself what that figure represents to you symbolically. For instance, if it is your grandmother, is she symbolic of childhood warmth and security? Is this lacking in your own behaviour? Perhaps your father is a strong, authoritarian figure and speaks to you of your own masculinity. It may be that a sibling shows themselves to you because they represent a conflict of power and rivalry which is reflected in an area of your life at the moment.

Usually our family unit is our first experience of the power of emotional ties and the strong responses we have to humans on every level. Therefore, if we grow up with unresolved family issues in our lives, it stands to reason that they will continue to replay themselves in our dreams until we sort them out. We gradually add non-blood ties into the mix as we grow up, although we often discover they are no less complicated! So it is natural that a lot of dreams may revolve around our everyday relationships. However, in our dreams we will be given the opportunity to see these people differently, provided we choose to see the signs and to work with them.

As you have been encouraged to do so far, you will want to continue treating members of your family in your dreams with the same all-encompassing, personal approach you have used with other elements that have appeared in your dreams. What is your mother or father in your dream trying to tell you about yourself? Stop trying to blame them for a situation in which you now find yourself; they come into your dreams to help you find solutions, not to confuse you further. Listen. Observe. Be willing to learn.

Notice how your family and your friends will change form in your dreams, because they manifest themselves to you differently in an attempt to have you understand them better. They may appear in a different mode of dress, at a different age, perhaps in a more gentle manner than you have seen them before. Conversely, they may appear more angry than you were expecting. What is this saying about your own feelings towards them? If they have different clothes on, really look at these clothes and analyse what they say to you.

There will also be people you have never met before and you will want to understand why they have come into your dream. There are occasions when a figure will be a guide manifesting itself to you or some wise teacher who has come to help you. However, the majority of the time this other person you are seeing who you do not recognize is likely to be a part of yourself that you are not acknowledging at present. In other words, this strange person you encounter is just part of you, being shown to you as a separate entity so that you may learn how to acknowledge part of yourself in a more powerful way. Always, whenever you greet a strange person in your dreams, stop to consider if part of you really is this person. Notice how they are dressed, how they behave, how they seem to be feeling. Closely observe their surroundings and see what they mean to you. Relate it to your own life. Does this person represent a figure of authority or someone who is cowed and subservient? Ask them what they are trying to say to you.

People often dream of having a new baby but this is not necessarily an indication of a new birth or a desire to become a parent. It can refer to your own babyhood or an issue regarding your vulnerability. Perhaps it symbolizes your need to return to innocence and uncomplicated living. Depending upon the dream, it may mean a new beginning. A young child can show you a need for purity of thought, for not analysing and being too critical of an aspect of your life. People often talk of finding their 'inner child': that pure, spiritual quality within them. How does that make you feel?

Our family relationships are so individual and so intensely personal that it is hard to generalize about them in dreams. It really is up to you to decide for yourself what different family members represent to you, then allow them to change form in your dreams and see what that teaches you. Remember the location of your dreams is also very important. Use that as a means of complementing your understanding.

Animals and other creatures

Lastly, let us now look at animals and other creatures, including what we might call monsters. It can be hard to find a quick and powerful interpretation for many of them. You may already have developed a relationship with certain animals through your work with your animal guides. You may want to take this experience with you into dreamwork or you may choose to let it go. As you read the next section, try not to anticipate what you ought to feel but simply enjoy the process of letting your mind run free.

There are dreams where you reacquaint yourself with animals you have known. You may want to put different interpretations on such meetings. The animals may be coming simply to say 'hello'; you may feel they are guides offering you wisdom; you may know you have some unresolved issue with them and want to use your dream to rectify this. You can determine which it is from the setting – for example, do you meet them in a particular room in a house? What does that room mean to you? – and emotions connected with the dream. Observe, too, the condition of the animals in your dream. Are they showing themselves to you at a different age from when they passed over? What is their general demeanour? You may even be able to speak to them and get them to respond. You may indeed realize that they are there to present a part of yourself to you. You will develop your own understanding of what this means.

However, there will also be many occasions when animals and creatures crop up that you do not know and you can't understand what they mean. You need to form a closer association with what each animal represents to you before you can understand them in your dreams. Start focusing on different animals. There may be some you feel more drawn to than others. You may also feel a dislike of certain creatures and apathy towards others. Notice what your first reaction is and make a note of it. Try to delve deeper once you acknowledge your first response. We'll begin with domestic animals and progress to wild creatures.

Consider the **cat**. Does this mean sensuality and femininity to you? Perhaps it means independence and inscrutability. You may be drawn to cats or feel uncomfortable with them. Whatever you feel about them will determine the meaning when one appears in your dream. Ask yourself what your response says about your own personality.

For instance, if you find cats aloof and uninterested in people, where does this behaviour manifest itself in you?

A **dog** is often called man's best friend. How do you react to this statement? Dogs are frequently associated with loyalty and blind devotion. Perhaps you feel faintly contemptuous of this animal or inexplicably drawn to it. Relate this back to you. Sometimes we are attracted by opposites. Sometimes we are repelled by something only because it truly reflects a part of us that we are avoiding. Determine what is going on with you in relation to animals and your perception of their individual personalities.

A **rabbit** is often linked to fertility and reproduction. It can represent the feminine and Mother Earth within us. Remember, we all have both the masculine and feminine within our psyche. A man acknowledging his feminine side is not questioning his sexuality but is balancing himself in a holistic way. (Our brain, for example, is often described as having two halves. We know the left-hand side of our brain controls the logical, analytical part of us. The right side controls the intuitive and instinctive parts of our being. The left is called the masculine – symbolized by the sun – and the right the feminine – symbolized by the moon. We all need both halves of our brain, just as we need both the sun and moon.) If you have a rabbit in your dream, think about what it might say about you. How balanced are you with both the logical and intuitive aspects of your personality?

A **horse** is often considered a powerful symbol, connected with great energy. What is your personal feeling about horses? Do you love riding them or watching them run free in open fields? Do you think of them as free spirits or under the domination of man, as beasts of burden and work? Think of a horse with flaring nostrils, neighing as it paws the ground. Imagine a horse standing quietly in a field, grazing. Imagine being a horse and how you would feel. Create your own personal relationship with this creature. If you aren't certain how you feel, spend some time observing horses in a field. Get to understand them better and always remember to relate your observations back to yourself. Keep a note of your first feelings about them to refer back to later.

What about **rodents**? Think now about a mouse. Make your mind focus on this tiny creature. There is the expression 'quiet as a mouse'. Are you a quiet personality? Are you drawn to these delicate creatures or are you frightened of them? Do they make you feel uncomfortable? Why? Think about how shy they are, how they scuttle away from humans. Compare and contrast your behaviour with that of a mouse. Imagine being a tiny mouse and how the rest of the world would seem. Could you learn from a mouse's behaviour? Now turn the mouse into a rat and observe your reaction. Why is it so different?

Let your thoughts move on to an **elephant**. See this enormous creature standing in front of you. What does an elephant symbolize to you? Many would say strength and endurance. Elephants also possess a phenomenal memory. They are one of the few animals that cry tears. They honour any death of their own kind with a ritual akin to a funeral. Where can you find an affiliation between yourself and an elephant? Imagine riding on top of one or becoming one, moving through the forest, swaying your trunk in front of you. Elephants are considered a very grounding symbol because of their massive weight and size. In certain faiths, they are related to the base chakra. They also represent spiritual wisdom in other cultures. What does all this mean to you?

There are many different types of **birds** and you might have any number of them come into your dreams. Why is a vulture so different in energy from a dove? What would a hummingbird mean to you as opposed to a chicken? Most birds can fly. Is this important in your dream? What sort of flight is it? What aspect of your life is revealed in that journey? Perhaps the bird can't fly. What does that mean to you? Is the bird a beautiful representation or a frightening image? Is it telling you about a part of yourself that you are apprehensive about looking into? Is it coming to you as a symbol of peace and protection, reminding you that you can fly away and release earthly pressure when you need to by retreating upwards to your spiritual world? Remember, you don't have to take these interpretations on board; think about them and then create your own. Jot down a few species of bird that you can think of and notice the first feeling that comes into your mind. Think about the image of a tamed bird, a caged bird, a wild bird. Relate these to different aspects of your life. If a bird had a damaged wing, how could you personalize that and make it apply to you?

The **lion** makes many of us think of control and dignity but also of imposing anger when aroused. Is this an appealing or uncomfortable image? Think about where in your own life you can find dignity and control. Think about what happens when you get angry. Think about a caged lion and then a lion running wild in its natural habitat. Can you relate yourself to either of these states? Allow yourself the sensation of becoming a lion. Notice how you feel. People often talk about a lion having enormous pride. Do you think you have a sense of pride? How would you describe your own ego?

The image of a **snake** tends to bring up strong emotions in people. What does it do for you? Many associate the snake with negative energy such as deviousness, cunning and even death. It is often linked with sexuality because of its shape and historical references. Try to let go of these concepts and ask yourself what the snake really means to you. It has been taken to represent spiritual awakening. The all-powerful latent psychic energy contained within us, called kundalini, is symbolized as a coiled serpent waiting to release itself. The snake can represent inner ambition and drive. DNA, the fundamental ingredient of life, is represented by two snakes coiled around a staff. Challenge your preconceptions about the snake and delve deeper into your own psychological make-up to understand what it really means to you.

There are many other animals and reptiles we could discuss, but there isn't room to go into them all. You now have the tools to go on and question your attitude to different creatures. Every time you find an animal cropping up in your dreams, ask yourself what it means given your present relationship and understanding of that animal. Notice how your awareness grows over time as you are shown different aspects of this animal in your dreams.

Monsters and mythical creatures

Let's move on to look at mythical creatures and how we feel about them. You may be looking at a variety of possibilities here. Historical creatures you may not have seen before may enter your dreams. If this happens frequently, you might want to consider acquiring a reference book on mythological creatures because it may become a fundamentally important aspect of your spiritual growth. If you love Egyptian or Greek history, you may find gods and deities from that period coming into your dreams. If you are a science fiction fan, you may find aliens entering your dreams. This simply means your higher awareness is trying to show you something in a way that will best enable you to identify the scenario. Always, always, relate the creature to some aspect of yourself and see how that makes you feel. You may have more work to do in this area because it may not be as easily understood as your relationships with some animals. Be prepared to put in extra time and effort. You might find it yields the greatest breakthrough.

If you find a monster coming into your dreams, remember this is likely to be purely a representation of some dark fear inside you. Although such an image can be frightening in dreams, it can be just as frightening to face an aspect of our lives we would rather avoid. If we spend too much time avoiding important challenges, those energies more wise and loving than ourselves will try to find more and more powerful ways of helping us through our dreams. If some frightening creature does come into your dreams, remember you have called it into your energy and you do have something to learn from it, other than simply finding it frightening! Delve deeper. Take a good look at this monster. By not being frightened to confront it, you take away its negative effect on you and then learn from it.

Nightmares

This is an appropriate point to have a brief discussion about nightmares and what they mean. For most people, a nightmare simply means a bad dream which leaves us feeling upset. Usually it represents a negative aspect of our lives. The more we have avoided an important issue, the more that issue will crop up in our dreams, although it may come disguised in different scenarios. Higher awareness and our spiritual guides are quite inventive! They will not give up on us just because in our physical life we are not following through on some important aspect of our development. We may use blocking tactics when we are conscious but, when we drift into sleep, we cannot escape our destiny and what we are meant to learn.

Until we heed our dreams and take the messages from them, we will continue to dream those dreams. Therefore, nightmares are really just an extension of that: a dream replayed in a different way to hopefully make us sit up and pay attention.

The more resistant you are to change, the more you are likely to suffer from recurrent nightmares. If there are people or situations you resent in your life, that strong emotion will create blocks for you. If you open your heart to the possibility of change occurring in your life, even if you do not know which way to turn or what to do for the best, you will find your nightmares receding into less threatening experiences. They are only there so that you may become aware. Higher energies and spirit guides will never chastise us for not knowing the answers to everything and they are unconditionally loving and compassionate in their actions. Nightmares are, if you like, their last resort in their desire to help you! Therefore, be willing to change and your dreams will change with you.

When you wake up after a nightmare, remember to use your tools for cleansing and closing down. Often, after experiencing such a dream, we wake up feeling vulnerable and frightened. You can wash away this fear in your Cleansing Sanctuary. You can also use whichever technique you favour to get rid of it, either burning it, washing it away, seeing it whisked into the cosmos in your rocket or having it evaporate in the sunlight. You do not have to carry the sensation of the nightmare around with you during the day. Let it go and know you will return to deal with this issue when you have the time to do so. Put an extra thick cloak of protection around yourself for the day. Ask your Guide of Protection to stay with you for a while.

Once you have uncovered the meaning behind what you might call a nightmare, you may go back over your Dream Diary and notice other recurring dreams you have had (although they were not disturbing or frightening) and realize they are all variations on that same theme. Until we resolve an area of our life, it will return in dreams for us to look at and analyse.

Using Free Association

There is not room here to go through each of the other objects and situations that will crop up in your dreams. The purpose of this chapter is to enable you to start questioning your dreams and work out their meaning for you.

The techniques you have applied to thinking more deeply about buildings, transport, water, people, and other creatures can be used with anything you encounter in your dreams. The approach is always the same. Be willing to see every creature and object as a manifestation of part of you or your life and listen to what it is saying to you. Observe everything.

There will naturally be occasions when you feel stuck with your interpretation, no matter how much you try to see a way through it. If so, why not try a different approach, such as the Freudian concept of free association? This is an easy tool to use. Take a single word from a scenario in which you are trying to gain some helpful insight. It can be any word and any part of the setting. Let us use an example. Perhaps you have a situation where a hooded figure is sitting in front of a fire. Take the word 'hood' and free associate with it. To do this, say the word and then the next word that comes into your mind. What your mind throws up does not have to be logical or sensible. In fact, it is better if it isn't because you are trying to relax your mind into behaving without anxiety or blockages. Keep going from word to word until you feel the strong urge to stop and examine the last word. This may be a quick process or go on for a while.

A free association exercise based on the word 'hood' might go something like this – hood, coat, dog, kill, loss, pain. For this person, the connection may refer back to the pain of their dog being killed many years before. The hood is representative of their shutting out the hurt. Someone else will free associate entirely differently, perhaps this way: hood, could, never, retreat, forest, calm, silence. In this instance, the hood symbolizes the individual's need for some time of peaceful retreat. Using this technique every person will respond differently to the same word. Free association proves conclusively how unique we all are.

Given the scenario of the hooded figure seated in front of a fire, you might have chosen the word 'fire' instead of 'hood'. Your free asociation might go this way: fire, liar, deceit, anger, red, burn. You can draw your own conclusions as to what this might mean. Someone else might come up with this: fire, warm, swarm, bees, busy, full, glass, drink, many, happy, sad, alone, empty, gone. What started out with happy associations suddenly shifted half-way through to something darker. That is the power of free association; your emotions go on a roller coaster as you stop analysing and deep, inner truths may emerge. Use the technique of free association next time you are stuck in a scenario and see if it helps you.

With the different approach you have been asked to take with your dreams in this chapter, now is a good time for you to look back over your Dream Diary and see what new insights have come to you. Perhaps you will want to make some more notes about your previous dreams. Do you remember it was mentioned earlier that you might want to leave a whole blank page marked 'Space for Later Thoughts'? Perhaps now you will understand why.

After you finish reading this chapter and absorbing its contents, make a note of having done so in your Dream Diary and observe how your dreams then change. It is highly likely that you will find yourself dreaming in more detail and noticing much more about what is happening to you and around you in your dreams. You will probably also remember a great deal more of your dreams afterwards.

This is just because you are putting into practice what we talked about in the very beginning: having a clear commitment to your dreamwork. The clearer you are about wanting to learn, the more there will be made available for you to understand.

One more word before we leave this section. Do try to be honest at all times. Remember this is very personal work and not something you ever have to discuss with others. In this one area of your life, resolve that you will be utterly truthful. You can be vulnerable, open, receptive and completely yourself. No one else ever has to know what is going on in your dreams. If you are worried about someone else reading your Dream Diary, carry it with you or put a lock on the outside of it. Make yourself feel as safe as possible so that you can enjoy this new learning process. You are being given the opportunity to discover some wonderful, new aspects of yourself. Enjoy it!

As you study the content of your dreams in more detail, you may begin to realize that your dreams seem to have different functions. Some might seem to be about helping you with a particular issue in your life, some might seem to be prophetic, others might just seem to be very practical and unremarkable in content. Next, we are going to look at different types of dreams and how you can start to determine for yourself what category your dreams fall into, and through that process learn how to understand them better.

DIFFERENT TYPES OF DREAMS

You may feel you have progressed a fair way in dream analysis. It can be very enlightening to start seeing your dreams as a deeper manifestation of all of you and to work with that concept to reveal new insights.

You may also be feeling that understanding your dreams on a more profound level has made matters more complex. You can see that your dreams may be saying something about you, but how on Earth do you take that interpretation out into the real world and decide how best to use the information you have gleaned?

Part of the solution is to learn how to identify the type of dream you have had. Just as different things within the dream can reveal different parts of our selves, so the dream itself can show whether we are referring to a past experience, a present situation or even a possible future scenario – either positive or negative – that we might create.

Determining what type of dream we are having can be more difficult than simply relating parts of the dream to our selves, but nevertheless through practice we can learn to recognize what sort of dream we are having. Let's first of all look at a few different types of dreams and how we might respond to them. The list of possibilities is endless and you may decide that some of your dreams fall into yet different categories after you have read through the following. That is fine. This list is simply for you to start thinking in a more specific way about how a dream feels to you.

Sometimes you won't know how to analyse a particular dream until you look at how you feel about it and then decide which type of dream you were having. After the description of each dream below, there is a discussion about how you might want to think about this kind of dream and how you might interpret it. If you think you have had a particular dream, try applying what is suggested to it. If you feel stuck and can't move forward with your interpretation, then it is possible your dream falls into another category. Look at the possibilities and use what you understand of different kinds of dreams to help improve your own personal analysis technique.

Everyday Dreams

These are quite common and could be described as a reflection of your present, everyday life. In these dreams, you go through familiar events. Perhaps you replay scenes that happened earlier that day, only the circumstances may be slightly different. Perhaps your dream seems to be a collection of various parts of your day all jumbled up into a distorted mishmash.

A clue to recognizing this sort of dream is that it feels very matter-of-fact and tends not to arouse strong emotions in you. It is not filled with symbolic or confusing images. It could also be called a practical dream, as it tends to provide logical solutions. If you are someone who naturally uses more of the left-hand side of your brain (the logical, linear-thinking aspect of you), then such dreams may be frequent occurrences.

In looking at the significance of these dreams, we want to closely observe what is taking place and see whether a slight change of activity is showing us a different approach we can take. These everyday dreams are not filled with imagery, so take what you see in your dream at face value. What took place in this dream? Does it mean something important to you? What can you learn from it? You don't need to make this sort of dream deep and meaningful. Don't try to find hidden messages. (Remember, if you have very strong emotions in your dream, it is likely not to be an everyday dream.)

Of course, you can also choose to 'test' an everyday dream and see if there is a more profound meaning, too. For instance, if you dream that you are shopping for clothes, stop to consider whether your life is reflecting a surfeit of material concerns or if there is a part of your physical body that needs greater protection or nurturing.

Just remember that it is possible to over-analyse, so with everyday dreams always work initially with the apparent literal meaning before you try to delve deeper. Everyday dreams can often be just a pleasant reflection of our everyday life. You can enjoy them on that level alone. If you find that what appears to be an everyday dream keeps repeating itself or if you find flashes of it keep returning to your conscious memory, then you might want to ask yourself if you can also take it on a deeper level. If the memory of an everyday dream remains as a powerful image, chances are you are then experiencing a more complex dream.

Symbolic Dreams

This is a big category because there are many types of symbolic dreams. A strong indication of a symbolic dream is that it is full of emotion and a depth of feeling that everyday dreams do not give. Often the events in them are not logical to the dreamer. The location is not an everyday setting; you may not know the people or places shown. Images may appear which confuse or intrigue but they are not necessarily readily understandable.

Often a symbolic dream leaves a powerful impression, but you may find it hard to put its impact into words. You may feel strangely moved and a little troubled afterwards when you recall the dream. Some areas of symbolic dreams will seem vivid and stay in your conscious thought. Others seem intangible, vague and elude your conscious memory, although you also feel those details are important.

These dreams take the most analysing and are deeply personal in content. This is certainly a good time for you to look closely at all aspects of the dream and see which elements are the most revealing. Try not to take literal events in the dream as being literal; try to put them on to a more spiritual level and see what that tells you. Also, take the overall emotion from the symbolic dream as a good starting point for determining its message. What affected you most?

If an element in a symbolic dream is elusive, try the process of free association and see if it yields insights. If the dream remains a mystery, accept that its meaning may become clear later. Sometimes the significance of a symbolic dream is only revealed months after the dream took place. Make sure you have written down everything you can remember in your Dream Diary, because these are the sort of dreams you may want to return to on a number of occasions before their meaning is revealed to you.

Also remember with symbolic dreams that you might want to consider different objects within the dream as extensions of you. No matter how ridiculous the object, consider if it is a part of you. Perhaps a rusty pot is hanging over a fire. Does that rusty pot represent some component of you? Is it empty or is something cooking in it? What about that solitary tree in the park? Are you drawn to it in your dream? Why?

With symbolic dreams you often have to delve beneath your surface interpretation of something. In a symbolic dream, nothing is probably quite what it seems. If you use that as a starting point, then you are well on your way to working at a deeper level.

Anxiety Dreams

These are relatively simple to identify because the feeling of anxiety attaching to the dream is usually strong, whatever it may concern. Sometimes we can readily identify the situation and see what we are dreaming about it; on other occasions it may manifest itself in a more symbolic setting, so we are being encouraged to take a fresh approach to the solution. During the dream, the dreamer will feel agitated and often either frustrated or fearful. The dreamer may even wake up feeling as though their heart is pounding or that they have been crying. Anxiety dreams are different from nightmares in that often they end in a sense of futility, with the dreamer feeling trapped or ineffectual. Often we wake from these dreams with the bed clothes in disarray as our physical bodies have been thrashing about.

Anxiety dreams are usually a manifestation of the dreamer feeling inadequate or not in control in one particular area of their life. This can relate all the way back to childhood experiences (are you a child in the dream?) or may reflect a way in which the dreamer feels they are not conforming or behaving as expected. To analyse this dream, first, take the overall emotion in the dream and ask yourself what area of your life makes you feel this way. Only when you have done this should you look back at the dream's scenario and relate it to your 'real' life. You may find that, instead of replaying your obvious fears in your dreams, your subconscious has presented you with a quite different scenario because you are being shown how you can take a new attitude to this problem and approach it from a different angle.

The anxiety dream may also be showing you how unfounded your fears are or how they refer back to an earlier time in your life. Regard anxiety dreams as a valuable tool in revealing the true source of your anxiety and also for providing an outlet for pent-up emotion.

Frightening Dreams

We discussed nightmares at the end of the previous chapter, so hopefully you remember the salient points. In case you have not taken them in fully, we'll repeat them here. People naturally have such a strong reaction to nightmares that it is important to remind ourselves what they really are.

Nightmares are a manifestation of your own fears, usually unfounded, and usually based in the past, which cannot harm you now in the present. A nightmare is purely an opportunity for you to look at a fear that you have not yet dealt with. This doesn't make you a 'bad' person or a coward; it just means that you are being given the chance to look at a particular issue in a new light. If this issue manifests as a nightmare it is because we have held this fear for a long time and have kept burying it deeper and deeper within us. The only way for it to surface is for us to be forced to look at the issue once and for all.

Unless we have a strong reaction to something, we are unlikely to remember the dream, and, secondly, to want to work through it and understand it. We know once we have dealt with it, the nightmare will go away. Until we do, it will probably resurface in some guise or another. In other words, the strength of the nightmare reveals its true power.

Once you have woken from a nightmare, remember to put down what you felt straight away. It doesn't matter how shaky your writing is or how much your voice trembles. As you describe the dream, you will find the terror recedes. You will often realize that the dream itself was rather ridiculous and does not accurately reflect you or your life. The scenario is not necessarily realistic in any way. It is only the emotion that feels overpoweringly 'real'. Take a few deep breaths and remember that the true power of the dream lies in your ability to work through it and understand it.

Nightmares are not to be taken literally. If you dreamt you have been chased and are about to be shot, this does not mean it is going to happen to you in real life. The emotion attached to the dream is very important, however. That is why you have experienced it so keenly. Try to break down an emotion such as 'fear'. What else was going on for you? Were you feeling trapped? Were you feeling helpless? Powerless? Ask yourself what area of your life is affected by this emotion.

Remember, your spiritual guides are letting you have this nightmare only because their pure intention is for you to sort out this issue. They want to help you.

Nightmares have no power over you once you express a clear desire to understand their true meaning and to work through this new realization. Have your nightmares lose their terror by acknowledging them purely as a useful learning tool. The nightmares will stop once you have learnt how to analyse them and to appreciate them for what they are.

Wish-fulfilment Dreams

These occur when your physical life reflects a deep area of desire. It can be any strong urge, such as wanting more money, having a baby, getting married, being world champion in your favourite sport, or more altruistic cravings such as world peace or ending world hunger.

This dream always contains a feeling of euphoria, the realization that you have achieved something wonderful. Often this sensation remains with you when you wake up and for a moment you feel as though it has actually happened. These dreams often feel so very 'real' and natural that there can then be an overwhelming feeling of let-down and depression when the truth dawns and you realize that you have not really experienced what occurred in your dream. Sometimes, this feeling of failure can stay with you throughout the day. Conversely, you can have a sense of believing it is possible to accomplish your wish because of the sensation of it having happened in your dream, and this provides you with a renewed optimism that lingers with you.

One could argue that this sort of dream does not need much analysis and that you simply want what isn't in your life at present. However, you can take a different approach. First, ask yourself why this wish is so important to you. What part of your life is it connected to? Is it about wanting to make yourself feel more important/powerful/successful/superior? What would it cost you and others should this wish come true?

A wish is usually connected to our own ego in some very significant way. Look at the dream and notice what part of your ego is being satisfied by the wish being enacted. Also observe others closely in the wish-fulfilment dream. Is everyone so pleased for you? What have you sacrificed along the way to accomplish your goal? There may be images in the background, waiting for you to notice them.

Also realize that a wish-fulfilment dream may be there to show you how best to create this outcome. What are you doing or not doing at present that is preventing you from attaining this goal? You will have to watch your dream closely to gain any clues as to its true message. If you find your dream uplifting and inspirational, let that carry you forward.

Next time you have a wish-fulfilment dream, note how it is different. Those changes may provide a clue for your future actions. This is where your Dream Diary becomes an invaluable part of your progress. You will have the memory written in detail, so you know it is accurate.

Recurring Dreams

Many of us have what we call recurring dreams. Often they have been with us since childhood, although we may only start remembering them at a certain point in our life. They may vary a little in content or apparent length but the theme remains the same throughout. For instance, you are being chased and can't run away fast enough. The setting in which you are being chased may change, the image chasing you may alter, but the fundamental action remains the same. Perhaps you are trying to swim towards the shore. The setting on the shore may change, the body of water may change, but the action is the same. Or perhaps you are trying to get through some aperture but your body won't quite go through. The hole may change, it might be a cat flap, a metal tube or a window, but the action is the same. These are recurring dreams.

There is always one reason and one reason only for recurring dreams. There is some lesson in life you are not heeding. This doesn't mean 'lesson' in the sense that you are being bad or stupid and need to be taught a lesson. It means you have access to some wisdom, some insight, that you are not yet seeing or are blocking out for some reason. The recurring dream is purely there to remind you of the lesson that is waiting for you at all times, when you choose to acknowledge it.

Recurring dreams are wonderful in that they are a golden opportunity for us to really learn something about ourselves. Whenever you have a recurring dream, bless the fact that higher consciousness and higher awareness are not giving up on you! They are so determined that you will understand what is being offered to you and they are ensuring you keep having the opportunity shown to you in your dreams, knowing that at some point you will take their gift.

You will understand your recurring dream when you are able to analyse it in the most powerful way and to act upon it. It is important to remember that a recurring dream no longer recurs when you have learnt the lesson from it. Of course it can be frustrating when either thinking you know what the dream means, or not having a clue what the dream means, doesn't seem to get you anywhere. Remember, higher consciousness is very inventive. They will show us different approaches in our dreams to give us every chance of understanding. They will not give up on us!

To work with recurring dreams, first ask yourself if there is an unresolved issue in your life (and there will be!). Take the time to be honest with yourself. You may find some revelation suddenly confronts and upsets you. Whatever you feel upset about is probably the issue you need most to confront. If you think you know what issue is most difficult for you, then and only then apply it to your recurring dream. For instance, if you have an unresolved issue with another person, where is that person represented in your dream? Are they the monster, the body of water, the enclosure from which you are trying to escape? Why have they been manifested in that form? What does that form mean to you?

It is all right if you feel uncomfortable about this. Realize that the dream is recurring because this unresolved issue has been with you for so long. The deep-seated issues are the most difficult to deal with. Often we have buried them deep inside and hoped they will go away. They won't.

Be gentle when you work with your recurring dreams. Always remember to acknowledge that they have happened because you have something to learn. Remember that spiritual guides are always loving and nurturing and that they will gently enable you to see what is the truth behind a scenario and help you to move forward. A recurring dream is not bad; it is a positive sign that there is something you can do about an area of your life that has been troubling you. Welcome recurring dreams and know that you will gain wisdom from them, if you allow yourself some space and unconditional love in the process.

Prophetic Dreams

There are some well documented prophetic dreams. It is known that Abraham Lincoln dreamt of his own funeral shortly before he was assassinated. Shortly before facing a fight with Jimmy Doyle, the boxer Sugar Ray Robinson dreamt that he inadvertently killed his opponent with a punch. Sadly, that event did indeed come to pass. Many other prophetic dreams have been recorded. However, the ones that receive publicity tend to be those pertaining to major world events or shocking incidents.

Suppose we also dream regularly about things that come to pass, although on a much less dramatic scale than the examples just given?

Many people believe we do. Often someone will exclaim, 'Oh, that's broken my dream' or 'Hey, I dreamt about this'. You may have experienced a prophetic dream yourself. The only way for you to determine whether you have indeed had a prophetic dream or just imagined that you have is to make a note in your Dream Diary of what happened. Remember to be as specific as possible. Don't elaborate or exaggerate.

You may notice that in many, small ways your dreams are prophetic. One night you may dream that someone phoned you and the next day they get in touch. Perhaps you dream of an object and the next day you see it out somewhere. It is quite possible that our dreams are much more of a representation of our life as a whole than we expected. The only way we can prove this to our selves is to keep a detailed Dream Diary that allows us to make comparisons. You will need to do this for a few months before you will truly have an accurate picture of what sort of prophetic dreams you are having. Always remember to be honest with yourself.

Keeping a separate notebook in which you jot down any predictions may make checking back easier. Always put the date beside each dream so you are sure what night it took place. It is all too easy to dream one night about something after it has taken place.

It is important not to fall into the trap of thinking that all dreams are prophetic in some way. As you should know by now, there are so many different kinds of dreams. It is unhealthy to start becoming obsessed with just one kind and to want to put all your dreams into one category. For instance, if you dream of a death of someone close to you, do not be tempted to try to read into it that this person is going to die. You know dreams can be taken on many different levels and it is far more likely to be symbolic than literal. Do not, under any circumstances, tell that person what you dreamt. It would be upsetting for them and might even panic them unnecessarily. Remember to apply sensitivity to your dreamwork, just as you do in other areas of spiritual work.

Divine Dreams

A specific emotion accompanying divine dreams is what sets them apart from other types of dreams. There is always a deeply spiritual – or you might say reverential – sensation attached to a divine dream. By divine dream, we mean an experience whereby you come into contact with some energy or force that you would not call earthly. You could say it is divine in nature, or spiritual or religious. It is hard to describe this sort of dream in everyday language because the experience transcends anything earthly or physical.

If you know you have never had such a dream, where you come into contact with a form of higher consciousness and where you feel pleasantly overwhelmed as a result, do not worry or think there is something wrong with you. This doesn't mean it won't happen at some point in the future. It also doesn't matter if it never happens to you. Divine dreams are very personal and often occur when someone is in need of some proof of higher spiritual awareness. If you know that you already feel connected powerfully in some way to higher forms, then one could argue that you do not need to have this experience because it would only be expressing something you already know.

A divine dream is a wonderful occurrence and you will no doubt feel very blessed if you have already had one. Whilst proof of higher spiritual awareness and great wisdom is the most frequent expression of a divine dream, it can also take the form of healing.

Again, this is hard to explain but divine healing could be described as the sensation of a warm balm settling over and through you. For each individual, this is a very personal experience, so it is hard to generalize. You may want to give this a religious name if there is a deity whom you worship or, if you do not follow any organized religion, you may want to create your own name for the energy.

People who have been recorded as going to bed ill and waking up cured could argue that they have had a divine dream of healing. Whether this has taken place on a physical, mental, emotional or spiritual level is hard to prove, but what is irrefutable is that they are 'cured' of the affliction they took to bed with them. Of course, it is hard to analyse what is occurring during this process, but as long as a positive act of faith and healing has taken place, perhaps it is not necessary to delve any deeper.

Divine dreams are very beautiful and probably not a common occurrence for many people. Start to notice if they crop up in your dreamwork and appreciate them if they do. Whatever insights you receive during them, make sure that you take their special message with you out into the real world in the most positive and powerful way you can find.

Past-life Dreams

We have already talked about the concept of reincarnation and what it means in a spiritual realm. A past-life dream is where you are taken back and shown a past life which you have lived, usually with the express purpose of your being able to better understand a situation that is troubling you in the present day.

Often a past-life dream will have the sensation of an old cine-film being played out in front of us. (Perhaps this is the way in which our brain can best assimilate and understand the scenario being shown to us.) You may not at first realize that one of the people in the scene is you. The whole scene may have to unfold in front of you before you realize that one of them is actually you. It is also possible you will 'know' at that same moment that someone else in the dream is also now reincarnated as someone you know in this lifetime.

These dreams are very powerful and often insightful in a way that other dreams are not. You are moving into the realms of 'knowing' something without having to really understand it. In a past-life dream, logical reasoning is not required. You 'know' something with a deep, inner conviction that touches you on a soul level, rather than a physical or earthly level.

Within past-life dreams we may also experience what we referred to earlier as 'archetypes'. Archetypes could also be called 'soul memories'. As a consequence of our work with karmic influences and looking at why we may have chosen to reincarnate into the body we are presently in, you may be able to accept that memories of past lives, or knowledge of earlier civilizations and ancient spiritual practices, may be locked somewhere deep within the recesses of your unconscious mind. Archetypes could be described as a haunting image of part of that past memory. Interpretation of archetypes requires a deeply committed approach and cannot be accomplished easily. You might need the services of a spiritual guru to help you in this practice.

If you never have one of these dreams, it does not mean that you are missing out in any way. It means that you do not need to know the information in that dream in order to be able to progress in your present life. Alternatively, it may mean that now is not the appropriate time to work at this level.

(If you want to follow this experience through on a conscious level, there are reputable past-life therapists who can work with hypnosis and deep relaxation and encourage you to return to previous lives, so that you may better understand your present state. There is no guaranteed measure of success with this technique, but you may find it interesting.)

Do you now feel you have had other kinds of dreams and want to redefine some of the dreams you have already experienced? That is fine. There is no right or wrong way to categorize your dreams.

Defining different types of dreams is only valuable in so far as it enables you to understand more about what is happening with your own dreamwork. A word of warning: do not be tempted to decide that all your dreams fall into one easy category. It just isn't feasible. Dreamwork is very complex. The more you understand, the more there is to be understood! If you enjoy the knowledge that dreams are complicated and endlessly fascinating, it makes it easier to accept that it isn't possible to necessarily interpret them all, all of the time. Dreams are a constant challenge but we can enjoy that challenge nevertheless.

At this point, it might be helpful to recap on the questions that we can usefully apply to our dreams. These will vary according to the dream you have had, of course. Not all the questions will apply but you might find the following a useful summary.

Questions about dreamwork

- What date it is?
- Approximately what time did I dream it?
- What happened to me during the day before I went to sleep?
- What did I do differently as I was getting ready for bed?
- What influencing factors were around – TV, radio, books, etc?
- What pressing issues are there in my life right now?
- What was my state of mind as I drifted off to sleep?
- Did I make a clear affirmation about wanting to remember my dreams?
- Did I spend time relaxing before I drifted off to sleep?

Regarding the dream itself

- What was the overwhelming feeling attached to this dream?
- What factor do I remember most clearly?
- What actually happened during this dream?
- What does that mean to me – literally, symbolically?
- How is that a relevant reflection of some part of my life?
- Does this dream feel literal or symbolic?
- What does each part of my dream represent – is it a part of me?
- Who else came into my dream?
- What do they represent to me?
- What other objects were in the dream?
- What do those objects mean to me?
- What can I learn from this dream?
- What do I want to learn about myself through this dream?
- Have I been completely honest about this?

In many ways, the most important question is the last one. It cannot be stressed too much that it is your own integrity and determination to be honest at all times that will determine your personal progress.

What you will also start to notice by working much more intensively with your dreams is that they start to become more vivid. You start to remember more of them. They start to mean more to you. Analysis becomes easier. Your interest and commitment to your dreamwork will start to impact positively in all areas of your life. You want to learn more, so you are given more opportunities to learn. It is exciting.

Something else may also start to happen to you around this time. You may notice through studying your dreams more intently that they are starting to change shape. Whilst you are in the dream state itself, you may even become aware that you are dreaming and even be able to manipulate certain aspects of your dream. This is a natural state called 'lucid dreaming'. We are going to look at this phenomenon and its implications next.

LUCID DREAMS

Let's be clear about what constitutes lucid dreaming. You are dreaming lucidly when, in the midst of a dream, you realize you are dreaming. This does not mean you then have to wake up straight away, although this may be your experience when you first start having lucid dreams. You can remain in the dream, knowing you are dreaming, and see what unfolds. In this state, strange things may occur, but you accept them because you know you are dreaming. You may think 'How ridiculous' as you're dreaming, but equally your dreaming self might think, 'Well, it is a dream after all, so anything is possible'. What is the implication of the second of these two responses? It may be that you need to test whether you are really dreaming. The mind then asks for something to occur that would not be possible in reality – for instance, to suddenly make you change shape or for an object to alter into something else in front of you.

If you are having a dream and your response is 'Well this is a dream, after all, so anything is possible', then you may be entering a deeper state of lucid dreaming when you progress to being able to manipulate your dream yourself. For instance, you may be having a dream that is not to your liking. If you are in a lucid dream state when this occurs, you have the ability to acknowledge how unpleasant it is and to say to yourself. 'I've had enough of this dream. I'll wake myself up.' Frequently, the dreamer does just that, and wakes up. You may have experienced this yourself, even if it was when you were a child. Evidence seems to show that children quite often have lucid dreams.

When we are in this lucid state we can also opt to stay within a dream and then manipulate the events within it as we wish. Flying dreams often come into this category (although flying dreams are not always lucid dreams). You may be somewhere in your dream and suddenly, realizing that you are dreaming, decide that you will have yourself fly because it is a dream and you can create whatever you wish within it. You will then take off and fly like a bird through whatever scenarios you choose or are shown to you. If you have ever experienced flying dreams, you will know how wonderful and liberating they can be. It is said that in a flying dream the dreamer discards their physical body and soars upwards and outwards to higher levels of consciousness.

It is not just the decision to fly that occurs when you start to shape your lucid dreams. You might be having an experience within the dream that you decide you want to alter. Perhaps you decide to conjure up a person to have a conversation with them. You might want to change the location or to have something happen that you enjoy. Sexual dreams can be shaped in this way too. Lucid dreams are most often used to transform a negative experience in a dream into a more positive outcome.

There is an implication here that lucid dreams can be very powerful indeed and can have far-reaching consequences. There have been examples such as the experience of a person who dreamed that they flew across the world to be with someone who was unwell; the next day the person who was ill reported being aware of the dreamer being with them. So the possibilities of astral travel (the state of leaving your physical body and travelling in spirit to other locations) can be said to come into play with lucid dreaming. If one considers one can have a great deal of power within a dreaming state, then the indication is that truly anything might be possible. For instance, could one call upon any spiritual guide, even 'God' (or the name of the deity you worship) and receive enlightenment? Is it possible to travel forward in time to predict or even influence certain world events? What are the implications if one were to go back in time?

The phenomenon of lucid dreaming throws up a number of interesting theories and questions about the power and purpose of dreaming. Whilst there is a great deal we do not yet understand about lucid dreaming, documented evidence shows that we have known about lucid dreaming for a very long time. Despite the fact that well-known analysts such as Freud and Jung practically ignored the concept of lucid dreaming, many others have not.

Going back to the 5th century AD, we can find references to lucid dreaming from St Augustine who, as was mentioned previously, described his dreams as a form of divine communication with God. The Tibetans, and many other Eastern peoples, are known for their ability to remain lucid during dreams to develop a better understanding of their soul's destiny. In Saint Denys's book 'Dreams and How to Guide Them', published in the latter half of the 19th century, much is made of the significance and value of lucid dreaming.

The term 'lucid dreaming' was not coined until the early 1900s, by the Dutchman Frederick van Eeden, who was himself a prolific lucid dreamer. Further research was carried out by a number of people, including Dr Keith Hearne, Stephen La Barge and Lynn Nagel. In the 1960s, the concept of lucid dreaming became more widely known in the West when a poll of a group of normal people (i.e. not selected dreamers) revealed that a surprising 73 percent of them could recall having lucid dreams at some point in their lives. Since then many psychic societies have taken a great interest, ostensibly to assess the possibility of using lucid dreaming to contact higher deities and thus attain greater spiritual awareness. Studies continue today into this fascinating subject.

Recalling your Lucid Dreams

So can you recall any lucid dreams? They may be from your past, you may often dream lucidly or you may never have had a conscious experience of this state. No matter, it is possible to encourage the process of lucid dreaming and make your dreamwork even more powerful.

It has to be stressed that lucid dreaming is not for the novice. You really will need to have worked for some time with your dream interpretation before you can move into this field. It is not a process you can rush.

If you have already experienced lucid dreams, the chances are that so far you will have found them to be infrequent and often frustrating. There is no guarantee that a lucid dream will remain a lucid dream. What that means is that you may be having a lucid dream and decide to manipulate it, at which point you will either wake up, or the dream will revert back into a dream without your being able to control it. In other words, your ability to acknowledge it as a dream can recede and you can feel very frustrated when you wake up. It's like the euphoria you feel when you are about to have a major breakthrough in some area of your life, and then the opportunity slowly and maddeningly fades away or alters into something else, leaving you deflated and undermined. It takes perseverance and commitment to learn how to dream lucidly.

So what is the starting point? As always with dream analysis, it is your intent to embark upon this new area and your commitment to working as effectively and honestly as you can. You need to express your desire to your spiritual guides. Let them know that you want to move into this new area; ask for their help.

When you go through your relaxation before you fall asleep, include a request to your guides to help you in this new endeavour. Let them know you want to learn; that you are ready to learn. Always remember to ask for protection and wisdom to handle this new phase to the best of your ability. This does not have to be a lengthy discourse; your sincerity will give it the necessary power. Make an affirmation and repeat it before you go to sleep. It can be a very simple sentence, such as 'I have lucid dreams'. Say it three times.

Also read as much as you can about lucid dreaming. Start thinking about the implication of how enlightening it could be. Think about what you might learn from it. Go back over your Dream Diary and notice if there have been any dreams or moments in dreams where you might have tipped into a lucid dream state. Ask yourself if you really believe it is possible to have lucid dreams. If you can't accept the possibility of them, you will find it hard to embrace the experience. Really think back to any dreams you may have had when you were younger. Can you remember flying (children often have this kind of dream) or a situation where you were having a nightmare and decided to wake yourself up?

Remember that lucid dreams are about taking control. Consider where in your life you are good at taking control and where you don't manage this so effectively. What could you do to improve your ability to take control and manage your life more effectively? Can you find examples of this issue in your Dream Diary? How did those dreams manifest themselves? What was your analysis of those dreams?

Ask yourself what the word 'control' signifies to you. Some people find it a domineering and aggressive word, others find it helpful and powerful. Decide what it means to you. Give it different interpretations and see how this helps you assess your own life and your relationship with this word.

Encouraging Lucid Dreams

Now think about the word 'lucid' and your understanding of its meaning. The dictionaries give a variety of words such as 'rational' and 'understandable'. However, it is also described as meaning 'wise' and 'bright', adjectives that bring us onto words such as 'enlightenment' and 'radiance'. How might this be relevant for a lucid dream?

Start to think closely about what might happen to you in a lucid dream. Think about what you might be able to create, about what could happen to you. Let your imagination soar during this flight of fancy. It is hard for many people to create a world with no boundaries. How does that thought make you feel: a world with no boundaries? Excited? Daunted? Free? Pressured? If you could create any scenario, what would you choose?

If there were just one issue in your life you could resolve, what would it be? (That's often a hard question! Most of us have more than one area of our life that we would like to 'make better'.) How do you think that enlightenment might manifest itself to you, if there were a clear solution to this one issue? Even if you don't know yourself how to solve the situation, think about a setting that might help you. It might be the presence of a spiritual guide, it might be calling upon a particular person to talk to you during your lucid dream, it might be being shown the way out of a distressing situation. Allow yourself to consider the way forward actually being shown to you.

This is quite powerful work and it will take some reflection on your part. These are not little issues and the more you start to consider the implications of lucid dreams, the more you enter into the concept of what is 'reality' and what is 'dreaming'. Do you remember the Chinese conundrum mentioned earlier (see page 246), about whether Chou dreamt he was a butterfly or whether he was but a figment of the butterfly's dream? Focusing on such ideas will force you to expand your thinking. They will open your mind to the possibilities of looking at life and reality on another scale. Embrace these thoughts.

Fundamentally, what we are talking about with lucid dreams is the concept of control. Very few of us learn how to control our dreaming world to any great extent. However, we have control to some degree in most other areas of our life. Let us take a look at this for a moment and then relate it to our dreaming world.

Physically, most of us learn enormous control over our bodies. Think about how helpless we are as babies and how gradually we learn to control different parts of our bodies so that we can talk, walk, consume food and drink and then eliminate it, hold a pen or pencil and then write, play sports, and so on. Most of our early life is about learning how to control various parts of our body.

Emotionally, too, we go through a roller coaster of experiences and end up learning a great deal about control. Think about how freely we express ourselves as young children. We don't stop to consider the feelings of others until we are taught to do so. We cry easily, laugh easily, shout easily. As we get older, we learn control in all these areas.

Mentally, too, we learn how to focus and to concentrate more effectively as we grow. As young children, our attention span is short. There is too much to explore, too little time in which to do it all. We go from one experience to the next, hungry for everything, impatient to learn, not wanting details but simply wanting to be able to do everything all at once. We learn how to control these attitudes as we mature. We learn how to study for longer periods at school and university. We progress from watching short cartoons and children's television to enjoying longer pieces of entertainment. We learn that prolonged application can be rewarding and can improve our working life and opportunities for promotion.

Spiritually – well, what do we learn to control spiritually as we mature? The truth is that so many of us, particularly in Western society, know so little about our own spiritual path that we feel we have little or no control over it. We have learnt how meditation and working with our spiritual guides might increase our understanding of who we are spiritually and what we are meant to accomplish this time on Earth. However, control of our spirituality? That seems a rather foreign idea, doesn't it?

Perhaps by learning to control our dreaming world, we can gain not only understanding but also control over our spiritual selves. This may be a new idea for you, so take some time to digest what is being proposed.

During your work so far with dreams, we have been discussing how dreams can refer to different parts of you and your development to understanding all of you and your life in a more profound and helpful way. You have been encouraged to see images in dreams as being more than mere figments of your imagination, to put seemingly unimportant scenes into a more meaningful framework.

Would you therefore acknowledge that you have come to understand yourself spiritually on a deeper level through your dreamwork? Perhaps you feel this hasn't happened to you yet, perhaps you feel you have only just started, or perhaps you feel you have travelled some distance down this path. Whatever stage you have reached, that is right for you.

Taking Control of your Spirituality

What we want now, by encouraging lucid dreaming, is for you to learn how you might be able to take control of aspects of your spirituality to better understand your personal destiny in life and to be able to shape it. The process by which you achieve this is gradual and gentle; you will not see amazing results overnight. However, if you commit yourself to this next part of your dreamwork, you may learn how to dream lucidly and gain some insights and control as a result.

Let us be clear about the word 'control', which has negative as well as positive connotations. Do not be tempted to use lucid dreaming as a means of gaining control over others. While working with your spiritual guides, you will have come to understand that manipulation of others is not a comfortable karma to live with. You need to concentrate on your own life, not try to decide how others should live. Unless you accept others as they are, you cannot move forward with your own life.

Manipulation of others comes under the category of not accepting others as they are. Any attempts you make, therefore, to manipulate others during lucid dreaming will backfire uncomfortably on you. Your dreams are about your progress. Take responsibility for yourself, not others. Let other people get on with their own spiritual path and try not to judge or condemn them. Focus on yourself.

You have been given a lot of ideas to help increase your ability to have lucid dreams. If your intention is clear enough and it is the right time, then you will start to experience lucid dreams, slowly and gradually. When this happens, you will first of all realize you are dreaming. This will probably happen with increasingly regularity, as your Dream Diary should confirm.

However, the process of dreaming more lucidly does not immediately give you control over your dreams. Initially what happens is that you start to notice that you are dreaming as you dream. The clues may be various. You may know you are in dream mode because you can see things happening that aren't 'normal'. It may be that you have a sensation of control that isn't usual. Sometimes, it just hits you with a pleasing sense of 'This is good, I can have fun now'. It may be you are not enjoying the dream and want to change it, so you become aware you are dreaming in order to do so.

Stage One

The early stage of lucid dreaming is a pleasant state to find yourself in. It is rather as though you have been given a new toy which, although you aren't quite sure what to do with it, you know is going to be fun to play with! However, having a new game and knowing how to play it are two different things.

You now have to learn the game of Lucid Dreaming – and the rules aren't that clear cut. They can change, according to the individual. You will partly have to make up your own rules, and learn the consequences as you go along. That is why working with lucid dreams really is only for adults who can accept responsibility and its repercussions.

You may find as soon as you discover you are dreaming lucidly that you wake up. This is normal and it may take you a while to train yourself out of this. As soon as you realize it is a lucid dream, try saying to yourself, 'I will not wake up. I will stay in this dream.' You can train yourself to stay asleep but it may take a while for you to pass on from this stage.

You may then find that when you fall asleep again, lucid dreams escape you for a while. Trust that they will return. You may reach a stage where lucid dreaming causes you to wake up, but when you fall asleep again you return to the dream and can continue as before.

Stage Two

Once you have found yourself able to stay in a lucid dream without waking up, you can slowly progress to the next stage, which is learning how to control the dream in some way. It is suggested that you start by manipulating small areas of the dream first. For instance, if you are dreaming about someone in a particular scenario, don't decide that you will change the person into someone else and change the setting completely. You will find trying to create big changes frustrating because you won't probably be able to gain that degree of control initially and the effort of trying to do so will only prompt you to wake up.

Look at a small area within the dream and see if you can change it. By making small alterations, you are learning gradually how to take control. Perhaps you might decide that you want to make that chair a little bigger, or place a cushion upon it. Maybe you want to make a chocolate bar suddenly appear in front of you. It can be a relatively trivial change, one you find fun rather than profound. When you do accomplish some small act of control within the dream, remember to acknowledge that.

Be satisfied with what you have done, rather than immediately wanting more. Be content to learn slowly. If you try to rush this process, whatever you try to do will backfire because you will keep waking yourself up. It is also possible to slip back into dreaming mode whereby you go out of the lucid dreaming state. You might go from knowing you are dreaming to finding yourself back in another dream and not able to recognize it as a dream or to take control in any way.

There are no hard and fast rules for lucid dreaming. You will work at your own speed and in your own way. All you can be assured of is that the more slowly and gently you take this process, the more successful you will be.

Lucid dreams can also be extremely profound, as we will discover. However, you may not want to reach this stage for a while. You may want to spend some time having fun first. Why not? You deserve to enjoy yourself and it really can be fun.

You can do all sorts of liberating things that are denied to you in normal everyday life. Try telling yourself you will fly. Let yourself soar upwards and outwards. See where your journey takes you. If you find you can't fly properly in one dream, try again on another occasion. Sometimes you will be able to fly and at other times you will find it hard or impossible. You might want to create a space-craft and let that take you up into the universe. Imagine a large bird coming into your dream, then sit upon its feathers and let it take you up into the sky. Dreams of flying and lifting yourself upwards and outwards are all about increasing your consciousness onto other levels. See what happens to you when you take this decision.

Whatever you have wanted to do in real life, you can try in your dreams. Have you wanted to climb a tall mountain or go rafting through rapids? Try it in your dream! Is there a dream person to whom you would love to be married? Conjure them up and see what happens. Perhaps you have always wanted to play your favourite sport with a sporting hero. Ask that they come and play a game with you.

Your lucid dreams can also become wish-fulfilment dreams. Enjoy it all. Always try to notice the point at which you no longer have control. There is always a point at which control is taken away from you. Make a note of it and then ask yourself why. What is your lesson to be learnt at that particular point?

Lucid dreams can also change direction suddenly and what you were thoroughly enjoying becomes less wonderful. How does this reflect an area of your 'real' life? Is someone else involved who you have been trying to manipulate? What do you have to learn from that?

Stage Three

Once you have experimented for a while and worked with the lighter, less demanding side of controlling dreams, you might want to progress to another level. Perhaps you are becoming aware that there is much more you can do through lucid dreaming, over and above indulging in enjoyable wish fulfilment. However, the latter is important because you need to know that control is possible and can have a positive outcome. You need to learn how to trust your own abilities before you move on.

Try to stop during a lucid dream and ask yourself what would be the most powerful thing to have happen in this dream. In other words, take the time to consider what would benefit you most. You are now progressing from letting your ego dictate a situation to trying to find a bigger, more insightful way forward. If you acknowledge you could have control but choose to relinquish that control to a higher and wiser source, that is the act of a truly spiritual being. This is a deep and difficult area into which to move and you may not choose to do this for some time.

When it is right for you, you will find yourself being led into this new area gently and kindly by your spiritual guides. They will give you an indication that the time is right and some of your dreams will enter a new realm as a result.

It is difficult to find words to express what this entails. Think of moments when you have had what could only be described as an unearthly experience, often involving great sorrow or joy or great emotion. This experience will be personal to you. Someone might remember the moment their child was born and equate it with that. Others might say a great sporting moment elated them beyond words. Someone might describe a great moment in their working life when, say, an ambition was achieved. For others, it might be paying off their mortgage, or being told their cancer has not returned and they have the 'all clear'. What might seem insignificant to you is of enormous importance to someone else.

You can experience those great moments in your dreams, on a spiritual level. This is where a lucid dream can lead you into the realms of a powerful divine dream. However, when you have a lucid dream that involves divine intervention, then you are talking about communication on a truly profound level. Not everyone will experience this in their dreams, but those who do recognize that they have been blessed and feel extremely privileged. You can call upon this sort of experience in lucid dreaming. How is this possible?

The answer lies in bringing together the three techniques we have been talking about throughout this book: meditation, spiritual guides and dreamwork. The final part takes us into this new realm of discovery and appreciation.

PART FOUR:

PUTTING IT ALL TOGETHER

THE POWER OF COMBINING

Why combine all three areas of development: meditation, contact with spiritual guides and dreamwork? This is a relevant question. We have already seen how meditation is quite separate from the energy required to work with spiritual guides and that dreamwork takes us into yet another realm. How can we possibly combine all three to make something even more powerful?

The answer is that we have already been doing this in certain respects but we are now going to look at the combining process in more detail and see just how powerful it can become.

We have already been combining some of these techniques, as you are no doubt aware. For instance, you were encouraged to learn how to relax for meditations, which helped you to contact your spiritual guides. It was also suggested that you use these relaxation techniques before you went to sleep. Relaxation is a constant theme running through this book.

Relaxation is inextricably linked to our breathing. We cannot relax unless we slow our breathing down and breathe more deeply. You have been asked to focus on your breathing during every part of your work with meditation, contact with spiritual guides and preparation for sleep and dreamtime. Hopefully, your appreciation of your own breathing system and how beautiful and wonderful it is has increased immeasurably since you began to pay more attention to how your body works.

Throughout this book you have been encouraged to appreciate your personal progress. Your first steps in meditation were basically a celebration of your appreciation of life in all spheres. Remember back to the Food Appreciation exercise (page 25) and then your meditations on shopping (page 53) and even rubbish (page 56). Perhaps you have now forgotten doing them, in which case why not revisit them and see what comes up for you now? Maybe you have taken their insights with you and incorporated them into your daily life. How often do you do your Waking Up exercise (page 45)? Do you stop to appreciate aspects of nature and beautiful things around you much more than you used to? Have you been improving the quality of your life through frequent mini meditations?

When you started your communication with spiritual guides you were constantly reminded to thank them for presenting themselves to you and to truly appreciate their energies and their unconditional love. Have you remembered to continue this state of appreciation? Do you always say 'thank you', do you always remember to feel gratitude for what is being given to you? It is easy to forget sometimes. Did you stop during your spiritual guide work and realize how far you had come? Can you remember back to when you felt very little contact with anything or anyone? Can you remember how you felt when you began to forge links, no matter how tenuous? Have you forgotten to acknowledge yourself for this?

With your dreamwork, you have been asked to enjoy going at your own pace and to remember to keep acknowledging your progress without needing to compare it to that of others. You have been reminded to keep your Dream Diary up to date and to constantly check back and see how far you have come: for example, how much more you remember, how easier your dreams are becoming to analyse.

It is so important that you take the time to stop and appreciate your progress and also to thank and appreciate what is around you. The more you accept where you are right now, without striving to be somewhere else, the more you pave the way to move forward and to progress to greater understanding and awareness on all levels. Acceptance and appreciation are powerful tools in your personal development.

Your commitment is vital to progress in the three areas you have been working with. You will probably notice that whichever area you have shown the greatest interest in and have found the most useful will be the one where you have seen the best progress. The more you are clear about your commitment to learning something, the more you want to learn, and the more effort you are willing to put into it, the greater your reward. The areas in which you have shown the greatest hesitation or scepticism are likely to have yielded the least results. Your whole approach to a scenario determines how powerful the outcome will be.

We can relate this to a personal sphere and say that if you have an issue in your life you want to resolve, your commitment to resolving it has to be rock solid. Then you are likely to find your solution. If you approach the situation full of doubts, cynicism, or with an attitude of 'There probably isn't a solution to this, but I suppose I ought to try', the outcome will probably not be very rewarding.

What areas have you had doubts about during your study of these subjects? Have you stopped to really ask yourself why you feel this way? So often we let our lives be dictated by old, redundant thoughts running around inside our head. We were brought up to believe a certain thing, so therefore we are conditioned to believe that is the only way to think. It is hard for us to erase our old thoughts and record new ones.

Yet you are the sole owner of these thoughts, they are only yours. You can choose to exchange your thought processes; you can choose to embrace new concepts and to learn from them. You stopped the progress; you can also decide to start it again.

That is why affirmations may be very useful for you. We only brought affirmations into use during Part Three but they can be valuable in any area of your progress. Say, for example, that you were very clear about wishing to communicate with a particular spiritual guide. Why not use a powerful affirmation to call upon them before you go into your meditation?

If you were to go through your day saying 'I am calm and relaxed', how do you think that might impact on your day? Of course, initially this might feel very false, particularly if you are rushing from one task to another. However, reprogramming our thoughts does take time and effort, so be prepared to persevere.

Effort can be synonymous with commitment. By effort I don't mean straining and struggling; I mean your degree of commitment. Given your life style, perhaps finding ten minutes a day to relax and meditate is an effort. To someone else, their effort might be finding an hour because that is what is suitable for them. Your degree of effort shows your degree of commitment. This does not mean you are a lesser person if you find less time to meditate than someone else. What matters is that you set your own standards and don't compare them to others'. The truth is you know your own situation best. You know yourself whether you can find regular periods of time for daily meditations without it being a great problem.

The other attitude you have been asked to adopt throughout is one of honesty. You have been encouraged to just be yourself throughout all these exercises, nothing else. This personal work is about letting go of our outer barriers and shedding the face we present to the world. We can just be ourselves, warts and all, whether we are meditating, contacting spiritual guides or interpreting our very personal dreams. Unless we are honest, we can't really progress onto better levels of understanding.

Of course, we shouldn't forget that it is often necessary for us to protect ourselves out there in the 'real' world, especially if we work in vulnerable professions such as policing, nursing or other public services. When we travel on crowded public transport and interact constantly with a wide cross-section of society, we have to be able to bring our cloak of protection about us when needed. We have to know how to shut off safely. Often we have to put on a bright face when necessary in front of work colleagues, children or people whose needs are greater than our own.

However, the process of going on to shed all those layers and just becoming ourselves again can become more difficult. Often we have built up so many different defence mechanisms that we have virtually forgotten how to let go of them. This is where our personal development comes into practice. To be truly powerful in our spiritual growth, we have no choice but to truly be ourselves. Our soul never lies. Sometimes we might want to hide from the truth, which is when we put up blocks and prevent ourselves from seeing the truth.

It is when we have the courage to let those blocks melt away and to move past our fears and insecurities that we allow ourselves to work powerfully. This is true of whatever realm we are working in, although it could be argued that in our dreams our true selves are always being revealed. Yet we know we won't see ourselves that way unless we choose to analyse our dreams properly. Even when we have the chance to see something clearly for what it is, we can still put up blocks to try to protect ourselves. Likewise, a spiritual guide might come to us with a specific message relating to a particular issue we are facing. Yet we may choose to misinterpret that message or take it on another level and thereby miss the point of the message.

In other words, our own honesty and integrity determine to a large extent how well we progress. No matter how much spiritual work you do, no matter how often you meditate, no matter how many guides you contact, or how many vivid, insightful dreams you may recall, it all comes to very little if you are not honest about the information you receive.

Another factor that creeps into these different techniques is something we have not mentioned so far – laziness. This does not mean that you may not bother to meditate or you may forget to keep your Dream Diary up to date. Laziness refers to our methods of working, and getting into bad habits with them.

You can compare it to driving. Most people who are drivers can remember when they took their test. You are so nervous, with every part of you straining to do everything right. You take enormous care with every manoeuvre, painstakingly putting all your efforts into that test because you care so very much. What happens once you have passed and your initial nervousness about being a novice driver wears off? If we are honest (that word again!) most of us would have to acknowledge that we let ourselves slip into bad habits.

So it is with personal development. If we do not keep applying what we have learnt to our everyday life, we forget. You may think you have absorbed a great deal of information and that you are now quite well versed in the three areas we have been working on. Below is a quiz for you. See how you fare.

What Have You Absorbed?

- How many major chakras are there? Describe each one: where it is in your body, its associated colour and meaning. Then write down how you personally feel about each one.

- What essential oils might be beneficial in meditation or working with spiritual guides? What are essential oils?

- What is the purported use of the celestine crystal? Name other crystals that might enhance your personal development.

- What exactly is a lucid dream? How many have you had? Check back through your Dream Diary.

- Describe in detail every aspect of your private Cleansing Sanctuary, going through sight, smell, taste, touch, hearing. Do the same with your personal cloak of protection.

• What is a mantra? How often do you use one? How is it different from a yantra? When was the last time you worked with a yantra?

• Write down what you think of the concept of reincarnation. Be honest. How many other books have you read on this subject?

• List twenty things in your present life that you appreciate and for which you give thanks. Do this within three minutes. Time yourself!

• When was the last time you used sound during your meditations and dreamwork? How many different kinds of sound appreciation have you experimented with?

• Describe, in detail, how the breathing system works in the human body. Draw yourself a rough diagram of how it appears to you.

• Describe what the word 'karma' means. What have you learnt about your own karmic path through the personal development work you have done so far?

Did you find some of these questions surprisingly hard? Congratulations if you answered them all easily: you're a real scholar! If you could answer only a few of them, don't worry. The purpose of the quiz was not to make you feel inferior or inadequate. It is simply to show you that we all become lazy. We forget to use information we have been given or we take what is shown to us and then forget how to apply it in the most effective way. We all tend to do this; it is human nature. The quiz is purely to point out to you areas of your development that you may have forgotten to use fully.

How did you get on with the very first question? For many people the chakras are a very grey area in their development. Many people say that the chakras are all rather complicated and they can't actually feel them in their body anyway, so how powerful can they be? As long as you breathe properly, you are opening up and therefore receptive to outside energies. This is true, of course, but also ask yourself what else you are missing out on because you are only choosing to be on one particular level of awareness.

The chakras are the most powerful information centre we possess. Many aware people would describe the chakras as their door from the physical world to higher spiritual realms. If you spend very little or no time focusing on the chakras and tuning in to them, how can you expect to receive powerful insights? You have to choose to locate these doors, open them up and then step outside. You also have to open them to enable your spiritual guides to come through and communicate meaningfully with you. If you have not yet developed a strong relationship with your chakras, don't worry; we are going to do more work with them during the next chapter.

As you can see, there are many common threads running through the different techniques we have been exploring. If we try to integrate them even more, what will this do for us? How can it make us more effective?

The best way for us to discover this is to go ahead and try it. We are going to look first at integrating meditation and spiritual guides.

MEDITATION AND SPIRITUAL GUIDES

Some of you will no doubt be thinking there is an obvious connection between these two areas because when you contact a spiritual guide you are basically entering a meditative state. In other words, the two are parts of a whole and you are using them in conjunction with each other already. They cannot be separated.

This is certainly true, but it is only part of the story. You are indeed going into a meditative state when you communicate with your spiritual guides. However, there are degrees of meditation and there are degrees of contact with spiritual guides. What we want to look at now is how we can work more deeply on both levels and, by truly combining the two, forge much stronger links with ourselves and our spiritual guides.

To work truly powerfully with both meditation and communication with spiritual guides, you have to be willing to let yourself sink even deeper into a relaxed state. This is more difficult for some than others. You may feel you are already relaxing properly, but there are always greater depths of meditation into which you can delve.

First and foremost, you have to increase your focus and to release all current, outside factors and any worrying thoughts nagging you. Go back and spend time on some of the earlier exercises we worked with, such as Playing with Numbers (page 79) and the Candle Flame (page 81). You want to be able to really lose your conscious self as we move into this new area, and to greet your higher self or enter a state of greater awareness with a clear, empty mind and body.

To help this process, here is yet another breathing technique, yogic in origin, which should help your concentration. It has some similarities to the Alternate Nostril Breathing (page 117) but you use both nostrils without restriction. If you find this exercise too difficult or it makes you feel light-headed or dizzy, keep the count low. As always, you need some time alone and undisturbed for this to be effective, so make sure you are not going to be disturbed. If you are congested nasally in any way, blow your nose before you start. You must breathe in and out through your nose, not your mouth, during this exercise.

Two to one breathing

Go into your favourite, quiet location and give yourself time to relax. Make sure your body is physically comfortable. Close your eyes.

This breathing is based on a 2:1 ratio. This means that as we count, the first number is always twice the second number. Start with a simple 2:1 ratio as follows.

Breathe in slowly and comfortably to a silent, slow count of two. Hold your breath in for one count. Breathe out to the count of two. Hold your breathe out for one count. Then repeat for as long as you feel comfortable. Stop if you feel dizzy. The exercise is summarized as follows:

Breathe in for two.
Hold breath for one.
Breathe out for two.
Hold out for one.

Remember to count silently and very slowly. The slower your count, the more space you will allow yourself to relax and to slow your body's mechanism. You can use the ticking of a clock if you want to make sure you keep your breathing even throughout. Your attention should only be on the breathing itself and the counting. This is an excellent way of ridding yourself of the day's stresses and encouraging a deeper state of relaxation.

Now try a 4:2 count, the ratio you really want to work with. When you feel ready, try: breathing in for four; holding in for two; breathing out for four; holding out for two. Repeat.

Do you find the 4:2 count too difficult? Return to the 2:1 ratio for a few weeks and don't try to increase the count until you feel more relaxed and ready to do so. Once you have reached 4:2 without a struggle, stay at this level for at least a month or two. Remember to keep the count slow and steady. Then, when you feel ready, you can try 6:3:6:3. If you try this and find it difficult, return to the 4:2 ratio. There are higher ratios – for example, 8:4, 10:5, 12:6 and so on – and you might want to try working towards them. If you do, go very slowly and gently, otherwise you may feel dizzy.

The object of this breathing is not to struggle to hold your breath for long periods because the essence of meditation is relaxation, not struggle. The joy of working slowly and gently with this breathing technique is that you gradually come to realize that you can slow your breathing down more and more and it is not an effort. You find yourself breathing deeply and fully and it becomes a wonderful sensation.

That is the point of this exercise. You are encouraging yourself to slow down even more, physically, and by breathing even more deeply, you are giving yourself the opportunity of discovering yet deeper realms of relaxation.

At the end of each breathing session, make sure you give yourself a few minutes to withdraw your focus from your breath. If you have spent some time in this relaxed state, you may find it a bit of an effort to withdraw yourself. Do this by stopping the counting and focusing on your physical body. Notice how heavy it feels and which parts of your body are resting against a solid surface. Wriggle your toes and fingers and then gradually stretch and flex your muscles. Open your eyes and focus on an object for a few minutes. Get up slowly.

If at any point you find yourself struggling with this exercise or not enjoying it, try returning to the Alternate Nostril Breathing (page 117) exercise for a while. This is particularly useful to balancing your energies and may help better prepare you for the Two to One Breathing. If you want to deepen the breathing, use your mind: envisage your lungs positioned somewhere deep in your stomach area, as discussed during the Stomach Breathing exercise (page 37).

Make sure you work with this Two to One Breathing technique for at least a month before you move on to work with the next set of exercises. This exercise should help you to discover an even deeper, darker, more velvety level of peace inside of you. If this is happening, then you are ready to progress to another level and will indeed be able to do so.

The Chakras

On this new level we're going to work with our chakras. As we discussed at the end of the last chapter, most of us forget how fundamental the chakras are to our personal development. Because we in the West have only recently discovered the existence of the chakras (although they have been acknowledged in Eastern cultures for thousands of years), they feel as though they are a relatively new phenomenon and somewhat mystical and unfathomable.

You may have found your eyes glazing over as you were reading about the description of each chakra in Part One. Perhaps you found yourself skipping over this section or just taking the bare essentials from it and then not thinking much more about the chakras. This is quite a natural reaction, and some novices would probably acknowledge that they often feel a sense of vague irritation when teachers harp on about the significance and power of the chakras. You may feel you will let other people enjoy the power of them but you can't help the fact that they elude you!

A way of helping you through this barrier is to spend some time focusing on the areas of your body where the chakras reside and to let the sensation of each chakra draw you into a meditation. We are also going to allow a spiritual guide to come into this with us to try to strengthen our relationship with each chakra and to help increase our own understanding of this complex energy system.

For these exercises, you are not going to have to concentrate on what you think you ought to know about each chakra. You are going to be encouraged to let all that preconceived knowledge fly away and see what insights come to you when you experience the chakras on a personal basis. Reading what other scholars tell you the chakras mean is likely to leave you feeling nonplussed by them! By personalizing the chakra experience, you may finally realize how wonderful and powerful they can be tools to enhance higher awareness.

These exercises are quite freeing in the sense that they are about experiencing on a deeper level of consciousness, without preconceived ideas and without trying to achieve anything tangible. In previous meditations, you have often been asked to look at a specific issue in your life, or to focus on a word, picture, image or feeling. Now you are going to let that go. As long as you have been using the various breathing techniques to prepare you, you should be ready for this new experience.

You may not want to work through all the chakras in one sitting. You may find some chakras more challenging or more emotional than others. If you aren't able to work deeply with certain chakras, that is fine, as long as you are gentle with yourself and allow healing to come through from your guides to help you in this respect. If you have already started a Chakra Diary, as was previously suggested, you can use the outcome of these exercises to add to your understanding.

By now you should be more than familiar with your process of preparation for meditation. But have you become lazy over this? Look back over the Meditation check list on page 60. Have you been following these points on a regular basis? You may only be guilty of some slight omission such as not drinking water afterwards, or not always wearing loose, comfortable clothing but these are still key factors that can influence your success. How much have you been working with outside influences such as sound and scents? Have you been using different incense or trying different sounds? If not, experiment now. It is never too late to try.

For each of the chakras, decide you will try a different piece of music or a different kind of sound. Don't spend a long time deliberating over it, simply choose what instinctively feels right. If you start your meditation and the sound is distracting, then change it or opt for silence. Also try different incense or oils, again using your intuition to see what feels right for each chakra. Make a note of what you use so that you can compare results. If you want to try a different position or location for each meditation, that is fine, too, as long as you are not going to be disturbed.

First and foremost with these exercises, your intention is to clear your mind and to let yourself simply 'be'. This means do not try to relax, do not try to breathe deeply, do not try to concentrate intently on the area of your body in question, do not try to do anything. Simply let all your troubles melt away and 'be'. When ready, start with the base chakra.

Base chakra meditation with guide

Take time to relax in your chosen position. Focus on your breathing. Let everything else float away into the background and gradually disappear altogether.

Now take your focus into your body to the base of your spine. Feel yourself melt into this area of your body and fuse with it. Your mind and the base of your spine are as one. Rest in this state of awareness. Become finely attuned to the energy at the base of your spine. Don't try to experience anything. Let yourself melt into it.

If a feeling comes into your consciousness, float with that feeling without consciously trying to analyse it. If a scent or sound comes into you, become that smell or noise. You are part of everything and flow with it. Melt into everything. If there is a taste in your mouth, become that taste. Explore this space without effort. Feel your own personal energy pulse with the base of your spine. Realize they are one and the same thing.

Let your awareness of this area deepen yet further. Notice what you are experiencing without questioning it. Let the sensations wash over you without trying to create anything yourself. You are being, not trying to be.

Realize there is an opening within this space; it may be a door, a window, a funnel of light or a large tube. This is personal to you. It is an opening that is bright and inviting. You are the keeper of this opening. You decide when it is open or closed. What is it now? Decide it should be wide open. Open the space and let light enter.

As you rest in this state of relaxed awareness, allow your base chakra guide to come into this new space you have found. Don't force them to come. Don't ask them to be with you. Simply trust. The opening is there, ready for them to enter through. Let them come into your base chakra. You are ready for their wisdom. Allow them to appear.

Do not decide what they will look like. Let yourself have no preconceived ideas. When they enter, however they manifest themselves, welcome them. They are here to help you with their unconditional love. Know they will not hurt you, whatever their shape or size. Rest quietly in this state with them. They may speak, they may communicate telepathically or they may be silent, simply making you feel comfortable and safe in their presence. Appreciate them being with you. Thank them for spending time with you.

They will know when it is time for them to go. They will leave through the same opening and fade into the light beyond. Let them go, but know that they will return when the time is right.

As soon as they have gone, then close the opening, firmly. Remember you hold the key to this opening, no one else. You decide when you will open and close it. Close it now. Lock it.

Now bring your awareness back to your everyday life. Let your focus pull back from the base of your spine and acknowledge your whole body. Stretch out your limbs slowly, wriggle your fingers and toes. Remember where you are resting, in which room, in which building. Think about what day of the week it is, what time it is.

Open your eyes when you feel ready. Are you feeling grounded? Does your body feel heavy? If everything feels very light and bright, then you may not be closed down properly. Remember to cleanse and protect yourself. Keep your cloak of protection around you for the rest of the day. Keep checking it is with you and you have not let it slip away.

When you have returned to your everyday reality, remember to make notes about what happened to you during this exercise. If you leave it too long, the details may fade from your memory, just as your dream recall tends to do. Try to be specific about what you felt, saw, etc. If you saw any particular colours, then note down what they were. Always be honest. If you did not like some of what you experienced, that is fine.

Our chakras go through different phases, just as we do in other areas of our life. There are times when certain chakras may feel blocked or when they may feel open wide as though they are leaking energy. They may feel hot or cold, tight or relaxed. Perhaps they feel bright and 'zingy' one day and dull and lethargic the next. Perhaps some chakras feel dark and mysterious, others light and happy. What adjectives apply to your base chakra after the previous exercise? (One of the many positive benefits of articulating our experiences in personal development is that we rediscover so many adjectives that we have forgotten how to use!)

If you found yourself being taken on a journey during the exercise, try to remember the details of the journey you went on. Did you travel out through the opening of your chakra? If not, where were you taken?

Remember to really question what happened to you during this free meditation. Make clear notes about your base chakra guide and how they made you feel. It is all right if you weren't immediately drawn to them. Your own relationship with your base chakra will be reflected in how they chose to present themselves to you. All the work you have done on your dream analysis may now help you as you analyse what happened during this meditation. Always acknowledge the emotion that accompanied each experience, particularly as your guide approached. Be honest.

Your intention during the meditation was not to force anything or to try to take control in any way. Do you think you honestly accomplished this? Your only task was to take responsibility for the opening and closing of your chakra. Was this difficult for you or did it happen without effort? If you know there were moments when you chose to take control during the meditation and you slipped back into a more shallow state of consciousness, that is fine. Make a note about when this happened and why it might have been.

Remember that working with the chakras makes us vulnerable. As well as keeping your cloak of protection around you for the rest of the day, notice if you feel more emotional than usual. If you do, you have probably not closed down properly or cleansed enough. Ensure you do this more thoroughly next time. When you are ready, move on to the next chakra.

Navel chakra meditation with guide

Remember to take your time to relax and open up. Spend some time concentrating on your breathing. Do not force anything. Let yourself relax. Enjoy the process.

Bring your attention to the area just below your navel (belly button). Feel your consciousness melt into this area. Move right through into your body and let your focus go out the back somewhere through your lower spine. Now let your focus be drawn to an area somewhere in the middle between these two points, somewhere deep in the heart of your lower stomach. Rest in this space.

Do not question anything. Let your mind focus on this area and then melt into it, become as one. Flow into the pulsing beat of this area. Let your senses run free. See what is being shown to you, hear it, feel it, smell it, touch it, taste it. Wallow in the experience. Become it. You and your navel chakra are one.

Let sensations come and go. Do not hold on to them. Bury your awareness deeper and deeper in this area. Really experience what it is like. If you are floating back and forth between the front and back of your body in this area, that is fine. Just observe what is happening to you.

Now feel this area opening both front and back. Sense it in the way that is appropriate for you. Allow it to open wide, knowing you are safe and secure.

Now allow your navel chakra guide to come into this space. Become open and receptive, without conditions. You are calm and relaxed as you wait quietly. You are floating in a state of knowing that they will come to you.

When they approach, observe through which opening they appear, either front or back. Welcome them. However they manifest themselves, welcome their presence. Allow them to communicate with you in their chosen method. Whatever happens, it is right for you at this time. If you simply rest silently together in this space you have discovered, that is enough. Thank them for being there.

They will know when the time is right for them to go. As they leave, notice which opening they retreat through. Let them fade into the light beyond and know they will return.

Take your focus away from your navel area and pull back to acknowledge all of your body. Feel how heavy and relaxed it is. Wriggle your body a little, stretch your arms overhead. Open your eyes and notice if you are grounded. Cleanse and protect yourself.

As you make notes in your Chakra Diary also notice the difference between the two chakra exercises. They will probably have been very different experiences. Try to understand why they were so distinct. How did the guides differ? What was similar about them? Remember to note down any particular colours, sensations or revelations that occurred.

As has been mentioned before, the navel chakra is a particular hotbed of emotion and can be quite difficult to penetrate. If you feel you have not progressed as well with this chakra as with the base chakra, do not worry or feel that something is wrong with you. Many memories are stored within this chakra, including issues we may find confrontational. Work at your own pace.

Once you have done two different chakra exercises, you then have a better means through which you can appreciate how different these energies are within you. If you work through all the chakras and have a similar response to them all, then you know you are not working at a deep level. Once you let go of your preconceived ideas and let yourself flow into the energy of each chakra, you can truly appreciate how wonderful and how complex your subtle energy system is. If you can release yourself from old concepts, it is inspiring how insights can flow into and through your chakras. It is a very liberating and joyful experience.

If you have trouble at any point identifying the exact part of your physical body to which each chakra corresponds, look back over the diagram of the chakras on page 136 and refresh your memory. You can also try running your hand lightly over that area of your body. Where do you feel the energies change, either becoming more powerful or simply different in some way? Use your own innate awareness to help you. Move on to the next chakra when you feel ready.

Solar plexus chakra meditation with guide

Give yourself time to settle and relax. Focus on your breathing. As you feel yourself relax deeper and deeper, tell yourself that you will not let your thoughts interfere with this meditation. Allow yourself to be free to just 'be' without conditions.

Now let yourself sink into the area of your body just below your ribcage. Melt into it. Drift into the new consciousness. There are again two openings, front and back. Let yourself float back and forth between each until you find a velvety area you want to sink into. Then let yourself sink even deeper. Deeper. Become one with this area. Experience it completely. Notice what surfaces without your having to do anything. Let yourself ebb and flow with the sensations. If conscious thoughts drift into this area, wash them away. Then return back to your wonderfully inky depths of relaxation. Observe what comes and go without judging.

Become aware that both openings are now open. Allow your solar plexus spiritual guide to come to you. Don't ask. Just let it be. Thank them as they approach, however they manifest themselves. Become the experience of them. Don't question. Don't think. Just be. Enjoy what they are communicating to you.

As they eventually move away again into the outer realms of consciousness, notice through which opening they leave. Then close the opening firmly and lock it after them. Close the other opening as well. Feel safe and secure.

Now let yourself return to your everyday life. Retreat from your solar plexus area. Focus on all of your body and its present position. Stretch your muscles slowly. Open your eyes. Rest quietly for a while before you get up. Remember to cleanse, close and protect yourself.

As you work your way up through the chakras, you will start to notice more and more how each chakra has a completely different energy. You will wonder why you haven't been so aware of it before (unless you have already been spending a lot of time on your chakra awareness, in which case you should acknowledge yourself for that).

Make notes of what this chakra felt like. Did you notice more conscious thought creeping in at this level? Perhaps you noticed less. Try to remember everything you can and jot it down as soon as possible.

As we move on to the next chakra, acknowledge that the energies are becoming finer, lighter and brighter now. Accept that they will feel differently without prejudging how they ought to feel. Remain committed to not letting your everyday thoughts intrude into your meditation.

Heart chakra meditation with guide

> You know this is a very powerful chakra and can arouse strong emotions. Make sure you are not going to be disturbed and have plenty of time for this meditation. Give yourself a little extra time for your breathing and relaxation. Choose your position with care. Ensure you are deeply relaxed before you continue.
>
> Now let yourself sink into the area above your chest and in the middle of your breastbone. Slide into this energy without effort and conscious thought. You may immediately feel yourself awash with various sensations. Go with that, if it happens. Let yourself become those sensations without worrying about them. Feel yourself fall deeper into the experience.
>
> Do not become personally involved. Let yourself float back and forth without owning any feelings. Just become them and then let them recede and allow other experiences to wash over you. You are an empty receptacle who fills with a sensation and then allows it to empty again. You are everything and are nothing. You do not judge or place conditions on experiences. You simply become them and then move on and change again as the next experience comes upon you, like a chameleon.

Now become aware of the two openings, one on each side of you. Let both of them open wide. Know you are safe. Allow your heart chakra spiritual guide to come into your heart chakra. However they appear, thank them for coming to you. Rest in their presence. Don't ask them questions or place needs on them, simply be. Let them do whatever is right and rest in a position of trust.

As they turn to go, thank them again. The experience may have been powerful for you, but whatever you absorbed, remember to let it bob away again, like a small boat bobbing on a large sea. You are an empty vessel. As they leave, close both openings after them.

Now you are ready to return to your other life. Withdraw from your heart chakra. You might find this difficult if it was a powerful meditation and you felt strongly drawn to your guide, but remember it is time to take control again. Withdraw from your heart chakra and return your focus to your physical body. Stretch and flex your muscles. Wriggle toes and fingers. As you open your eyes, remember which room you are in, what day it is, what hour of the day.

Take special care to cleanse and close down after this chakra. The heart chakra can open so easily on a variety of occasions and you need to remember to protect it properly. Keep your cloak of protection around you for the rest of the day. If any sensations linger after this exercise, make sure you keep cleansing them away using your favourite technique.

If you find you have more to say about this chakra, good. Some of you may have less to say but have felt stronger emotions without necessarily understanding them. Notice, as you fill in your Chakra Diary, whether your analysis is really happening now or whether you tried to analyse things during your meditation itself. Did you let your conscious thoughts slip in and interfere? It doesn't mean you are 'bad' if they did! What matters is that you acknowledge what went on and record it truthfully.

How powerful a figure was your heart chakra guide? This chakra houses so much emotional activity that often people find their guide in this area is particularly clear or strong as an image. If nothing happened for you, that is also fine.

It is worth mentioning here that if you are discovering chakras where there seem to be no guides, that is also fine. It doesn't mean they aren't there; it just means you are not necessarily allowing them the space into which they can come and join you. Another way to put this is that the guides are there for you, but at this stage you are not able to 'see' them. Simply make a note if this is happening and try on another occasion to see if you can allow your guide to come through to you.

It might also help you to be reminded that your guides can manifest themselves in different ways. If you are still trying to 'see' them, you may be disappointed. It is possible that with different chakras, you may only be able to sense a guide or to hear but not see a guide, or that they come to you in a guise you do not recognize. That is why it is important, however they manifest themselves, to give thanks and to appreciate them exactly as they have shown themselves to you.

It is also not necessary to have names for your guides. If you know who they are, whether it is through sound, smell, hearing or seeing, why do you need to imbue them with earthly names? Your guides are personal to you, so there is no need for you to discuss them with others, which is possibly the only other reason why you would need to have names for them. In the early stages, you may have needed to know their name to call upon them, but now at this deeper level of working you know you can bring them into your energy through your thought processes alone, without having to endow them with an earthly name.

As we work at these deeper levels, you want to be encouraged to let go of your ego and to see how it can trap you into earthly, human behaviour. This is not to say there is anything wrong with that, of course. We are here on Earth to live as humans and have all those human experiences. However, when you want to lift yourself in order to reach spiritual realms, anything you can do to divert your thoughts from everyday concerns will help. You are no doubt aware that the very physical and human parts of you are so easily called up that it is hard to shed some of them, even temporarily.

Since we are now working higher up the chakra system and reaching more and more into these spiritual realms of consciousness, it might be helpful to think more about how you can shed, albeit fleetingly, some of your very physical responses to life. Move on to the next chakra when you feel ready.

Throat chakra meditation with guide

The energies are becoming finer now as we move up the chakra system. If you find it more difficult to feel the chakras at these higher vibrations, try cupping the front of your throat gently with your two hands. Move them gently up and down your throat. When can you feel the energy change? Move a hand around to the back of your neck and slowly move it up and down. Can you feel any area where the energy changes?

Let your hands fall to your sides. (Have you chosen an appropriate scent and sound for this meditation?) Close your eyes and settle into your chosen position. Spend time on your breathing, focusing on it and letting yourself sink deeper and deeper into a relaxed state. When you have let everyday worries float away and your body is comfortable and heavy, you are ready to continue.

Let your awareness close in on your throat chakra. Enter through into your aura and delve deeply into it. You feel yourself melt into this area. Go through and feel yourself floating back and forth between the two openings. Float for as long as you wish, free from restrictions and physical constraints. Allow yourself just to be. Sink deeper. Whatever occurs, let the images and feelings come and go. You are not in control. You are experiencing everything through just 'being'. Go even deeper.

Let yourself become aware that there are two openings, front and back. Let them both open wide. Rest in your velvety softness and allow your throat chakra spiritual guide to come to you. Trust. Relax. As they approach, acknowledge and thank them for coming to you. See which opening they appear through, then rest in their presence without expecting anything more from them. Feel yourself merge with their consciousness without trying. Rest in that awareness.

When they eventually slip away from you, observe which opening they retreat into, then firmly close both openings. Lock them.

Now it is time for you to retreat. Pull your thoughts away from your throat. Bring your awareness back to your whole physical body and where it is resting. Wriggle, stretch your arms and legs. When you are ready, open your eyes. Make sure you cleanse away anything left within your energy, then close down and protect yourself.

If you felt less in this area, that is all right. Perhaps you felt it was all very different, but found it hard to explain why. Write down your thoughts as soon as you finish. Are you remembering to include any colours, sights, scents or feelings that ran through you during the meditation? Describe your spiritual guide and the sensations that came with their presence.

If you have the experience of a guide returning to you from a previous chakra, ask yourself if this is because you were not focusing on a particular area, or if there is a direct link between these two chakras. What might this link be? For instance, are you doing something in one area of your life that is directly impacting on another area? Is this same guide trying to show you in two different ways what is really going on with you? If you are struggling to understand the reasons and nothing feels quite right, don't worry and don't dwell upon it. You can return to it on another occasion. When you are ready, move on to the next chakra.

Brow chakra meditation with guide

Take your time to settle and focus your thoughts. Make sure you have chosen incense or oil and some music for this exercise. The brow chakra often responds particularly well to this sort of stimulation. If, as you start, it feels wrong, then try another oil or a different piece of music. If it jars with you, it won't help your meditation. (You might find at some later date that your initial choice works well. There was probably a good reason why you chose it in the first place but you may simply have been a little premature in your actions! As we progress with our meditations, so our tastes can vary and become more refined.) Remember to take your time as you relax and concentrate on your breathing.

When you feel relaxed and ready, take your focus to the area in the middle of your forehead, between and above your eyes. This is a powerful area. If you feel strong sensations or see sharp colours, just let them come and go without judging or analysing them.

Be gentle as you let your consciousness sink through this physical area into the subtle energies beyond. Move with sensitivity and don't rush. Notice what comes and goes without getting caught up in it. Let yourself sink deeper and deeper into the warm, dark depths of your brow chakra. Don't try to be anything. Just let yourself 'be'.

Become aware that there are two openings front and back. They are wide open and are inviting your brow chakra spiritual guide to join you. Allow your guide to come through to you, and see which opening they choose. Greet them, thank them for being with you. Sit in their presence without expectation. Allow yourself simply to 'be' with them. If they communicate in any way, thank them.

As they leave, notice which opening they have chosen. Close the opening firmly after them; make sure the other opening is also shut.

When you have done that, the time is right for you to withdraw and return to daily life. Take your focus from your brow chakra and pull it back to encompass your whole body. Notice how you feel physically. Wriggle your body. Cleanse and close down. Protect yourself. Check that you feel grounded again. How heavy are you feeling now? Slowly open your eyes. Does the room feel abnormally bright and clear? You may not be closed and grounded properly. Close down again. Protect yourself. Make sure your body feels heavy and relaxed before you get up and continue with your day.

You will notice you were asked to really look at how grounded you were at the end of this exercise. Because the brow chakra is vibrating at a very high frequency it is easy to feel quite light-headed and 'out' of your body when you probe into this area. This can happen without your realizing it. Often it is when you first open your eyes again that you can tell how 'back to earth' you are. If the room feels very light and bright, you are still up in your brow chakra and not properly grounded. When you do this exercise again, make sure you always take those extra few minutes to reorientate yourself at the end.

Make notes in your Chakra Diary about the brow chakra and what you experienced. Have you noticed if the openings in the chakras always manifest themselves in the same way? It is quite possible different chakras will seem to have different openings. That is fine. In fact, that is good observation because it means your conscious mind is learning how to differentiate between the different energies of the chakras. Visual images help us to make those distinctions. You may hear separate sounds, if you are essentially an aural person, or feel different emotions, if you relate naturally in a kinaesthetic way. (Refer back to the NLP exercise on page 229 if you have forgotten into which category you predominantly fall.)

We are about to move on to the crown chakra now, the seventh chakra and often the one that people describe as the most elusive, the least tangible of chakras. Whatever you may personally feel about the crown chakra, it is again important that you let those preconceived ideas go for the purposes of the next exercise. Simply open yourself to the possibilities of what might be there for you to experience, rather than deciding it is going to be a difficult journey. Refuse to create any blocks before you start. We all know that below the crown chakra is the brain, that wonderful and relatively unknown part of our body. Remember to release your conceptions about your brain and how it works. Read through the exercise when you are ready. Ensure you have plenty of time for this chakra.

Crown chakra meditation with guide

Start with your usual relaxation and breathing awareness. Notice whether you feel right about the incense and music you have chosen. Change either of them before you start if you find yourself distracted. Check that your body feels comfortable and relaxed before you continue.

Now bring your focus to the top of your head. Gently move your awareness until you feel the pulsing energy of your crown chakra, then very gently, very slowly move your awareness through from your physical body down into your subtle body and inside the crown chakra. Sink down into this awareness. Sink deeper and deeper. Let the warm, velvety darkness engulf you. Melt into it. Experience the sensation of becoming one with your crown chakra. Observe the sensations that sweep over and through you as you allow this to happen. Let yourself ebb and flow with the waves. If you find yourself being taken on a journey, let yourself go with this experience without judging it or expecting anything from it. Allow yourself to go even deeper.

The crown chakra opening is in front of you: a bright, beautiful light that opens upwards to the heavens. Bathe in the beauty of this iridescent light. Allow it to permeate every part of you. Allow the opening to widen further. Notice how much stronger and more beautiful the light becomes. Experience everything that is happening. 'Be' the experience, stand in the middle of it. You and the heavenly light are one, there is no division, you are blending inextricably.

Now your crown chakra spiritual guide is with you, beside you. Melt into this guide and become one with it. Experience it. Words are not necessary. You are living the experience with every part of you fully absorbed. Do not try to analyse the feelings, soar with them. You are somewhere you have never been before. That is fine. You are safe.

As your guide takes their leave, watch them melt out through the chakra opening and disappear into the white light beyond. Then close the chakra firmly. It is time for you to leave.

This may feel difficult. You may not want to leave. Pull your focus back from the crown chakra and feel the whole of your body in its chosen relaxation position. Start to concentrate on different parts of you: feet, legs, buttocks, back, front, arms, hands, neck and head. Wriggle all of you, stretch slowly and fully. Notice how your body starts to feel very heavy again. Cleanse and close down. Protect yourself. If, when you open your eyes, you feel light-headed, then close down again. Concentrate on your feet and how heavy they feel. Imagine roots coming out of the soles of your feet and anchoring you deep into the ground, right down to the Earth's core.

Don't get up until you feel grounded and ready to continue your day. Ensure you drink a glass of water when you finish.

How have you found working at this deeper level? If you have noticed little effect, it is probably because you are not yet breathing as deeply and as fully as you might. Breathing techniques take a long time to develop. Unfortunately the majority of us spend our lives breathing shallowly and not learning how to fully experience breathing in all its joy and complexities. All the deeper work you do will require a certain discipline of breath. If you feel you are still struggling to understand the deeper levels of you, it is time for you to return to your breathing exercises and to continue strengthening control of your breathing.

If you find you cannot spare regular time each day for a short meditation, you can always incorporate breathing into your everyday activities; nobody needs to know what you are doing. Next time you are on crowded public transport or stuck in a traffic jam, do one of your breathing exercises. You can be standing in the queue at the supermarket or Post Office and practise too. You do not need any special equipment or private time to practise breathing; get into the habit of focusing on your breathing at different times during the day. As you clean your teeth or tidy your home, are you doing so mindfully, with attention to your breathing and with appreciation of what you have?

Perhaps you find everyday awareness of your breathing and mini meditations easy but when it comes to the more esoteric studies such as the chakras, you still feel very much 'in the dark'. It might help you to remind yourself of something we discussed earlier in this book: that in ancient traditions, thousands of years ago, many scholars were taught about the chakras by wise gurus and they often spent an entire lifetime grasping the true significance of just one chakra. They lived with an implicit understanding of reincarnation and accepted that they would study the other chakras during other lifetimes. So, if we are dealing with subtle energies that are so complex, it is no wonder that you may sometimes feel you are not making much headway.

There was much talk during these exercises of just 'being'. Many people find this a hard concept to work with and to apply. It is the attitude of letting go of preconceived thoughts and of not expecting, thinking, judging or consciously responding to anything but letting yourself ebb and flow with the current of whatever energy you are experiencing.

You might find it helpful to think of an analogy here – say, of a cork bobbing on water. The cork follows the current of the water, is swirled along and taken to different areas; it may be drawn under the water briefly, but it always bobs back to the surface, and its resilient material means that it completes the journey in the same physical shape as it began. So it is when you just 'be'. Many people would say a relaxing holiday is the chance to be just that and that is why a relaxing holiday can be a vital ingredient in keeping us healthy. On holiday many people choose just to 'be', whether it's lying in the sun or floating on an inflatable raft in the water. It is the act of relinquishing all decisions, stresses and conditions, which enables us to truly relax. Just 'being' determines the power of these meditations and how much you can learn from them.

However much you feel you are learning, there is always another level to reach, more to aspire to, greater depths of understanding available for us to tap into. The truth is that meditation and work with our spiritual guides is a perpetual, ongoing voyage of discovery. The more we accept that we are just at the beginning of our journey, the more we realize how much more we can embrace, when we are ready to do so.

How much stronger was your contact with your spiritual guides by working through your chakras? Did you find some of the spiritual guides you have already met came back to greet you? What was the difference, if any, in your communication now? How many were new guides? Were they possibly the same energies but in a different form? Were there any guides who came through two or more chakras?

It is up to you to put your own personal interpretation on what you experienced with your chakras. However, there is an interesting experiment you can now conduct. Go back to your notes regarding your base chakra. Summarize what you felt you understood from that meditation. Now go back and reread the previous sections in which we discussed the base chakra, on pages 149 and 325. How do they compare? It is fine if they gave different results. As we have already said, there is no right or wrong way to work with your chakras. There is only your way. You will probably find there are some similarities, or you may find that your recent meditation enabled you to see an aspect of yourself in a different light. This is very personal work so you cannot make sweeping generalizations for everyone.

However, if there were areas of your last chakra meditation which confused you, try to apply what you experienced to what you know traditionally of the base chakra, such as your need for physical energy, your survival instincts, your sense of being rooted in reality. Did any aspect of that reveal itself to you in an insightful way during the last meditation sessions?

Go back through all your chakra meditations and compare them to your earlier understanding of each chakra. How are they related? Are they completely different? Can you find common ground between your earlier thoughts on the chakras and your latest understanding? The more you explore, the more you will realize there is to explore and the less you will feel you know! That is fine. Simply remember to acknowledge yourself and how well you are progressing. As Marie Curie put it:

'One never notices what has been done;
one only notices what remains to be done.'

You have done some very intensive work during this chapter and been encouraged to increase your understanding even more by delving into deep, dark areas of your subconsciousness. It seems only right that we should end with a little light relaxation. Why not invite your angel of relaxation to come into your meditation? Try the following exercise:

Angel of relaxation meditation

Find a really comfortable position for this exercise. It is suggested that you lie flat unless you know you will fall asleep so quickly that the benefit of the meditation will be lost.

Close your eyes and start to relax. Focus on your breathing, but do not work through any of your usual breathing techniques. Simply observe your breath coming and going and don't try to alter it. This is not about learning or trying; this is just about 'being'.

As you feel yourself sinking deeper and deeper into a relaxed state, you are not required to work in any way or focus on anything in particular. Enjoy the feeling of release. Feel yourself unwinding even more. You don't have to prove yourself to anyone right now or to minister to anyone else's needs; you can simply be yourself. Relax. Sink further and further into your wonderful, velvety, soft darkness.

As you do so, your angel guide of relaxation comes to join you. They bring with them a sense of calm, peace, gentle love and infinite relaxation. As they come into your subtle energy field, feel the small tensions and stresses leaking out from your body in all spheres: physically, mentally, emotionally and spiritually. Because your angel of relaxation is so wise and loving, they know exactly what is needed for you to relax fully. Let them float over and through you. Feel their presence in whatever way is right for you and enjoy all the sensations. Notice how all of you is sinking further and further into a wonderfully relaxed state.

You don't even need to thank your angel of relaxation. No effort is required on your part because their task is purely to assist you. That is their function and reason for being there. As you appreciate this, feel yourself sink still deeper and deeper into heavenly warmth and comfort.

You may not notice when your angel of relaxation has gone. They will float away quietly and gently, without disturbing you in any way. You may just realize they have gone and your whole being is feeling relaxed and yet refreshed at the same time.

Give yourself some time to readjust as you return to daily life. Lie there for a while, appreciating your sense of well being. Then slowly start to move your body. Give a long, slow stretch, letting your arms come over your head, and stretch from the tips of your fingers to the tips of your toes. Then relax. Feel all your muscles expanding and contracting as you do this. Give your shoulders a little wriggle. Notice how much looser they feel. Open your eyes and look at an

> object in front of you for a while. When you feel ready, sit up slowly. Drink a big glass of water. Have another stretch when you get up.
>
> At this stage, just before you continue with your daily tasks, you might choose to silently thank your angel of relaxation. Although they came to us without expectation of gratitude and purely to assist you, it is always a positive act to acknowledge others.

Did you find that particularly restful and undemanding? Good! It is so important that you take time to remember the lighter aspect of meditation and spiritual guides regarding your well-being in all areas of your life. You may have discovered that your angel of relaxation and your healing guide were perhaps similar, or even the same energy in a different form.

When we work so deeply with spiritual practices, it is easy to forget that we are physical beings and that we need to acknowledge our earthly selves as well. Pleasure comes into the category of earthly emotion. Always remember when you meditate to give yourself the opportunity to relax and enjoy yourself. Don't always be striving to understand or seeking to solve some particular issues in your life.

Purely relaxing meditations, with or without any spiritual guides, help to unblock any stagnant energy within us and often afford us great insights later that day or the day after. By allowing ourselves just to be ourselves and not trying to alter anything, we can end up creating some wonderfully positive changes. Have you been spending some time in your forest, garden or beach as per the meditations on pages 162–67? You may have created another setting that you find wonderfully restful. Remember to return to them regularly and allow yourself true 'breathing space'.

Hopefully you are now seeing how a stronger link can be forged between meditations and spiritual guides and how the process of just 'being' in a meditation can create further insights for you in all aspects of your life. Your chakra guides can help you a great deal in this area. Revisit them as often as you can.

This process of just 'being' is summed up by an anonymous quote that is quite inspirational. (Substitute for the word 'God' any deity of your choice, if you wish.)

Part Four: Putting it all Together

'Prayer is speaking to God;
Meditation is listening to God.'

Now we want to move on to look at how combining our dreamwork with spiritual guides can take us into yet another new realm of discovery and appreciation.

DREAMWORK AND SPIRITUAL GUIDES

You may feel you have already experienced this combination of your spiritual guides coming into your dreams, particularly if you have had what might be called divine dreams. This is wonderful if it is has happened to you and no doubt you feel richer for the experience.

However, spiritual guides do not only have to come into divine dreams. Without you realizing, they may already have come into an everyday dream or a symbolic dream. You may even find that the monster who chased you in a nightmare is purely a guide in disguise and you are not seeing the value in their presence.

This is not to say that every person in your dream represents a spiritual guide. It can be tempting to start thinking that way, but the chances are there have been some guides who have already come to you and you simply didn't acknowledge them as such.

The converse of this is also true. Our dreaming mind can be cunning and manipulative and play great tricks on us. That is why we have spent so much time explaining the importance of applying honesty to everything we do. It is possible someone you thought was a guide and encouraging you to do something may in fact have been an aspect of your own personality manifesting itself.

We are going to spend time looking at when a spiritual guide may appear in your dreams or when you might be misleading yourself. This is an important distinction to learn and it may take a little application before you can be sure of the difference. This awareness has not arisen before, with waking meditations, because we know our conscious mind is sifting through the information as we receive it. We have less opportunity to deceive ourselves when we are awake.

However, our sleeping, unconscious mind is capable of wonderful tricks, which is of course why so many gloriously freeing and fantastical events can occur when we are in a dreaming state. You need some tools to enable you to determine when a true guide is coming to advise you in your dreams and when you might be misleading yourself.

If someone appears in a dream and you think it is a spiritual guide, why might you be wrong? Who or what else might this someone be? We have talked briefly before about our own ego and how it can get in the way of our spiritual progress, hence the need for honesty and applying it to everything we do.

Our ego is purely the earthly part of us. We use our ego to push ourselves ahead, either to grasp work opportunities or to further our personal goals. We use it to erect defences and give ourselves an outer confidence. It enables us to survive in a competitive world.

However, our ego is a hindrance to spiritual awareness. Just as earlier we talked about letting ourselves 'be' and bringing down our barriers during personal development work, so we need to rid ourselves of our ego, too, if we want to be effective. Why is it so important to do this? If a person comes through in our dreams who is not a spiritual guide, the chances are they will be part of our ego in some form or another.

If your ego wants you to get a better-paid job because that will make you feel powerful and good about yourself, it may manifest itself in your dream as a wise figure, urging you to change your job and even showing you how this might be done. Does this make it a bad dream? Of course not. However, you were not having a spiritual experience with a guide. You were having a dream about yourself and your material life. You could say this doesn't matter, as long as you find a way of making it happen! Perhaps that is true, but there is the concept of karma and reincarnation to consider when you work with higher awareness.

You may know the expression 'Be careful what you ask for, because you may get it'. In this new world of working with your higher awareness, it's important that you take responsibility for your behaviour. Through powerful affirmations and strong inner desires, you can possibly make certain things happen to you. You might end up making a lot of money or garnering for yourself a lot of earthly power.

However, that comes with a price. Whatever you may do, if it takes place without integrity, without honesty and without sensitivity to others and their rightful place within the universe, it can only backfire on you. Material goods and earthly power have absolutely no effect in the spiritual world. This deserves repeating: *Material goods and earthly power have absolutely no effect in the spiritual world.*

This is why our relationship with our true spiritual guides affords us an inner world of riches with which no material world can compare. This is not to say that money or earthly power is a bad thing! It is simply to point out that it is the means by which you acquire your physical wealth or power that determines your own spiritual progress. If you work with your spiritual guides to understand your way forward on Earth, then you are working with integrity and honesty. When you listen to manifestations of your own ego, you are working to your own, selfish agenda.

So how can you tell the difference? You might be looking back through your Dream Diary now and suddenly wondering if every time you thought you had a divine experience, it was nothing more than a part of your own ego speaking to you, wrapped up in a seemingly spiritual package. It is an unnerving aspect to consider.

So, to begin with, look back through your Dream Diary and study the different people and images you have noted in them. Were there some that you immediately identified as a guide? Why? How was their energy or presence different from others? Did they speak to you in the dream or did it take another form of communication? Make some notes about the guides you feel you have met in your dreams already and how they manifested themselves to you. Notice if a guide appeared on more than one occasion and what you think the issue was in each instance. If you don't think any guides have come through in your dreams so far, that is fine. Be honest with yourself.

When you have made some notes, start questioning each dream on a deeper level. What was the meaning of the dream? Did it relate very much to physical, earthly matters? Was it about some area of personal gain for you or was it about others? Was it related to a spiritual aspect? Did the advice you received in the dream urge you to take an action that would result in your own personal desires being fulfilled or would it also involve others in a positive outcome as well? (Be careful when answering this question that you don't decide what others might want for you or want for themselves. If you don't know, don't make assumptions. Be honest.) Ask yourself if this dream involved your ulterior motives. It is fine if it does; just allow yourself to be truthful.

Now look at the emotion involved in the dream. Did you record it as uplifting or enlightening? Did you wake up inspired and touched without quite being able to define it? Were you left with an overwhelming ability to see some aspect of life in a much wider context? Did the effect or images of the dream stay with you for a long time and did you find yourself reflecting on it at different times during the next few days? Did you feel privileged to have experienced the dream?

Perhaps your responses were different. Did it simply make you feel good about yourself? Were you spurred on to some strong action, without stopping to consider its repercussions for others? Did it imbue you with a strong feeling of urgency and energy but no sense of wonderment or awe? Did the desire of the dream stay with you but not the beauty of it?

You want to question yourself very closely. Really think about the answers. If this process makes you stop and reassess your own behaviour as a result, that is fine. Remember, the object of this self-assessment is not to criticize yourself or your experience in your dreams; it is for you to further deepen your understanding of yourself and where you lie in the realms of honesty and self-awareness. If, upon reflection, some of your behaviour does not satisfy you, all it means is that you have learned something positive about yourself and you have the opportunity to change your attitude at any time when you so desire.

We have mentioned before that personal development work can be an emotional and soul-searching experience. If, through considering your spiritual guides in dreams and also your own ego, you have come to some uncomfortable conclusions, try not to castigate yourself. Our personal development is much more powerful when we have the ability to keep acknowledging our behaviour and to learn from it. We're here to learn, not to keep covering our true selves with layers of illusion. You choose the speed at which you progress. You decide how gently you want to remove some of the layers. Discovering our true spiritual guides in our dreams is just about revealing another layer.

Now, whatever your response was to the close questions about your dreams, and whatever contact you feel you have already had with guides in your dreams, you are going to conduct an experiment. See how you fare.

Reassessing your Progress

First, embrace the possibility of your true spiritual guides coming into your dreams and being able to help you. A good starting point would be a simple affirmation every night before you drift off to sleep such as 'My spiritual guides always come to me in my dreams'. You want to open your conscious thoughts to this realm and to let your subconscious know that you are ready for this experience.

Start thinking about your spiritual guides on a daily basis and reflect upon how they might help in your dreamwork. Where would you most like them to appear? In what kind of dream might they be most powerful? What issue in your life would you most like to look at and which guide would you like to help you in this matter? (This does not mean you can call upon them at will; spiritual guides don't respond to our demands! But by sending out a request or resting in a state of awareness, you are letting them know you would welcome their presence.)

Really consider how you would describe your current state of communication with your spiritual guides. Choose one response from the list below.

- non-existent
- intermittent
- frequent
- constant

If you consider yourself to be still in the first category, don't lose hope! There is every chance that through bringing spiritual guides into your dreams, you will be able to create a meaningful level of contact with your guides. If you can choose any of the other categories, then you are doing extremely well and can look forward to improving further.

Now consider how you would describe the level at which you communicate with your spiritual guides. Which of the following is accurate for you?

- often unfathomable
- often understandable but tends to relate to trivial issues
- seems to be meaningful but then fades away without any resolution
- often profound and insightful

You might want to describe that level as a combination of all four at different times. If there have been any occasions when you would opt for the last as an answer, you should stop and acknowledge how far you have come. It takes a certain commitment and application to create a relationship as powerful as that. You have obviously been doing a lot of work on yourself and your spiritual progress to have come this far.

This mini quiz is simply here to help you reassess your progress. You may discover you have done better than you thought you would. We prefer criticising ourselves to being pleased with how much we have done, as Marie Curie's quote in the previous chapter shows.

Your dreams will help to improve your communication with spiritual guides, especially if you are someone who has struggled with the concept of just 'being' during your waking meditations. Dreams allow the subconscious to take away some of the pressure of just 'being' and also relieve us of some of our old inhibitions.

In other words, so often in dreams you can just 'be' and this is the ideal time for your spiritual guides to come to you with messages. The strength lies in our ability, firstly, to remember their presence in our dreams and, secondly, to be able to interpret their messages powerfully and truthfully. You have been working on these two techniques all through Part Three, so hopefully you are now ready to face this new phase.

Now you have chosen to think about your spiritual guides and your dreams and how they can be a more powerful combination, make sure you note this date down in your Dream Diary. If you start your affirmation tonight, make a note of it.

This does not mean that you will immediately start to forge a strong link with your spiritual guides in your dreams. You are just opening the doors, so to speak, to enable this process to begin. There is a lot more you can do to improve contact further.

During your waking meditations, start to introduce your willingness to learn on another, deeper level. When you do communicate with your guides, ask if they will come to you in your dreams. Let them know that you would value their presence to help you improve your progress.

You might choose to resort to some other physical tools as well. Do you have a small piece of celestine? Have you kept it beside your bed or under your pillow? Have you ever tried holding it in your hand and drifting off to sleep? Have you recorded the effects of any of this in your Dream Diary? Did any of the other recommended crystals have any effect on your dreams, such as the jade, jasper, lapis lazuli, opal or sodalite?

Spend some time looking around a crystal shop and gently holding a few different pieces of crystal. You might find another piece inspirational, such as howlite or moonstone. There is no such thing as a wrong or right piece of crystal. Further develop your relationship with them and explore other possibilities. Has a guide ever come to you with a particular colour? What crystal can be found in that colour? Would it help you?

Perhaps you have found certain colours generally to be more inspirational than others. It doesn't mean you have to go out and buy an expensive set of new bed linen to enjoy that colour. Have your lampshade next to your bed in that colour, or even buy a low watt light bulb with a hint of that colour in it.

If you have actually seen one of your spiritual guides and have the ability to draw or paint, why not do a small sketch of them and prop it up near your bed? Likewise, if you associate a particular sound with a guide, such as dolphin sounds with a water guide, then you might choose to play dolphin sounds as you drift off to sleep. If a particular guide has a scent attached to them, dab a few drops of that essential oil onto a cotton wool ball and place it by your pillow.

If you have the time and money, explore your relationship with scents a little further and see how they might enhance your communication with your guides during sleep. We talked about oils during meditation and mentioned lavender as a useful soporific to precede dreamwork, and we mentioned sage and angelica as being helpful for communication with spiritual guides. However, there are other oils you might also want to try and which are considered beneficial for encouraging euphoric emotions and divine inspiration; basil, chamomile and clary sage are examples. Smell a tester in a shop and see how you respond.

Certain flowers and herbs are also said to increase spiritual communication. We talked about some earlier in relation to meditation and also spiritual guide communication (St John's Wort and Violet) but there are others. For instance, did you know that the simple dandelion is considered to have properties that aid spiritual contact and divine experiences? You might find it surprising that a common and often much-disliked weed could be imbued with such power, but perhaps there is a lesson here about the wisdom of not being too hasty or shallow in our judgements! You might also want to try other herbs and flowers considered inspirational, such as agrimony, eyebright, jasmine, passion flower, purslane, saffron, thistle and willow.

There is a variety of strong scents that may simply make you feel wonderful, release tension and open you to other, higher influences. We mentioned some of them earlier but they are worth repeating here. A bowl of sweet smelling roses can be so therapeutic and enable you to slow your over-active metabolism down. The pungent aroma of arum lilies or lily-of-the-valley may help you, or a vase of lilac blossom or freesias. There is a large number of wonderfully fragrant flowers available to us, often year-round. Take advantage of this availability when you can afford it and enjoy the beauty of scents. Place a vase next to your bed one night and see how you respond during the night in your dreams.

Pay particular attention to your dreams in the forthcoming weeks. Make notes as soon as you wake up. If your intention and commitment is clear, you will probably find that entities of some description are coming into your dreams with more frequency. This can be encouraging and also confusing. You may still be feeling uncertain, because of our earlier discussion, about whether you are experiencing a spiritual guide or whether it is a part of you that is manifesting itself in your dreams.

A good clue is how you feel when you wake up. If your first sensation upon waking is a kind of unearthly euphoria or wonderment, if you feel a sense of well being you can't explain, if you are filled with an inner contentment or even excitement, then you are more likely to have had spiritual contact.

Next, look at the content of the dream closely. Begin with a silent affirmation: 'I am honest in all my dream analysis'. By sending this clear message to your unconscious mind that you do not want to be tricked in any way, you are clearing the old sludge of self-deception and opening the gates to honesty. The joy of dream analysis is that no one else need ever know what you are finding out, so you can allow yourself to be completely vulnerable and open.

After a few sessions of this, you will begin to understand quite quickly what is happening. As long as you listen to your gut reaction, you will know if what you experienced was divine or earthly in content. Once you make a clear commitment to banishing self-deception, it is amazing how quickly spiritual truths are allowed to come through to you. It is often not as painful or as emotional as we expect it to be.

The difficult moment comes in the very first realization that we all deceive ourselves about our true selves in some fashion or another. It is not comfortable to acknowledge that we are not truthful with ourselves all the time and that we suffer from very human emotions such as greed, jealousy, selfishness, anger and resentment, even in our dreams!

Yet it is by embracing this knowledge and understanding how human we are, that we allow ourselves to progress into higher spiritual awareness. We can appreciate the fact that we are human, especially when we can counter-balance it with our ever-deepening and ever-enriching spiritual awareness. It is all right to make mistakes in ignorance and out of fear. What is not all right is to continue that behaviour once we have enough conscious knowledge to eradicate our ignorance and fear.

The truth is that there is no retreating once you start out on your spiritual path. Although you might want to physically back away at times, you cannot 'undo' your knowledge. What is wonderfully uplifting is that, once you reach this stage of understanding, you will be given help by your spiritual guides. Their unconditional love will enrich you in a way that nothing earthly can. Again, this is not to diminish material support and earthly pleasures in any way, but merely to stress that both are complementary and parts of a whole. One without the other is not ultimately truly fulfilling. (When you finish your meditations and dreamwork, remember to take the time to hug, love and appreciate another physical being!)

To create balance in our lives, it is extremely important to know when these guides really are coming into our dreams and advising us. A good way to check this out is to 'test' them. Yes, it is all right if we want to test our guides; they will understand that we need proof before we can trust. So how can we test them?

When you wake from a dream that you believe contained a visitation from a spiritual guide, spend a moment before you get out of bed to ask that guide to give you some sort of proof, in your everyday life, that they are indeed your guide. Now this proof can come in any form provided you find it meaningful and conclusive. You cannot dictate what that proof should look like; guides do not respond to orders! However, by letting them know that you want to work more with them and want to grow to trust them, you are allowing the possibility of something to happen.

So what might this proof look like? Let us consider a few examples that will encourage you to consider the possibilities. Perhaps you have had a dream in which your guide comes to you with information and there is a distinct image somewhere in this dream that stays in your conscious mind. It could be something simple like a small brown dog or a book on a table about a particular subject. Once you have asked for proof, notice if something comes into your daily life which represents that image for you. You might be walking in a park and see that small brown dog or go past a shop window and see that book on a table. You will have to be living your daily life mindfully to see it. Your guides will not make everything crystal clear and easy for you. It is up to you to make it obvious that you want a sign and then to remain vigilant about seeing it.

Consider another dream. In it you are flying on the back of a beautiful white angel, soaring over mountains and oceans, filled with euphoric sensations and receiving wonderful insights. This would seem to be a clear indication of a divine dream and an enjoyable one at that. However, you still want proof from your angel. Ask for it when you wake up. Then go about your day mindfully. What happens that proves their presence to you? You might go into a shop and see a card with the image of an angel flying over a scenic vista. Perhaps you are out on a walk, look up and see a cloud in the shape of an angel. Maybe you are talking to a colleague at work and realize they are wearing an angel necklace. It does not matter how the proof manifests itself, as long as you register the sign and feel confident in the knowledge it is the proof you have asked for.

Continue to do this with your dreams for a month or so. Whenever you feel a guide has come into a dream, ask for proof. You may notice that your daily, waking communication with your spiritual guides improves as a result. You may also discover that your spiritual guides often have a good sense of humour. Be careful how much you test your guides, though! Once you have received sufficient proof, trust that when they next appear in your dreams, they are what they say they are. If you persist in demanding proof, they will not appreciate your cynicism. Doubt and scepticism has an energy of its own that is not particularly attractive.

You may find your guides refusing to constantly 'perform' for you or they may respond in a way that shows their humour. For instance, in the case of the first dream, perhaps if you keep asking for proof, they might choose to show you a small brown dog in the park who is angry and barking furiously at you!

You may also find the proof coming to you at unexpected times and reminding you of parts of a dream you had forgotten. Perhaps you woke up with a vague memory of a guide but not a clear picture of what took place. You ask for proof and also a clearer indication as to what the dream was about. You may take that thought with you throughout your day but still not remember anything more about it. By the evening, after a particularly busy day, you may even have forgotten your request of that morning. Then, late at night, as you flop down in an exhausted heap on your sofa, your eyes casually alight on a candlestick on the mantelpiece and you suddenly remember that your guide was holding that very candlestick in your dream. You realize your guide was talking about you finding the light within you by using the candle flame as a means of focus. Yes, the insight really can come as clearly and suddenly as that. It can also be as easy as that, once you open yourself to your guide's love and nurturing.

Once you become open to allowing spiritual guides to express their presence, you will start to see their influences everywhere. This is a good example of showing how your life becomes a waking and sleeping meditation, because you are constantly remaining open to the possibility of wonderful things happening around you.

When you feel confident that your guides are indeed coming to you in your dreams, then you can start to work powerfully with them. In the dreamstate we let go of so many preconceived ideas and conditional thoughts, enabling us to 'soar' better with the teachings and wisdom of our guides.

When you can apply a lucid state to a divine dream, then you are really working at a level that has immense repercussions. This is not necessarily something you will do with ease. To be able to call upon a spiritual guide in a lucid dream and to allow yourself to be freely guided by them is indeed advanced work. However, you can hold that in your heart as an ideal state to which you aspire.

There is another consideration when you work at a more powerful level with your spiritual guides. We mentioned earlier that making mistakes through ignorance is more acceptable than making mistakes wilfully and knowingly. Once you have ascertained that clear communication is possible with your spiritual guides, no matter who they are or how many or how few of them there are, you have to consider that you are choosing to become more aware and more responsible for your actions. So the more you learn from your guides, the greater is your sense of responsibility to act upon their guidance. This does not mean you will want to follow through on every suggestion offered to you, because you have your own free will.

However, when you are given a universal truth as an insight and you know it is there for you to learn from and to work with, it does mean you become more responsible for everything you say and do. You will find yourself doing something and then suddenly stopping and thinking about the intention and integrity behind this action. This development has both pros and cons.

It is wonderful to be able to understand everything you do in a much wider context and to understand the repercussions of your actions on a universal scale. It is also a nuisance at times, because we all know it is easier just to do something without first thinking about the consequences. The ultimate positive of this awareness is that you have the confidence of knowing you are acting responsibly and truthfully, with awareness and sensitivity, to others. That is a big reward.

Of course, we are jumping forward here, because many of you may find it takes a long time before you have any sustained communication with your spiritual guides during your dreams. If so, simply remain committed to your intention that this will happen. Continue with your affirmations and your frequent requests to your guides that they come to you in your dreams. Continue experimenting with all the outside influences that can help enhance your work, too. Know that the journey itself is also enjoyable, not just the arriving at a point where you think you want to be. Remember to thank your guides, always, for their presence. Remember to stop and feel gratitude for what they are choosing to come and teach you.

There are no simple exercises you can do to enhance this communication with your spiritual guides in your dreams because dreamwork and contact with spiritual guides are two very different energies, but it is highly recommended that you continue with your regular breathing exercises throughout all these experiments. It can never be stressed enough how beneficial they are.

Just after you wake up, after you have scribbled down your thoughts about your night's dreams, take just two minutes to do some gentle Alternate Nostril Breathing (page 117) or simply concentrate on each 'in' and 'out' breath, using the words 'in' and 'out' as a focus (page 78). Consider how much more you remember about your dreams after you have spent a few minutes of breathing awareness. It is almost inevitable that you will discover you have remembered something further that eluded you just a few minutes before. Experiment with different breathing awareness techniques in the morning and see which ones provide you with the best results in so far as remembering your dreams is concerned. This is a good way for you to prove conclusively to yourself that the deep breathing really does make a big difference to your well being.

In the next chapter we are going to look at how we can combine all three techniques that we have learnt about: meditation, communication with spiritual guides and dreamwork. We are going to see just how powerful this will enable us to become and why we might want to use this combination of awareness on a regular basis.

MEDITATION, DREAMWORK AND SPIRITUAL GUIDES

You have been encouraged to look at many deep issues through your work in these three areas of discussion: meditation, communication with spiritual guides and dreamwork. You may have found one field more helpful and/or inspirational than another. You may realize you have chosen, either consciously or unconsciously, to focus more of your attention on a particular subject because you felt a closer affinity with it.

You may still be someone who cannot remember much about their dreams, despite the work you have done in your Dream Diary; you may find communication with spiritual guides has mostly eluded you; you may think that meditation accomplishes very little apart from mildly relaxing you.

Whatever level you have reached in any of the areas, this is your opportunity to find a truly powerful way of using all three. You might find that one area on which you weren't so keen suddenly becomes more powerful when used in conjunction with the other two. This phenomenon is akin to what happens when we incorporate the physical, mental, emotional and spiritual realms in our lives. You have been encouraged to appreciate how our four separate bodies combine to create one whole. If we leave out one part of ourselves, we cannot function fully.

So how can we combine all three techniques into one big powerhouse of activity? The best way of explaining this would seem to be to encourage you to take one particular issue or theme running through your life and see how, by applying all three methods to the same issue, your insights become more profound.

Taking an Issue

Let's see how all this combining might work when it is applied to a basic question concerning us all: 'Why are we here?' The issue of trying to understand why we are alive is something probably everyone has asked themselves, and many philosophers and theologians have spent their whole lives trying to determine man's true purpose. Perhaps you have spent a lot of your life thinking about it and trying to understand it. Maybe it didn't cross your mind much until you started reading this book and now it is much more in your thoughts. Perhaps you feel you have reached a greater understanding through your work so far and some of your meditations or dreams have given you much clearer insights into your own personal significance. You may still find it so daunting a question that you haven't yet tackled it.

Whatever your thoughts so far, you are now going to take this subject and look at it using the different techniques we have learnt. This topic can create strong emotions and concerns in people. However, you have been encouraged to deal with a large number of major issues in this book. You have got this far, so there seems no good reason why you cannot take this next step and try to see your life in a much wider context. By being honest and applying what you already know to what is given to you, it is unlikely you will find this task so daunting. Re-read various sections if you need help with your interpretations – you are not expected to work out your life and its meaning totally on your own!

In Understanding Karma in Part Two we looked at your purpose in life. You are going to take a slightly different approach here and see what you can learn. In those earlier stages of meditation, you were working a great deal with conscious thought and letting it intrude, even though no doubt you weren't aware of it. As you have now been encouraged to see everything from outside your own ego, you can revisit this area from a different perspective and with greater understanding.

Your starting point is a new exercise dealing with releasing the ego and then bringing it back into yourself at the end. We need our ego for much of our daily life, but if we are to work more powerfully in meditation and with our guides, we have to learn to release it from our physical body for a short while. Work through the following exercise when you are ready.

Releasing the ego

Take up a comfortable relaxation position. Close your eyes. Give yourself some time to unwind and focus on your breathing. Then consciously open up your chakras, open by one, gently and slowly.

Sink down into your velvety darkness when you are ready. Let yourself go. Forget your daily persona, the face you show the world. Become you. Sink deep down into you. Rest in that state for a while.

Now bring the word 'ego' in your conscious thought. Meditate upon it. How does it manifest itself in you? Give it a shape, size, colour, smell, taste, sound. Create it as a recognizable, powerful image in front of you. Take your time. This is very personal. If you find yourself creating something that you do not like very much, redesign it in your mind's eye with compassion and unconditional love. Acknowledge that this part of you, this ego, you have had to create in order to protect yourself on a daily basis from all sorts of earthly pressures and fears. Don't be judgmental. Be loving. Make the image powerful.

Now see that this ego, although it is a part of you, is not physically attached to you. It is free moving and can be released from your energy field using your thought processes. First, attach a piece of strong string around your wrist, then attach the other end of the string to your image of your ego. When this is done, you can allow your ego to float out of you and go up into the air beyond. It is joined to a very long piece of string which is securely attached to your wrist and you can see your ego safely floating up into the distance. You know you can pull your string towards you and recapture your ego at any time. For now, let it bob peacefully up in the air, free from restrictions and demands.

Notice how this makes you feel, now you are free from your ego and its attendant responsibilities. Do you feel lighter, freer, happier? Perhaps you feel a little vulnerable. Bring some protection around you, either the golden light or your cloak of protection. Feel secure.

Rest for a while in this novel state of freedom. You are simply 'you'. No ego. Unfettered. Raw. Real. Relish the sensation. If your ego starts to float back towards you, gently push it away again. Watch it bob back up into the sky.

> When you are ready, slowly pull your ego back down towards you. Let it float back into your subtle body and notice where it rests. It may appear connected to one chakra in particular. Which one is it? How does your ego feel inside of you now? Know that you have it to protect yourself on Earth, that it is a necessary part of you and not to be disapproved of or criticized.
>
> Slowly withdraw your consciousness back to your whole physical body. Wriggle and stretch your muscles. Close down and cleanse. Protect yourself. Open your eyes. Rest a moment before you get up.

How did you get on? Did you find it easy to create your own ego in a shape and was it easy to let it go for a while? Perhaps you felt awkward as it first left your body and you wanted to pull it back. Perhaps you were glad to see it go. Maybe you worried that the string wouldn't be strong enough and your ego might disappear.

In fact, your ego is connected to you like a strong magnet. You do not really need a piece of string to keep it near you because your own ego is attracted to you magnetically and could not move away even if it, or you, wanted that to happen. If you feel secure in this knowledge, you do not need to hold your ego to you with a length of string; that was purely to enable you to learn to trust and relax in the whole process.

If you feel happy, next time you can release the ego with your thoughts and know it will return when you call upon it. You may find it returning when you did not expect, but it is up to you to push it away again gently.

You may also have discovered that your ego is more complex than you first thought. You may find that as you release it upwards, you realize there is more ego inside you which has to be released too. The more we focus on our ego the more we realize that it is not just one part of us but composed of many layers within our aura. Don't worry if it takes you several sessions before you begin to understand on a deeper level. It is suggested you practise with this technique for a few weeks before you go on to try the further exercises. The easier you find it to visualize your ego leaving your body for a short while, the easier it will be for you to progress further with the exercises coming up. When you feel you have worked at this exercise with a good degree of success, move on to the next exercise.

We now want to look at how releasing your ego will free your energies to work at a deeper level. We start with a meditation that takes us deeper into work with our spiritual guides and then tie that into our dreamwork.

Ego-less meditation with a guide

Go through your usual relaxation and opening up process. Make sure you take plenty of time; don't rush the experience. Cleanse thoroughly if you are carrying 'baggage' with you from your everyday life. You don't need that now. Make sure you open each chakra carefully and lovingly; notice how each responds to your awareness; don't try to change it in any way.

When you are ready, sink into the wonderful, deep, velvety darkness deep within you. Rest in this state for a while. Notice what state you are in today and how that is reflected in your thoughts. Acknowledge how you are without trying to alter it.

Now go through your ego-release meditation and let your ego float upwards and outwards, knowing it will return when you call it back. Enjoy the lighter sensation of being without your ego. Rest like this for a while.

Bring all your focus to your crown chakra and the beautiful white light pouring down from the divine source above. As you concentrate on the light, it becomes more radiant, stronger with every breath you breathe in and out. Feel it cascading through and over you. Enjoy its cleansing power. Sit in this comforting state for a while.

Is your ego still safely bobbing above you? Make sure it has not returned to your body again. Focus more and more on this beautiful white light. Feel it become stronger and stronger and more and more beautiful. As you do this, feel yourself blend with the light itself. Your energy merges into it and you become one.

Now allow yourself to float up into the white light and beyond. Allow your consciousness to shift upwards, following the source of this divine light. Feel yourself moving higher and higher up this beautiful beam of light. It is easy to do this, without your ego weighing you down. Follow this source, let yourself melt completely into the light and let yourself be taken effortlessly upwards, higher and higher. You may travel for some time. Be comfortable in this state, knowing you are secure, safe and unconditionally loved.

At some stage, you stop. You find yourself surrounded in beautiful light. You may not know your surroundings or they may be irrelevant. They may manifest themselves in a way that is personal and meaningful for you. You have stopped because you are now at a level of awareness that houses one of your guides. They are now here to be with you. As they come into your consciousness, thank them for bringing you to their 'home', their sphere of consciousness, and see what you have to learn in this new environment.

Without your ego, it is easier to learn and to understand what is being said or shown to you. You have now stepped into their 'world' to better comprehend their energy and their teachings. This has only been made possible by releasing your ego before you started on this journey.

You might want to ask your guide a question about your reasons for being on Earth at this time. You might simply want to experience their wisdom in this new environment. You may find everything brighter, sharper and easier to understand at this level. It may feel as though metaphorical clouds have lifted from your vision and you can embrace a new level of awareness. Enjoy this state.

When it is time, your guide will slowly release you back through the white light and return you to your everyday life. As you drift back through your layers of consciousness, you may find yourself resisting the return journey. Let that resistance go. There are many things you have still to learn from your earthly existence. Embrace them as well. Let yourself float gently downwards.

> As you float back down to join your physical body, allow your ego to float back with you. You may notice a sudden jolt as you return your consciousness to an earthly level. Your body may suddenly feel very heavy and awkward. Your ego may seem large and cumbersome. This is a normal reaction but it is essential you give yourself time to readjust.
>
> You must sit quietly, with your eyes closed, as you reorientate yourself. First, cleanse. Do this thoroughly in your Cleansing Sanctuary. Cleanse through every part of you. Now you want to close down your chakras, one by one. You may be surprised to feel how much they have opened and how vulnerable they suddenly feel. Start at your base and close them, slowly and gently. When they are all closed, then cleanse through again. Now give yourself protection. Make sure it is solid protection and suitable for you.
>
> Only once you have done all this, should you open your eyes. You may still feel light-headed. Go through your grounding exercise. Really focus on the roots coming out of the soles of your feet. Then sit quietly and drink your glass of water for a few minutes. Think about what you have experienced and notice how even thinking of it can send your thoughts soaring upwards. Close down again and ground yourself before you get up.

You may have been taken aback by how strong your experience was in this exercise. The more you work with understanding your own ego and how it can be separated from you for purposes of meditation, the more powerful and the 'deeper' your meditations become. Freeing yourself of your ego allows you to soar to levels you had previously only imagined and to truly understand yourself on a profound level.

What is essential is that you really do take that time to cleanse, close and ground yourself afterwards. You are probably tired of reading all those phrases about how you must focus on your chakras and close them, how you need to ground your body afterwards, but it is so important you take the time to do this. If you don't, you will be going back into the earthly world with a sense of unreality and a lack of physical awareness which may prove dangerous. Many accidents of all descriptions can happen when we are not properly 'grounded' on earth. Don't let yourself be a victim of that kind of experience. It is also lovely to have that quality time to reflect and relax when you finish meditating. Plain water never tastes as good as it does when you are slowly sipping a glassful as you readjust to everyday life!

Your first visit to the higher echelons of awareness may have thrown you somewhat. If that was the case for you, simply remember to give yourself time to reflect on your experience. You have read a great deal about how you can attain a higher degree of spiritual awareness; however, when it is then offered to you, it is somehow still quite a shock. You may find yourself wondering if what you experienced was indeed 'real'.

This sensation of leaving your ego behind and letting yourself soar upwards is wonderful but responsibility also comes with it, as we have talked about earlier. When you truly embrace spiritual teaching and leave your ego behind, it can fundamentally alter your perception of life and your role within it. Therefore, you are given a choice about your personal responsibility, integrity and lifestyle. The more you discover about who you really are, the more you will question what you do on a daily basis.

This doesn't mean to imply that your physical life is going to change radically as you become more spiritually aware. What it does mean is that your intention or thought processes behind what you do may alter. In other words, meditation becomes an experience that impacts positively on your daily life. You find yourself questioning your reasons behind your behaviour and perhaps that of others. This is not to say that you become more judgmental or critical, but rather that you try to understand what lies behind a situation or behaviour. Once we understand, we can learn to treat ourselves, and others, with greater compassion.

So now you have had your first experience of letting yourself soar upwards to higher consciousness, without your ego on board, your task is to repeat this exercise on a number of occasions and, on each one, to allow yourself to consider an aspect of your life. You may want to choose what you will focus on before you meditate or you may prefer to trust that whatever happens is meant to happen. Likewise, you may want to call upon a specific guide before you start the meditation, or simply trust that the appropriate guide will come to you.

It was suggested that you look at your soul's purpose in life during this new stage of meditation. If you still find this a little too daunting, it is all right to focus on another, less challenging area of your life. You may find that, despite your best efforts to avoid it, a particular topic will still come up in your meditation, or your guide will offer insights into what you are trying not to look at. This is because they may know what you do not: that you are indeed ready to deal with this area of your life.

If you went through the previous exercise and did not have a wonderfully revelatory experience and have been left wondering if you aren't doing it properly, rest in the knowledge you have plenty of time in which to move on to this level. Go back to the Releasing the Ego exercise (see page 359) and keep working through it. You may be someone who finds it difficult to trust or to let yourself be taken out of your own physical control. When you experience going into the divine light and letting yourself soar upwards, it does take a kind of trust before this can happen.

You might find it helpful to do a meditation on the meaning of the word 'trust' and see if the insights you receive help you to move forward.

Continue working with this exercise for at least a month or so and notice how your awareness deepens. You may find you are taken to a number of different levels and meet many guides, or you may find yourself always returning to one level and one particular energy. Whatever happens, enjoy the whole process. You may find you have to consciously keep letting your ego go and that it tends to return to you at odd moments. Even when you have soared upwards to higher awareness, you may discover your ego suddenly decides to pop back to say 'hello' again! The more this happens, the more you can practise releasing it again; this does become easier after a few sessions.

It would help you to make notes of these experiences and your own personal development. What you may notice is that it becomes harder and harder to find the right words to describe these higher states of awareness. You begin to appreciate that heightened consciousness goes beyond the realms of ordinary words. If this happens to you, that is wonderful. Don't try to describe the experience but use simple words to talk about who your guide was and what they imparted to you. Don't try to put the other emotions and sensations into words; you can feel them with your heart.

Conscious and Unconcious Thought

Are you still struggling to understand some or even quite a lot of what your guides are saying to you? This is a common problem that almost everyone experiences. Our guides are not here to make everything simple for us; we still have to do the work. They will not just come to you and explain everything in basic terms, or advise you clearly what you should do. They may appear to talk in riddles or to show you images that don't immediately make sense. Working out what they mean is part of your own personal development.

What we feel frustrated by in our conscious world, we can sometimes learn to understand better through our subconscious. We are now going to encourage our spiritual guides to come from our meditation into our dreamworld and see how we can make the unfathomable more readily understandable.

We have talked a lot about lucid dreams and how they can become quite powerful. We have said how we can encourage spiritual guides to come into those dreams. Now we are going to see just how much we can accomplish in this sphere.

To do this, we are going to spend just a short time where we start blurring the edges between reality and the spiritual realm. Did you feel that soaring up through the divine light without your ego was very much a non-real event? Did it feel as though it wasn't quite an earthly experience, even though you knew you were conscious throughout and that your physical body never actually left its chosen meditation position?

Conversely, when have you had physical things happen to you and felt them more on a spiritual level? This might be when you went through a deeply emotional experience, such as a birth or marriage. Did you feel a sense of heightened reality such that you couldn't quite believe the physicality of it all? Sometimes it feels as though we are looking at ourselves having experiences rather than actually having them ourselves.

The expression 'living a lie' may have more significance for you now after your deeper work with your ego and your own integrity. By 'living a lie' we often mean living in a way that is not true to your own spiritual path, or your own innate personality. How did it make you feel if you uncovered an area of your life that was like that? What other illusions could you let go of, if you so wished?

When you start to question your own reality, interesting images come and go. You find yourself considering time in a different way. Ancient meditation practitioners regularly and easily shifted back and forth between what we call reality and illusion without fear and with a different level of understanding. (It is beautifully expressed in the Chinese conundrum about the butterfly we talked about on page 246.) They lived their life in the light of spiritual knowledge; we have not. Therefore, when we try to grasp these larger truths it is quite difficult for us because we have not been steeped in them.

The comments and questions which follow are for you to reflect upon and use to further widen your understanding of the gap between conscious and unconscious thought, or between waking and sleeping states.

Have you ever had flying dreams? This is where you literally experience your body taking off and flying upwards into the sky. You may truly have the sensation that you can fly as this happens to you. Perhaps you are having these dreams now as study your dreamworld more closely. How did that sensation differ from your conscious meditation when you soared upwards into higher consciousness? Was it similar in any way? Which felt more 'real'? Perhaps the dream seemed real and the meditation seemed unreal. Perhaps both experiences were in a realm that you find difficult to explain. Think about what they really felt like to you. Define 'reality' in the context of those flying experiences.

How often do you live in your imagination? Do you often daydream? How do your imaginings and daydreams differ from meditation? How are they different again from your dreams? If you find it hard to differentiate between these states, ask yourself why. Examine your true feelings about what is 'real' for you. Do you sometimes feel as though your dreams are more real and more vivid than your daily, waking moments? You may find some surprising answers.

Think about great inventors and ask yourself how they invented objects. Did they not have to 'dream' them up in their imagination and then bring them into reality? They could not create them out of nothing. They had to have a dream from which to then create reality. So when does illusion become reality? Think of examples in your own life. It is also true in reverse. Reality becomes illusion. Again, think of an example from your life. What was once real for you and has now become an illusion?

If you go further back in your life and really question your beliefs, you may discover that you have a very long and deep relationship with reality and illusion stemming from early memories. Did you believe in Santa Claus, for example? Was he a truly real figure for you, who lived in your heart and mind? What happened when you were told he did not really exist? Where did that reality go? Perhaps you believed in fairies or Superman or spirit friends whom you were later told did not exist.

Maybe you regarded your parents or guardians as 'gods' who knew everything and were all-powerful. When did that reality become shattered? What happened as a result? How do you see your family now and what is your reality as far as they are concerned? Could it be shifted again if you allowed yourself to see them in a different way? How might your reality constantly keep shifting, expanding, growing and changing, if you allowed it to do so?

Look at physical objects around you and notice how they might physically change shape. For instance, think of water in its liquid form and then reflect upon it frozen into ice. It can also be boiled to evaporation. Which of these states is 'real', or are they all real? Can you see ice and then visualize it as nothing but moist air? Which is the true state and which is created? If water can exist and be 'real' in different states, within what different 'states' might humans also be 'real'?

If humans can exist in different states, is it possible our dreamstate is just as real as our waking state and is purely a different level of awareness?

Take all these questions and their possible answers with you as we progress to the next level. Now, your next task is to find time where you can meditate in the evening, shortly before going to bed. This is so that you have as short a time as possible between completing your meditation and preparing for sleep. Make a note in your Dream Diary of the date when you start this experiment.

An evening meditation

Find the time for your meditation as described earlier in this chapter. This time take into your meditation a clear issue that you would like to work on. Make it a simple but important issue for you. If you know there is a particular guide who would be a great help to you with this issue, then ask that they appear to you before you start.

When your resolve is clear, let yourself sink into the meditation. Really relax, really let go of your ego and really let yourself soar upwards to higher consciousness. Observe whatever happens during your time with your guide and reflect upon how this helps you with your issue.

When whichever of your guides is with you, directly ask that they come into your dream that night. Make a direct, simple request. Do not expect a promise that they will do so. Make sure your ego is not with you when you make this request. Your intention in asking this question needs to be very clear. If you are doing this just because you think it will be a fun experiment, it probably won't work. If you are doing it because you have a particular issue you want to work on and you have not found your guide's advice clear so far, tell them that. Explain that you wish to work on another level. If your intentions are pure, your guide will understand.

When you finish your meditation, note if there is a particular area of the meditation you would still like to understand better. You may, of course, have experienced a meditation which seems quite clear to you and which you have found helpful. If this is the case, then remember that there is always more you can learn about any subject.

As you prepare for bed, keep in your thoughts the issue you want to work on and your relationship with your spiritual guide. Focus your thoughts on your lucid dreaming state and how much success you have had so far in this field. Consider your true commitment to understanding more about yourself. Be honest in this assessment. Do you truly have a hunger to understand more about yourself and your true purpose in life? Ask yourself if you are ready for each new step you take. Check your own integrity with each question you ask yourself.

Leaf through your Dream Diary and note where the issue you want to examine has come up for you before. Read through what you have learnt from these previous dreams. What is the greatest success you have had with lucid dreaming so far? Have you ever experienced what you would consider a divine dream? Notice the conditions that led up to that dream and try to recreate them, if possible. As always, your intention is the best and most powerful tool you can have.

Then, before going to sleep, do the following exercise:

Preparing for divine dreams

Put on whatever music or sounds help you. Have any suitable incense by your bed. Close your eyes and let yourself relax into the bed. Feel all your muscles loosen. Feel your body settling heavily into the mattress. Breathe deeply. Relax.

Now, *without opening your chakras or concentrating on your physical body*, simply imagine the beautiful, divine light above you, pouring in through the ceiling and coming down onto you. Focus on this brilliant light and see it become stronger and stronger. Feel it pour over and through you, rejuvenating you and relaxing you at the same time. Feel it seep between every cell and fibre of your being, relaxing and nurturing you as it does so. Bathe in its radiance.

Now let your ego go and feel it float upwards and away from you. See it hovering gently in the distance, ready for you to call it back again when you need it. Enjoy its release. Feel lighter and more joyous as a result.

Then whisper the name of your guide silently to yourself. If you do not use names, then conjure up their image in the way that is right for you: see them, smell their scent, hear them, feel their presence. Focus on their presence.

As you drift off to sleep, allow the beautiful white light to continue shining down on you from above. Drift off to sleep with the divine light and your guide's presence in your conscious thoughts.

As soon as you wake up the next morning, make detailed notes about what has happened to you, before you forget it. Did you have a powerful dream? Was it a lucid dream? Would you call it divine in nature? Was your spiritual guide there or did someone else come into your dream?

Remember to be honest with yourself. Perhaps something occurred that was more vivid than you have experienced before. Perhaps a particularly strong image has stayed with you this time. Maybe you have woken up with some aspect of your life feeling lighter and less pressured than before. Try to be specific about what you feel.

You might wonder why you were asked not to open your chakras before you went off to sleep. This is because you are so vulnerable in your dreams and can experience so much in a spiritual realm that to consciously open your chakras can make the experience too intense. You will find your chakras do open during the dreamstate without your conscious intervention anyway. It is better to let this happen naturally during your dreams, rather than drift off to sleep with them consciously open.

If you feel overwhelmed by the strength of the dream and feel it has yielded a break-through for you in an area of your life, remember to give silent thanks to the spiritual guide who came into your dream and advised you. Acknowledge your progress, too, and how you are growing and learning.

Before you get up, consciously draw your ego back into you. It is more than likely that it will have returned of its own accord as you started writing in your Dream Diary. However, whatever you feel, take a moment to pull it back inside you and let it settle. Remember, also, to cleanse away anything you don't want from your dream. Pull a secure cloak of protection around you before you get up and start your day.

Once you regularly use this technique of consciously letting your ego go, meditating with your guide and then encouraging your guide into your dreams, you may discover you are working at a very different level. Your degree of success at this level is directly related to your commitment and your desire to want to learn more.

As always, with any stages of learning, we have phases where we seem to leap ahead and then times when we seem to be standing still or even slipping backwards.

Now you are working with releasing your ego, you are approaching very much the heart of you, your own soul, or your own true path in life. This work therefore becomes much more emotional and although it is often enlightening and uplifting, it can also be more demanding.

Whenever you feel you want a break, take one. If you find the work you have done during this chapter is too difficult or is making you feel too vulnerable or emotional, it is up to you to return to another level and work at that stage for as long as you like.

Remember, there is no right or wrong way to do this work. Once you start pulling all the different strands together, the work can become very powerful. Only you know whether you are ready for it yet. There is no shame in being aware enough to know the time is not yet right. On the contrary, there is enormous honesty and integrity in making a decision such as that, when you are listening to your own higher awareness.

We have left the process of releasing your ego until this late stage because it is an advanced concept to work with and many people find it daunting. It is impossible not to feel very vulnerable when you experience spiritual work at this level. If you are someone who has found it wonderfully liberating and deeply inspirational, that is excellent. As you continue working at this level, remember your pledge to be honest at all times.

If you can release your ego and honestly assess your work, you are indeed opening yourself up to the possibility of having profoundly rewarding spiritual experiences. Always remember to cleanse, close down and protect yourself afterwards.

FINAL THOUGHTS

If you have done only a small proportion of the exercises listed in this book, you have been working extremely hard! There is so much here for you to absorb and so much of what you experience on a spiritual level has to be done gradually and lovingly. It is impossible to rush the process.

It is very tempting to want to rush through certain parts. However, notice which areas you have tended to rush through, because it is usually those very areas from which we have the most to learn. We tend to run away, unconsciously, from what we are nervous or uncertain about. That is where our dreams can be so valuable in gently showing them to us. Meditation can give us the relaxation to enable us to move into the different spheres. Spiritual guides can help us in both dimensions.

As humans, we often get very caught up in the desire to get somewhere, without seeing that the journey itself is of the utmost importance and also very much part of the joy. How often have people, once they have attained a degree of material success or fame, talked about earlier stages in their life, when they were struggling to become so powerful, as being full of surprisingly happy memories?

We can see the journey of our spiritual growth that way, too. If we have our eyes fixed on the levels of awareness we want to attain, we will miss the enjoyment of the whole process. If we accept there are many good reasons for our being on Earth as physical beings, then should we not relish all aspects of daily life and live them to the full?

If we want everything, all at once, we are not really living in the present and regarding our daily life as a waking meditation. You have already spent time looking at how having your life full of mini meditations creates so many positive benefits, allowing you to truly 'be' and to accept exactly where you are right now as being the appropriate place for you to 'be'.

If you consider some of the greatest man-made monuments on this Earth, most of them religious or spiritual in content, it is interesting to note that the majority of them took longer than one lifetime to construct. A person diligently involved in the construction of one of these structures would probably not see it come to fruition in their own lifetime, yet they worked tirelessly upon it nevertheless. The same is true of the person who had the vision and designed the building in the first place. There have been many instances of a designer living with the illusion and never seeing the finished reality – at least not in an earthly sense. Reflect upon how they might have viewed it in another dimension, in a spiritual realm.

How do you feel about the idea of working on a project that you do not see come to fruition before the end of your present lifetime? You could say working with your soul's intended path is just such a task.

Perhaps that makes you feel a little sad: the thought of working on something and never seeing it finished. However, when you bring in the realms of higher consciousness and view the 'bigger picture', you can see your own soul's path illuminated and appreciate how your destiny is inter-woven with that of so many other people and factors. You can appreciate you are part of a whole and the more you understand the whole, the more you understand you and those around you.

That process of understanding your own 'destiny' is not an easy project. How far do you feel you have come since you first started reading this book? How do you measure your success so far? If you think you have accomplished very little, you have no doubt accomplished more than you realize. If you feel you have made great strides, you can be sure there are even greater strides to take.

Now you have come this far, it is good for you to have times when you meditate with your ego and without. It is helpful for you to notice the difference. Do the same with your dreams. Communicate with your spiritual guides in the way you find most powerful and do this with and without your ego on board. Experiment on different levels with the different exercises and see which provide the most profound results. From time to time, leaf back through this book and see which page your eye is drawn to. Reread it. What is the lesson for you to learn that you may have forgotten or not quite grasped the first time?

What is the exercise you liked least the first time around? Go back and experience it again. What do you learn from it this time?

Have you ever done the very first exercise in this book – The Camera – more than once? Let us revisit this exercise in a slightly different way. When you feel ready, work through the following:

The camera revisited

Take up a comfortable meditation position. Go through your usual relaxing and opening up process. Open up all your chakras and feel the energy coming and going from each of them. Feel the divine light from above pouring into your crown chakra and filling all of you. Sink deeper into your relaxed state.

Now let your ego go. See it float away from you and hover somewhere above you, bobbing contentedly in the distance.

As you rest in your relaxed state, you realize that the feather-light camera is once more in your hands. Your eye is trained to the lens and your finger is on the zoom button. You feel comfortable and secure and look forward to the journey that is about to start.

You look through the lens and see the same tiny ant in the grass. You pull back effortlessly and see the larger beetle beside it. As you keep pulling back, you see the different images in front of you: the bird, rabbit, cat, small dog, the large dog, the horse. Then you are resting on the head of the giraffe. You have visions of your own life, which you now see in this wider context. Let them come and go through your consciousness without trying to hold on to them.

Then you pull the zoom back further. You see the ever-widening vista in front of you. The giraffe is in a field, the field is surrounded by houses. You see more houses and more fields and people scurrying like ants through the scenery. You think of yourself in this context and realize you can understand yourself and others much better through what you have learnt. Acknowledge you have more still to learn. (Keep your ego at bay as these insights come to you.)

Now you pull back further and your speed increases. You find yourself being pulled swiftly up through the beautiful white light. As this happens, you realize that you and this camera are all part of the divine light. All the creatures and images and scenery you have seen are all part of the divine light and its consciousness.

The Earth is disappearing into a tiny ball in front of you as you keep your eye trained through the lens. You pass the moon and stars and other planets and galaxies you vaguely remember from your past.

You are travelling at speed but it is effortless, beautiful and inspiring. You keep your eye trained through the lens as you experience this wonderful journey, observing everything being shown to you.

After some time, the speed slows. You are coming to a halt. The zoom lens has come to the end of its power. Slowly, you let the camera drop into your lap and you take a look around you.

Where are you? Who else is with you? What sensations are there for you to experience? Allow yourself to feel blessed with this long journey you have taken. Realize there are more powerful cameras you may wish to own in the future. This is not the end of your journey; it is still the beginning. Rest a while in this beautiful place.

When it is time, you will be led back down through the white light and gently returned to your meditation position back in your room. If you feel a slight jolt as you return, remember that it is important for you to return to your daily life and to continue with your tasks on Earth. Give yourself plenty of time to readjust. Remember to let your ego come back and rest gently inside of you. Cleanse, close down and protect yourself. Sit quietly and reflect upon this exercise for a while before you get up and continue with your day.

What difference did you notice having done this second exercise with the camera? Were you taken aback by your new experiences? Were you disappointed? I think not. Whatever you experienced this time, it will be a direct reflection of your attitude towards spiritual work and the effort you have put in during your journey so far. What is certain is that your second visit will have afforded you a very different viewpoint from your first visit. It is impossible not to reassess your attitude towards spiritual awareness when you have been encouraged to do so through working on all the exercises in this book.

If you fundamentally work very much with the left-hand side of your brain – that is, through logical and linear thinking (and statistics shows a great many of us do work this way) –, you may still be finding yourself questioning the power of spiritual awareness in relation to everyday life. Even if you have spent considerable time on some of the more esoteric exercises and found them very useful, your left-hand side of your brain may still be telling you that you ought to be more sceptical!

It might be helpful for you to know that many eminent scientists and decidedly 'left-brain-dominant' people came to acknowledge the power of spiritual awareness through their work. For instance have you any idea who said the following?:

'I maintain that cosmic religious feeling is the strongest and noblest incitement to scientific research.'

Think also about who might have said the following:

'Pure logical thinking cannot yield us any knowledge of the empirical world; all knowledge or reality starts from experience and ends in it. Propositions arrived at by purely logical means are completely empty of reality.'

The person who gave us both quotes was none other than Albert Einstein (1879–1955). It truly is possible to embrace both your physical self and your spiritual self, as many eminent people have proved. All it takes is the refusal to go through life wearing blinkers.

Perhaps through reading this book you have spent so much time studying the spiritual aspects of you that you have let some of your everyday pleasures slip a little. Remember our discussions about the importance of balancing all of you? Are you good at giving yourself time to enjoy moments of fun and stress-free activity? This doesn't necessarily mean meditating all the time; what are your other favourite relaxations?

To honour all the work you have done in this book and as a reminder of the importance of balancing all aspects of ourselves, let us finish with a light and enjoyable meditation which encourages us to remember the lighter qualities we possess.

Your angel of fun

Close your eyes and settle into a comfortable position – perhaps lying down, provided you don't fall asleep! Breathe comfortably but don't spend a long time focusing on your breathing. Just relax and sink into your comfortable position. Feel your body unwinding.

As you do this, realize that a wonderful energy has just entered into your awareness. This is a light, frothy energy, unlike any other you have so far experienced. This energy is bright and instantly uplifting. You may see a sprightly figure as this happens or just hear, sense or smell in your own way. Whatever happens for you, it is very different from any other energy you have so far experienced.

It literally dances around and through you, making you want to laugh, making you want to smile. You feel yourself relax even more in the company of this new energy. You feel lighter, happier and can't stop smiling.

This is your angel of fun, come to lighten and brighten your day. Observe what they do. They may clown around or joke and make you laugh. They may just dance in front of you. Perhaps they are singing. Perhaps they want to play a silly game with you.

They may be showing you something that you could introduce into your own life to enjoy it more. Observe what they do without judging them. You might think they are silly; you might find them enchanting; you might find yourself wishing you could be more like them or realize you are a lot like them but you hardly ever show it or even that you are glad you are not like them! It doesn't matter what you think of them, as long as you enjoy their presence.

They will stay in your awareness for a while and they may then suddenly disappear without reason. They can literally disappear in a puff of smoke or a flash of light, or vanish in the blinking of an eye. Angels of fun come and go very quickly because their energy is so light. They are not grounded in any way.

When they have gone, give yourself time to ground your body. You may find yourself wanting to laugh or just feeling happy for a long time afterwards. That is wonderful, as long as you have reorientated yourself to everyday life before you get up and continue your day. Most people find it unnerving to encounter someone who is perpetually smiling and laughing for no apparent reason! Just give yourself a little time to readjust back to earthly energy when you finish.

Angels of fun are a delightful boost to our everyday life and can give us a much-needed injection of optimism and pleasure. Do you have an important business meeting coming up or are you dreading seeing someone who always gives you a hard time? Lighten your energy by inviting your angel of fun to visit you, even for a few minutes. Just a short time can really lift and enliven you.

You may have to work hard on all levels: physically with work, family, friends and home life; emotionally with anxieties and pressures; mentally with aspirations and concerns about different issues; and spiritually with trying to understand your soul's true path.

No matter how hard you work on these different levels, no matter how much you want to understand or how much you want to accomplish, it is not the end of the journey that is important, but the very process of the journey itself.

So whenever you feel that you are getting bogged down with responsibilities, on whatever level it may be, take a few minutes to stop, relax and invite your angel of fun to bring light and love into your energy.

You are the true master of your own destiny. Decide you will enjoy this process called life. See it not as something to be got through, but as a moment in time to be treasured, relished and enjoyed to the full.

CLOSING PRAYER

Divine Light,

help me to see the way forward with love, light and joy.

Show me how best to help others, as well as myself.

Let me spread your Divine Light through myself and others

without judgement, conditions or expectations.

Amen.